D0218341

Administering Windows Server® 2012 Exam 70-411

Lab Manual

Patrick Regan

WILEY

EXECUTIVE EDITOR	John Kane
EDITORIAL ASSISTANT	Allison Winkle
DIRECTOR OF SALES	Mitchell Beaton
EXECUTIVE MARKETING MANAGER	Chris Ruel
SENIOR PRODUCTION & MANUFACTURING MANAGER	Janis Soo
ASSOCIATE PRODUCTION MANAGER	Joel Balbin
PRODUCTION EDITOR	Eugenia Lee

www.wiley.com/college/microsoft

or

call the MOAC Toll-Free Number: 888-764-7001 (U.S. & Canada only)

ISBN 978-1-118-55082-3

Printed in the United States of America

10 9 8 7 6 5 4 3 2 1

BRIEF CONTENTS

CONTENTS

LAB 1
DEPLOYING AND MANAGING SERVER IMAGES

THIS LAB CONTAINS THE FOLLOWING EXERCISES AND ACTIVITIES:

Exercise 1.1	Installing and Configuring Windows Deployment Services
Exercise 1.2	Creating Windows Deployment Images
Exercise 1.3	Generating an Autounattend.xml file
Exercise 1.4	Deploying a Windows Image
Exercise 1.5	Updating a Windows Image
Lab Challenge	Adding Drivers to a Windows Image

BEFORE YOU BEGIN

The lab environment consists of student workstations connected to a local area network, along with a server that functions as the domain controller for a domain called *contoso.com*. The computers required for this lab are listed in Table 1-1.

Table 1-1
Computers Required for Lab 1

Computer	Operating System	Computer Name
Server (VM 1)	Windows Server 2012	RWDC01
Server (VM 2)	Windows Server 2012	Server01
Server (VM 3)	Windows Server 2012	Server02

In addition to the computers, you also require the software listed in Table 1-2 to complete Lab 1.

Table 1-2
Software Required for Lab 1

Software	Location
ISO of Windows Server 2012 installation disk	\\rwdc01\Software
Windows Assessment and Deployment Kit (ADK) for Windows 8	\\rwdc01\Software
Autounattend.xml file	\\rwdc01\Software
Windows8-RT-KB2769034-x64.msu	\\rwdc01\Software
Lab 1 student worksheet	Lab01_worksheet.docx (provided by instructor)

Working with Lab Worksheets

Each lab in this manual requires that you answer questions, take screen shots, and perform other activities that you will document in a worksheet named for the lab, such as Lab01_worksheet.docx. You will find these worksheets on the book companion site. It is recommended that you use a USB flash drive to store your worksheets, so you can submit them to your instructor for review. As you perform the exercises in each lab, open the appropriate worksheet file fill in the required information, and save the file to your flash drive.

After completing this lab, you will be able to:

- Install and configure Windows Deployment Services

- Deploy Windows servers using Windows Deployment Services

- Create and modify an Autounattend.xml file using Windows System Image Manager

- Update an offline Windows image

Estimated lab time: 100 minutes

Exercise 1.1	Installing and Configuring Windows Deployment Services
Overview	In this exercise, you first create a new server. You then install and configure Windows Deployment Services, so that you can quickly install Windows servers in the future.
Completion time	10 minutes

Mindset Question: **If you have a network infrastructure in place including a domain controller, a DNS server and a DHCP server, what are the general steps that you need to perform before you deploy Windows using WDS?**

1.   Log into Server01 as contoso\administrator with the password of Password01.

2.   On Server01, using the Server Manager console, open the Manage menu and click Add Roles and Features.

3.   When the Add Roles and Features Wizard starts, click Next.

4.   On the Select installation type page, click Next.

5.   On the Select destination server page, click Next.

6.   Scroll down and select Windows Deployment Services.

7.   When the Add Roles and Features Wizard dialog box opens, click Add Features. Then click Next.

8.   On the Select features page, click Next.

9.   On the WDS page, click Next.

10.   On the Select role services page, make sure that the Deployment Server option and the Transport Server option is selected, and then click Next.

11.   On the Confirm installation selections page, click Install.

12.   When the installation finishes, click Close.

13.   At the top of Server Manager, click Tools > Windows Deployment Services. The Windows Deployment Services console opens.

14.   Expand Servers, right-click the Server01.contoso.com, and then select Configure Server.

15.   When the Before You Begin page appears, click Next.

16.   On the Install Options page, select the Integrated with Active Directory option, and then click Next.

17.   On the Remote Installation Folder Location page, take a screen shot by pressing Alt+Prt Scr and then paste it into your Lab 1 worksheet file in the page provided by pressing Ctrl+V.

18.   On the Remote Installation page, click Next.

Question 1	*What is the default path for the remote installation folder?*

Question 2	Why is the default location not recommended?

19. When the system volume warning appears, click Yes.

20. On the PXE Server Initial Settings page, select *Respond to all client computers (known and unknown)*. Click Next.

21. When the task is completed, click to unselect the *Add images to the server now*

22. Take a screen shot of the Windows Deployment Services Configuration Wizard by pressing Alt+Prt Scr and then paste it into your Lab 1 worksheet file in the page provided by pressing Ctrl+V.

23. Click Finish.

24. Keep the Windows Deployment Services open for the next exercise.

End of exercise. You can leave the windows open for the next exercise.

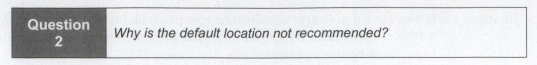

Exercise 1.2	Creating Windows Deployment Images
Overview	In this exercise, you prepare images (boot images and install images) that will be used to deploy Windows.
Completion time	20 minutes

1. On Server01, create the C:\Software folder.

2. On Server01, right-click the Start button, select Run and type **\\RWDC01\Software,** then click OK

3. Copy the ISO file for the Windows Server 2012 installation disk, the autounattend.xml file and the Windows8-RT-KB2769034-x64.msu file to the C:\Software folder.

4. On Server01, open the C:\Software folder.

5. Right-click the ISO file for Windows Server 2012 installation disk and select Mount.

Question 3	What drive letter was the ISO file mounted to?

6. From the Windows Deployment Services console, expand Servers, and expand Server01.contoso.com, so that you can see the Install Images folder and the Boot Images folders.

7. To add a boot image, right-click the Boot Images folder and choose Add Boot Image. The Add Image Wizard opens.

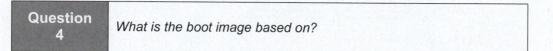

Question 4	*What is the boot image based on?*

8. Browse to the E:\Sources folder, and click the boot.wim file, and then click Open. Click Next.

9. On the Image Metadata page, click Next.

10. On the Summary page, click Next.

11. When the image is added to the server, click Finish.

12. Right-click the Install Images folder and select Add Install Image. The Add Image Wizard page opens.

13. On the Image Group page, the Create an image group named option is selected. Click Next.

14. Browse to the E:\Sources folder and double-click install.wim file, and then click Next.

15. On the Available Images page (as shown on Figure 1-1), deselect the following images:

- Windows Server 2012 SERVERSTANDARDCORE
- Windows Server 2012 SERVERDATACENTERCORE
- Windows Server 2012 SERVERDATACENTER

Be sure that Windows Sever 2012 SERVERSTANDARD is selected. Click Next.

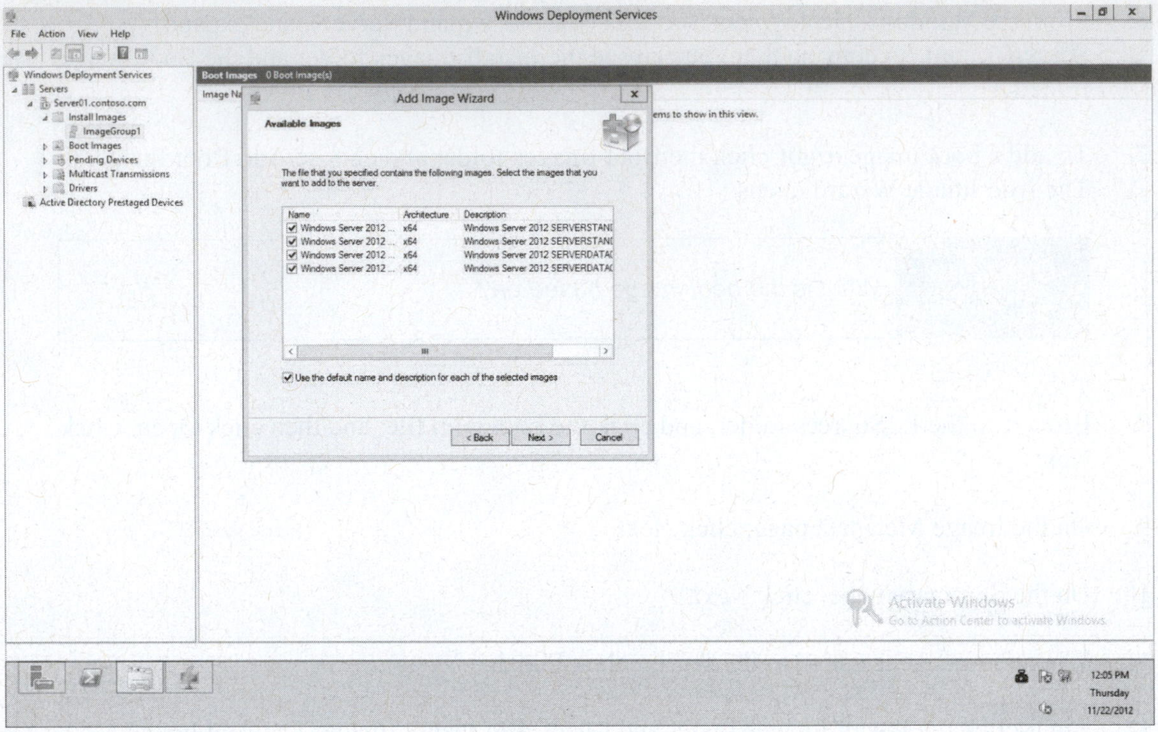

Figure 1-1
Selecting images to use

16. On the Summary page, click Next.

17. When the imageis added to the server, click Finish.

End of exercise. You can leave the windows open for the next exercise.

Exercise 1.3	Generating an Autounattend.xml File
Overview	You are ready to deploy Windows. However, if you install using WDS, you will have to interact with the Windows installation program by choosing applicable settings during the installation process. To help automate the installation, during this exercise, you create an Autoattend.xml file and check a provided Autounattend.xml file.
Completion time	20 minutes

Mindset Question: So far, you have installed and configured WDS. However, right now, the WDS server will only allow you to install Windows remotely just as if you booted from the Windows Server 2012 installation disk. What do you need to do to automate the installation?

Generating an Unattend.xml File

1. On Server01, right-click the Start button, select Run \\rwdc01\software then click OK. Copy the ADK folder to C:\Software folder.

2. Open the E:\Sources folder and copy the install.wim to the C:\Software folder.

3. On Server01, open the C:\Software\ADK folder.

Question 5	*What are the two ways to create or modify an unattend xml file?*

4. To start the installation of the Windows Assessment and Deployment Kit, double-click adksetup.exe. If it asks you to run this file, click Run.

5. On the Specify Location page, leave the default settings, and then click Next.

6. When you are prompted to join the Customer Experience Improvement Program (CEIP), click Next.

7. On the License Agreement page, click Accept.

8. Deselect all options except Deployment Tools and Windows Preinstallation Environment (Windows PE). Click Install.

9. When the installation is complete, click Close.

10. Using Windows Explorer, create a folder called C:\DistFold.

11. Click Start > Windows System Image Manager. The Windows System Image Manager console opens.

12. Click Tools > Create Distribution Share. The Create Distribution Share dialog box opens.

13. In the Folder name text box, type **C:\DistFold** folder and click Open.

14. Click File > Select Windows Image. The Select a Windows Image dialog box opens.

15. In the file name text box, type **C:\Software\install.wim** and click Open. Click Windows Server 2012 SERVERSTANDARD and click OK.

16. If you are prompted to create a catalog file, click Yes.

17. Click File > New Answer File. The answer file elements display in the Answer File pane.

18. In the Windows Image pane, expand Components. Then scroll down and right-click *amd64_Microsoft-Windows-International-Core-WinPE_6.2.9200. 16384_neutral* and click *Add Settings to Pass 1 WindowsPE*, as shown in Figure 1-2.

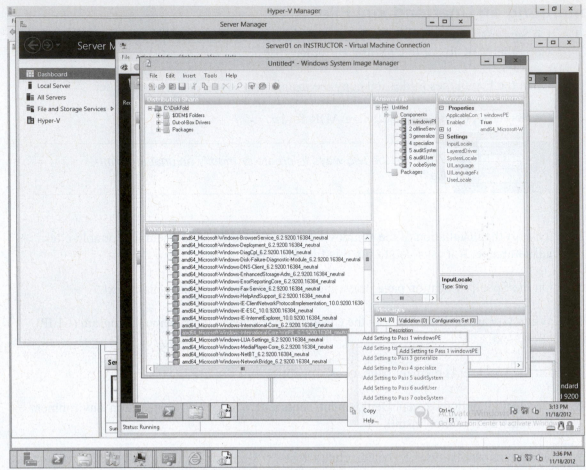

Figure 1-2
Adding Settings to Pass 1 WindowsPE

19. The Microsoft-Windows-International-Core-WinPE component specifies the default
language, locale, and other international settings to use during Windows Setup or
Windows Deployment Services installations. In the Answer File pane click
amd64_Microsoft-Windows-International-Core-WinPE_neutral, and fill in the language
settings as shown in Figure 1-3 as appropriate, such as **en-US**.

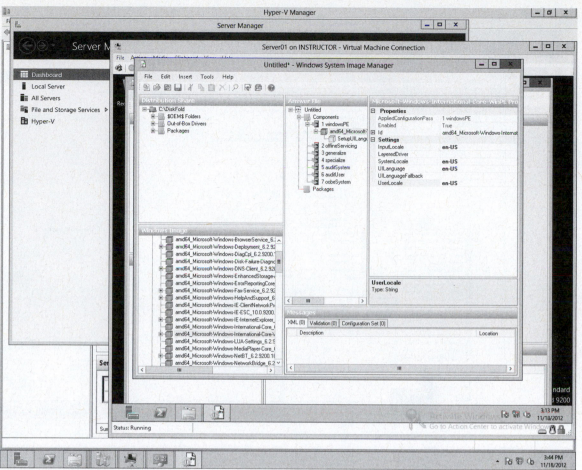

Figure 1-3
Specifying language settings

20. Expand *amd64_Microsoft-Windows-International-Core-WinPE_neutral* and click
    SetupUILanguage. Type **en-US** in the properties for UILanguage.

21. The Microsoft-Windows-Setup component contains settings that enable you to select the
    Windows image that you install, configure the disk that you install Windows to, and
    configure the Windows PE operating system. Under the Windows Image pane, right-click
    amd64_Microsoft-Windows-Setup_6.2.9200.16384_neutral, and click *Add Setting to Pass
    1 windowsPE*.

22. In the Answer File pane, expand *amd64_Microsoft-Windows-Setup_neutral,* right-click
    DiskConfiguration, and select Insert New Disk, as shown in Figure 1-4.

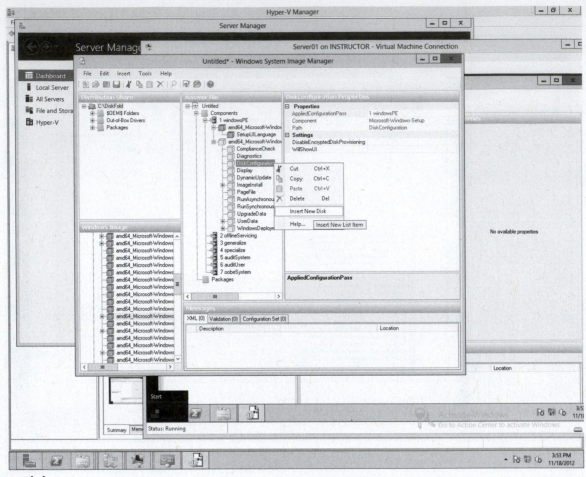

Figure 1-4
Inserting New Disk

23. In the Answer File pane, expand *amd64_Microsoft-Windows-Setup_neutral*, expand Disk, right-click CreatePartitions, and select Insert New CreatePartition.

24. Specify the order of **1**, size of **350**, and type of **Primary**, as shown in Figure 1-5.

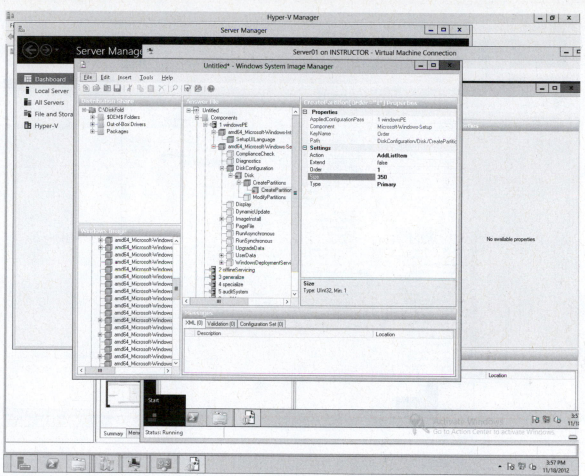

Figure 1-5
Specifying size of a partition

25. Right-click CreatePartitions and click Insert New CreatePartition. For the new CreatePartition entry, change the Extend property to true and set Order to **2**. Don't configure the size, as shown in Figure 1-6.

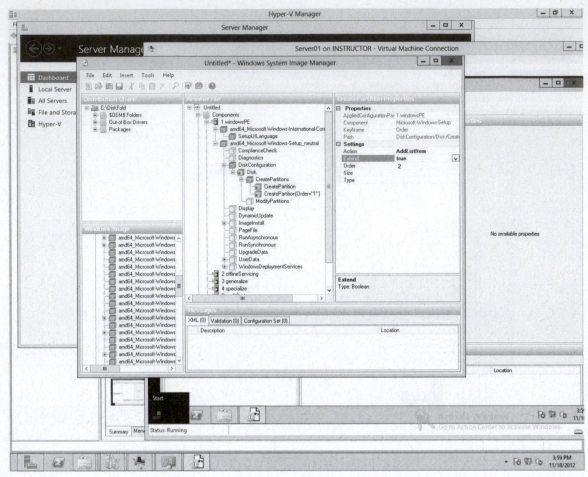

Figure 1-6
Extended a partition

26. In the Answer File pane, click Disk, then change the DiskID to **0** and WillWipeDisk to true, as shown in Figure 1-7.

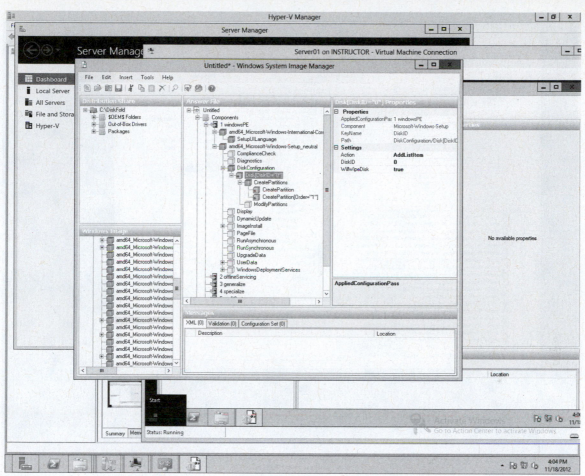

Figure 1-7
Specifying the Disk ID

27. Right-click ModifyPartitions and select Insert New ModifyPartition. Then specify the following, as shown in Figure 1-8:

   Active is **true**

   Format is **NTFS**

   Label is **Boot**

   Order is **1**

   PartitionID is **1**

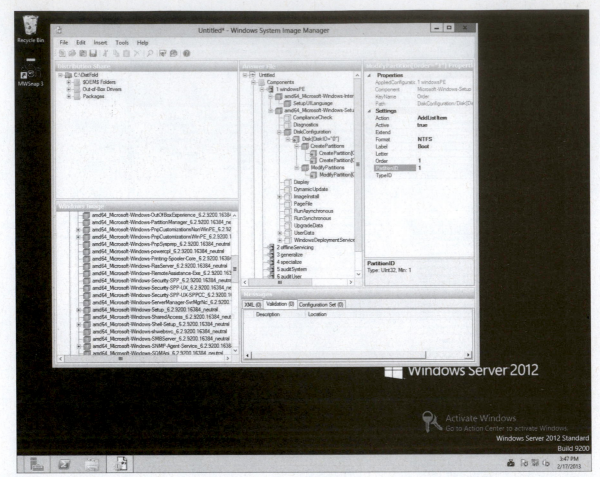

Figure 1-8
Specifying the Partition ID

28. Add a second ModifyPartitions and configure as the following:

    Format is **NTFS**

    Label is **System**

    Order is **2**

    PartitionID is **2**

29. In the Answer File pane, scroll down to and expand ImageInstall. Expand OSImage and right-click InstallFrom and select Insert New Metadata and configure the metadata as shown Figure 1-9.

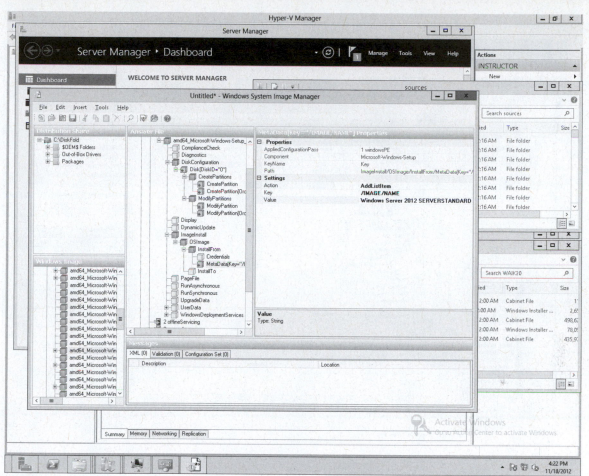

Figure 1-9
Specifying Which Image to Use

30. Click InstallTo and configure the DiskID to **0** and PartitionID to **2**, as shown in Figure 1-10.

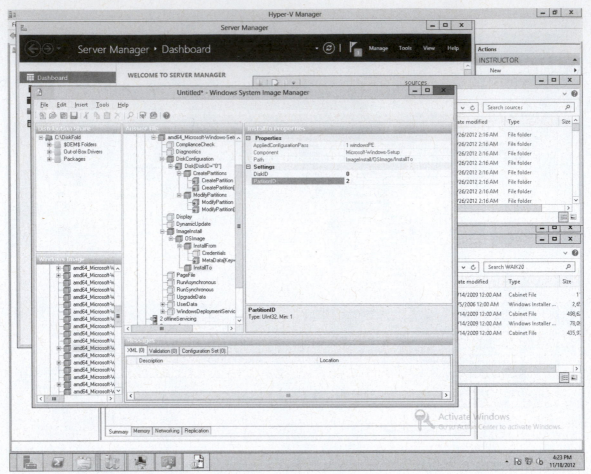

Figure 1-10
Specifying which disk and partition to install to

31. In the Answer File pane, click UserData. Then specify the following:

Accept EULA to **true**

FullName to **Student**

Organization to **Classroom**

32. Expand UserData and click ProductKey. If you have a key, you type the Windows key in the Key box. For this lab, leave it blank.

33. The Microsoft-Windows-Shell-Setup contains elements and settings that control how the shell of the Windows operating system is installed on a destination computer. In the Windows Image pane, right-click *amd64_Microsoft-Windows-Shell-Setup_6.2.9200.16384_neutral*, and click *Add Settings to Pass 4 specialize*.

34. In the Answer File pane, click on *amd64_Microsoft-Windows-Shell-Setup_neutral*. Here, you also enter the ProductKey. In addition, you can specify the ComputerName and TimeZone. For now, leave these blank.

35. In the Windows Image pane, right-click the *amd64_Microsoft-Windows-Shell-Setup_6.2.9200.16384_neutral* component and click *Add Settings to Pass 7 oobeSystem*.

36. In the Answer File pane, under *7 oobeSystem/amd64_Microsoft-Windows-Shell-Setup_neutral*, configure the following settings:

Registered Organization to **Classroom**

Registered Owner: **Student**

37. Open the File menu and select Save Answer File.

38. Browse to the C:\Software folder. For the File name text box, type **Unattend (Temp).xml** and click Save.

39. Open the File menu and click Close Answer File.

Checking a Current Autounattend.xml File

1. On Server01, using Windows System Image Manager, open the File menu and click Open Answer File. Select the autounattend.xml from the C:\Software folder. Click Open.

2. Open the Tools menu and click Validate Answer File.

3. In the Messages pane, make sure there are no errors. Warnings will appear, which are common.

4. Take a screen shot of the Windows System Image Manager interface by pressing Alt+Prt Scr and then paste it into your Lab 1 worksheet file in the page provided by pressing Ctrl+V.

5. In the Answer File pane, expand the structure and view the various settings.

6. Close the Windows System Image Manager.

7. Open the C:\Software folder.

8. Right-click the autounattend.xml file and click Open with and click Notepad.

9. Scroll through the document and review the various settings.

10. Close Notepad.

End of exercise. You can leave the windows open for the next exercise.

Exercise 1.4	Deploying a Windows Image
Overview	During this exercise, you deploy a Windows image from the WDS server while using the autounattended.xml file.
Completion time	10 minutes

1. On Server01, copy the C:\Software\autounattend.xml file to the C:\RemoteInstall folder.

2. If Windows Deployment Services is not open, on the Server Manager console, open the Tools menu and click Windows Deployment Services. The Windows Deployment Services console opens.

3. Expand Servers. Then right-click Server01.contoso.com and choose Properties. The server's Properties dialog box opens.

4. Click the Client tab.

5. Select the Enable unattended installation check box. Click the Browse button corresponding to the x64 architecture, and browse C:\RemoteInstall\autounattend.xml. Click Open. When completed, the Client tab should look like Figure 1-11.

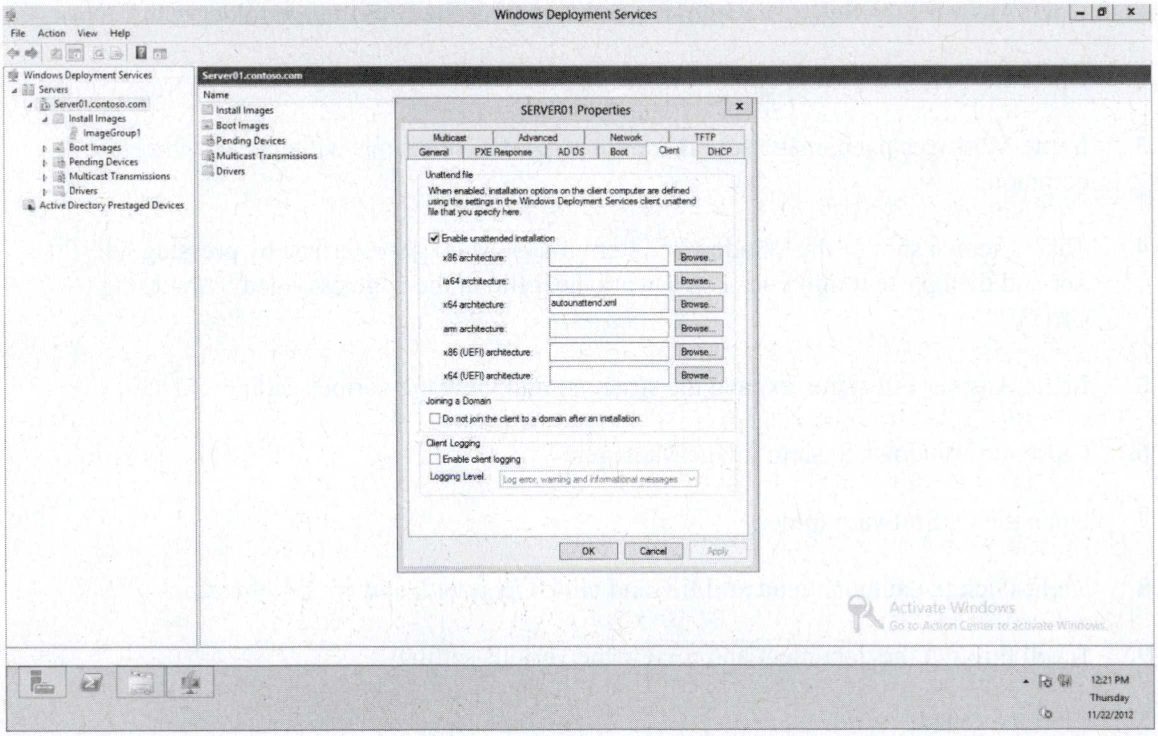

Figure 1-11
Configure the Client settings

6. Click OK to close the server's Properties sheet.

7. Expand the Server01.contoso.com node, expand the Install Images node, and click ImageGroup1.

8. Right-click the Windows Server 2012 SERVERSTANDARD image click Properties. The Image Properties dialog box opens.

9. Click to select the *Allow image to install in unattended mode* check box.

10. Click Select File. The Select Unattend File dialog box opens.

11. Browse to the C:\RemoteInstall\autounattend.xml, and then click Open, then click OK.

12. Click OK to accept your settings and to close the Image Properties dialog box. You are now ready to perform a PXE boot on a new server and perform an installation of Windows Server 2012.

13. Close Wndows Deployment Services and any explorer folders you have open.

End of exercise. You can leave the windows open for the next exercise.

Exercise 1.5	Updating a Windows Image
Overview	From time to time, you need to patch a Windows image. During this execise, you add a Windows update package to the install.wim file
Completion time	20 minutes

Mindset Question: **You need to update a Windows Image with a critical patch. What are the general steps to add the patch to the Windows image?**

1. On Server01, create a **C:\Package** folder.

2. Create a folder called **C:\Offline**.

3. Right-click the Start Menu button and click Command Prompt (Admin).

4. To change to the C:\Software folder, execute the following command at the command prompt:

```
cd\Software
```

5. To extract the cab files from the Windows8-RT-KB2769034-x64.msu file, execute the following command:

```
Windows8-RT-KB2769034-x64.msu /extract:C:\Package
```

6. Using Windows Explorer, view the content of the C:\Package folder.

7. Take a screen shot of the Package folder by pressing Alt+Prt Scr and then paste it into your Lab 1 worksheet file in the page provided by pressing Ctrl+V.

8. Open Windows Deployment Services.

9. Navigate to the ImageGroup1 node, which is under Install Images.

10. In the ImageGroup1 pane, right-click the *Windows Server 2012 SERVERSTANDARD* image and click Disable.

11. Right-click the Windows Server 2012 SERVERSTANDARD image and click Export Image.

12. When the Export As dialog box opens, type **C:\Software\install.wim** in the File name text box. Click Save. If it asks you to continue, click Yes.

13. On the Administrator: Command Prompt window, to mount the c:\Software\install.wim, execute the following command:

```
dism /Mount-Wim /WimFile:C:\Software\install.wim /index:1
/MountDir:C:\Offline
```

14. To get information about the WIM file, execute the following command:

```
dism /Get-WimInfo /WimFile:C:\software\install.wim /index:1
```

15. To add the package to the wim image, execute the following command:

```
dism /image:C:\Offline /Add-Package
/Packagepath:C:\Package\Windows8-RT-KB2769034-x64.cab
```

16. To commit the changes to the wim file, execute the following command:

```
dism /Commit-Wim /MountDir:C:\Offline
```

17. To dismount the WIM file, execute the following command:

```
dism /Unmount-Wim /MountDir:C:\Offline /commit
```

18. Take a screen shot of the Command Prompt by pressing Alt+Prt Scr and then paste it into your Lab 1 worksheet file in the page provided by pressing Ctrl+V.

19. Go back to Windows Deployment Services console.

20. Right-click the Windows Server 2012 SERVERSTANDARD image and click Replace Image.

21. When the Replace Install Image Wizard dialog box opens, use the Browse button to browse to the **C:\Software\install.wim** file and click Next.

22. On the Available Images page, click Next.

23. On the Image Metadata page, click Next.

24. On the Summary page, click Next.

25. When the image is replaced, click Finish. The image is automatically enabled.

26. Close the Administrator: Command Prompt windows and Windows Deployment Services.

End of exercise.

LAB REVIEW QUESTIONS

Completion time	10 minutes

1. In Exercise 1.1, what program did you use to install WDS?

2. In Exercise 1.2, what two images did you have to add to the WDS server to handle the Windows installation?

3. In Exercise 1.3, what program did you use to create the unattend file?

4. In Exercise 1.3, what program should you use to verify a unattend file?

5. In Exercise 1.3, how was the Windows System Image Manager installed?

6. In Exercise 1.4, what two places did you have to define an unattend file?

7. In Exercise 1.5, what program did you use to modify a Windows image?

Lab Challenge	Adding Drivers to a Windows Image
Overview	To complete this challenge, you must demonstrate how to add drivers to a Windows image by writing the steps to complete the tasks described in the scenerio. Since the class servers do not have drivers to add, just write the steps as if the drivers actually existed.
Completion time	10 minutes

Over the last couple of months, you have been using WDS to deploy Windows Server 2012. Recently, you started to purchase new servers that require additional drivers that are not included with Windows installation. You need to ensure that WDS will deploy these drivers. What should you do?

Write out the steps you performed to complete the challenge.

End of lab.

LAB 2
IMPLEMENTING PATCH MANAGEMENT

THIS LAB CONTAINS THE FOLLOWING EXERCISES AND ACTIVITIES:

Exercise 2.1	Installing WSUS
Exercise 2.2	Configuring WSUS
Exercise 2.3	Configuring Clients
Exercise 2.4	Approving Updates
Lab Challenge	Running WSUS Reports

BEFORE YOU BEGIN

The lab environment consists of student workstations connected to a local area network, along with a server that functions as the domain controller for a domain called *contoso.com*. The computers required for this lab are listed in Table 2-1.

Table 2-1
Computers Required for Lab 2

Computer	Operating System	Computer Name
Server (VM 1)	Windows Server 2012	RWDC01
Server (VM 2)	Windows Server 2012	Server01
Server (VM 3)	Windows Server 2012	Server02

In addition to the computers, you also require the software listed in Table 2-2 to complete Lab 2.

Table 2-2
Software Required for Lab 2

Software	Location
Lab 2 student worksheet	Lab02_worksheet.docx (provided by instructor)

Working with Lab Worksheets

Each lab in this manual requires that you answer questions, take screen shots, and perform other activities that you will document in a worksheet named for the lab, such as Lab02_worksheet.docx. You will find these worksheets on the book companion site. It is recommended that you use a USB flash drive to store your worksheets, so you can submit them to your instructor for review. As you perform the exercises in each lab, open the appropriate worksheet file fill in the required information, and save the file to your flash drive.

After completing this lab, you will be able to:

- Install and configure WSUS

- Deploy updates to client computers

Estimated lab time: 60 minutes

Exercise 2.1	Installing WSUS
Overview	In this exercise, you use Server Manager to install WSUS. Because this is a test environment, you use the standard internal database
Completion time	10 minutes

Mindset Question: **When planning WSUS, what factors must you consider when deciding which server to place the WSUS on?**

1.   Log into Server01 as **contoso\administrator** with the password of **Password01**.

2.   Using File Explorer, create a **C:\Updates** folder.

3.   To deploy WSUS, Network Services needs to have Full Control to the %windir%\Microsoft.NET\Framework\v2.0.50727\Temporary ASP.NET Files and %windir%\Temp folder. Open the %windir% folder.

Question 1	What folder does the %windir% folder represent?

4.   Right-click the Temp folder and select Properties.

5.   When the Properties dialog box opens, click the Security tab.

6.   Click the Edit button.

7.   When the Permissions for Temp folder open, click Add.

8.   When the Select Users, Computers, Service Accounts, or Groups dialog box opens, type **network service** in the Enter the object names to select text box and press the Enter key.

9.   While NETWORK SERVICE is selected, click the Allow Full control.

10. Take a screen shot of the Permissions for Temp dialog box by pressing Alt+Prt Scr and then paste it into your Lab 2 worksheet file in the page provided by pressing Ctrl+V.

11. Click OK to close the Permissions for Temp. If it asks you are about to change the permissions settings on system folders, click Yes.

12. Click OK to close the Properties dialog box.**12.** If Server Manager is not open, open Server Manager.

13. At the top of Server Manager, click Manage > Add Roles and Features. The Add Roles and Feature Wizard displays.

14. On the Before you begin page, click Next.

15. Select *Role-based or feature-based installation* and then click Next.

16. On the Select destination server page, click Next.

17. Scroll down and select Windows Server Update Services.

18. When the Add Roles and Features Wizard opens, click Add Features.

19. Back on the Select server roles screen, click Next.

20. On the Select features page, click Next.

21. On the Windows Server Update Services page, click Next.

22. By default, the WID database and WSUS Services are selected as shown in Figure 2-1. Answer the new question, and Click **Next**.

Question 2	*What option would you pick to store the database on a dedicated SQL server?*

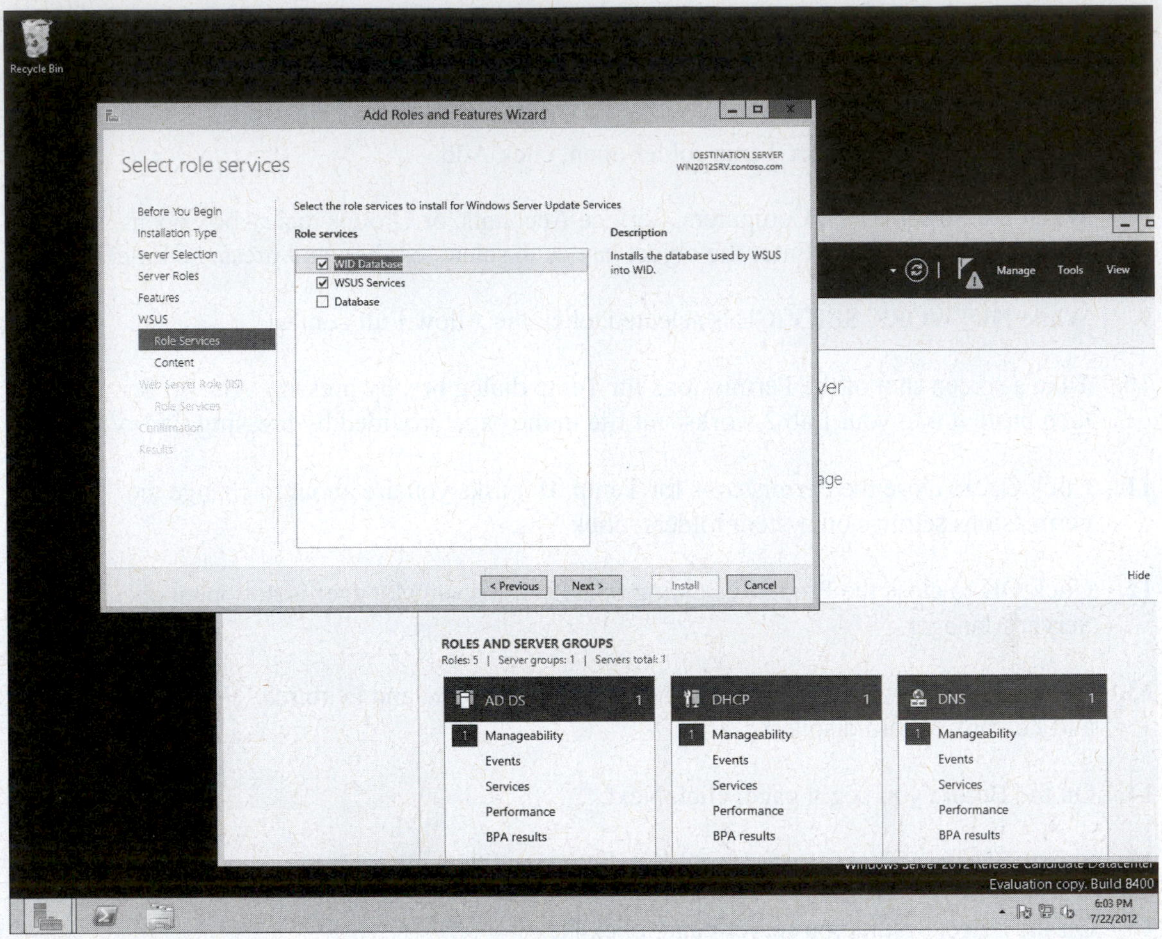

Figure 2-1
Selecting the WSUS components

23. On the Current Location selection, type **C:\Updates** (as shown in Figure 2-2), and then click Next.

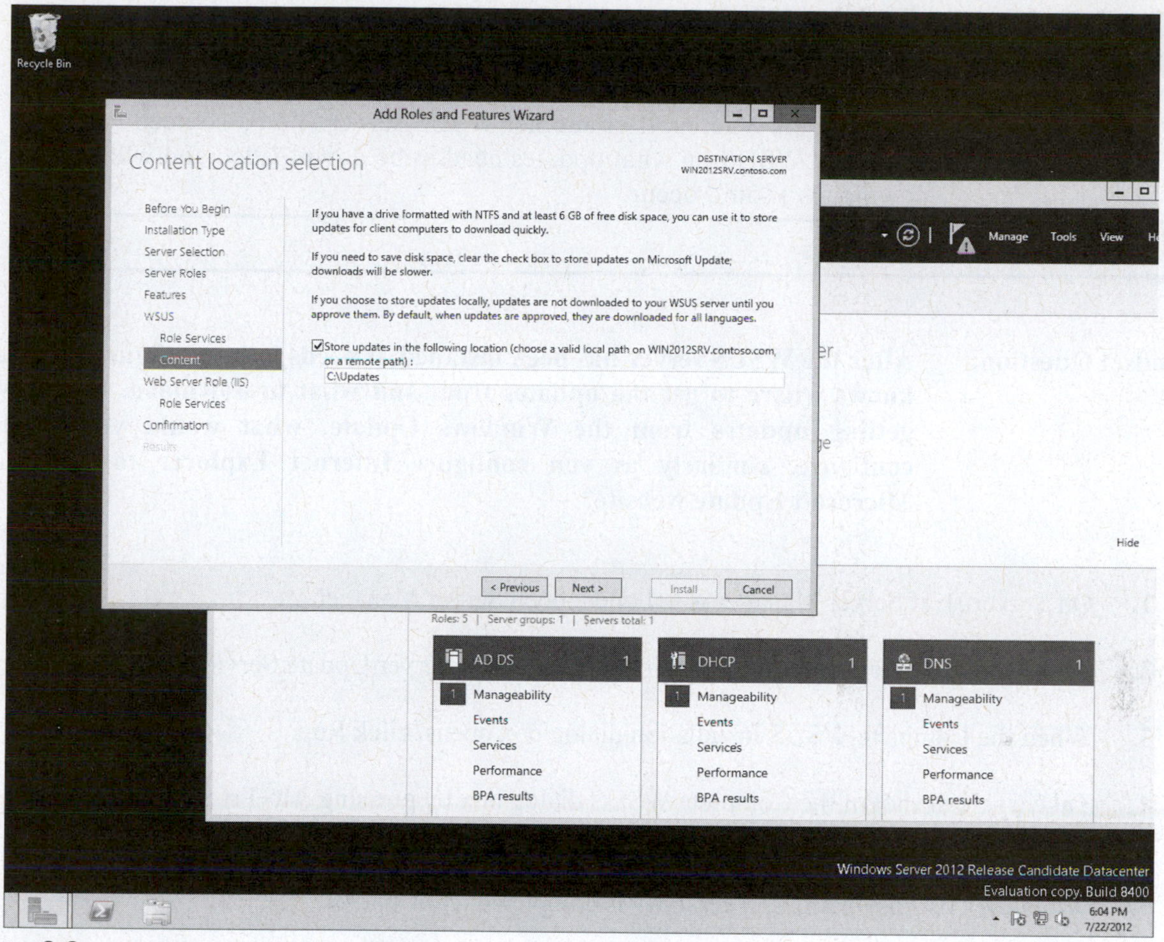

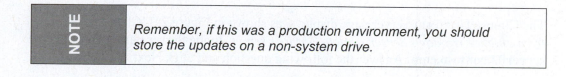

Figure 2-2
Specifying where to store the updates

> **NOTE**
>
> *Remember, if this was a production environment, you should store the updates on a non-system drive.*

24. On the Web Server Role (IIS) page, click Next.

25. On the Select Role services page, click Next.

26. On the Confirm installation selections page, click Install.

27. When the installation is done, click Close.

End of exercise.

Exercise 2.2	Configuring WSUS
Overview	After you install WSUS, you must configure WSUS so that it retrieves updates from Microsoft or another WSUS server. You also need to configure WSUS on what updates need to be downloaded and when the downloads should occur.
Completion time	20 minutes

Mindset Question: **After the WSUS server has been installed, it needs to be configured so that it knows where to get the updates from and what to download. If you were getting updates from the Windows Update, what would you need to configure, similarly as you configure Internet Explorer to access the Microsoft Update website?**

1. On Server01, if Server Manager is not open, open Server Manager.

2. At the top of Server Manager, click Tools > Windows Server Update Services.

3. When the Complete WSUS Installation dialog box opens, click Run.

4. Take a screen shot of the Complete WSUS dialog box by pressing Alt+Prt Scr and then paste it into your Lab 2 worksheet file in the page provided by pressing Ctrl+V.

5. When the post-installation successfully is completed, click Close.

6. When the Before You Begin page opens, click Next.

7. On the *Join the Microsoft Update Improvement Program* page, click Next.

8. The Choose Upstream Server page displays, as shown in Figure 2-3. Click *Synchronize from another Windows Server Update Services server*. In the Server name text box, type **server02.contoso.com**. Answer the following question and click Next.

Question 3	*After synchronizing from another WSUS server, what default port is used?*

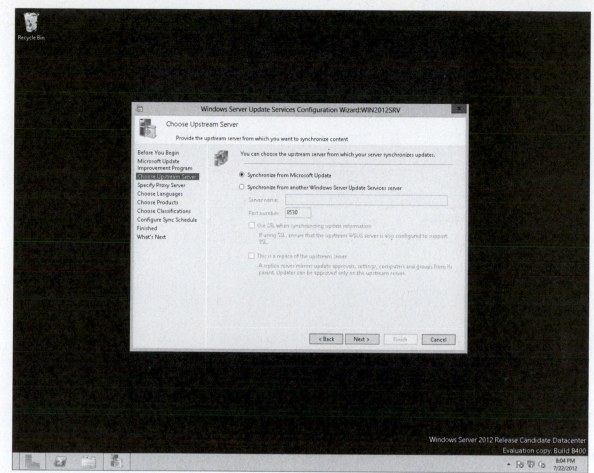

Figure 2-3
Specifying where to get the updates from

9. On the Specify Proxy Server page, click Next.

10. On the Connect to Upstream Server page, click Start Connecting.

11. When the connection is complete, click Next.

12. On the Choose Languages page, choose one language that you need to support, and then click Next.

> **NOTE**
>
> *If you were updating directly from Microsoft, you would choose which products and which classifications to download. However, because you are downloading from another WSUS server, you automatically get the products and classifications used on the upstream server.*

13. On the Set Sync Schedule page (see Figure 2-4), click Next.

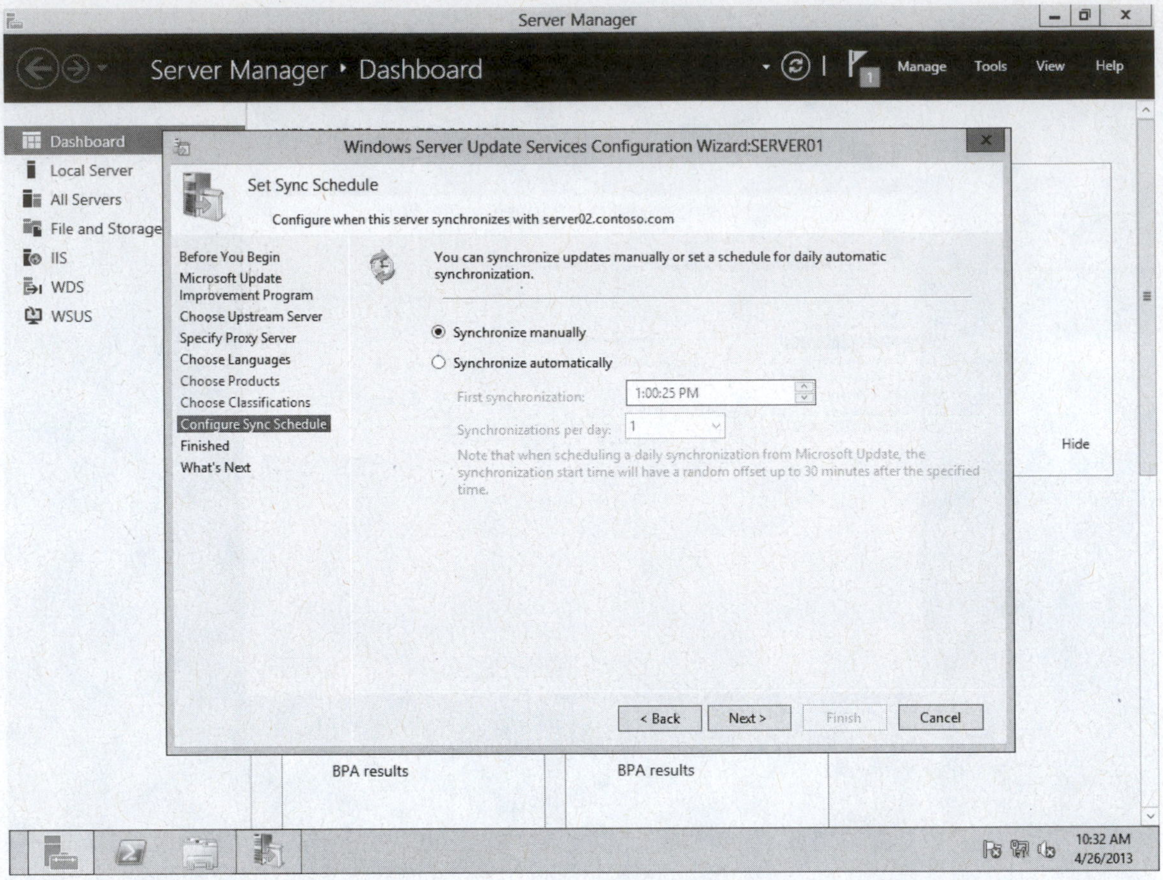

Figure 2-4
Specifying when to sync updates

14. On the Finished page, select Begin initial synchronization and then click Next.

15. On the What's Next page, click Finish.

16. On the WSUS console, expand Server01, and click Synchronizations.

17. Take a screen shot of the Update Services console by pressing Alt+Prt Scr and then paste it into your Lab 2 worksheet file in the page provided by pressing Ctrl+V.

18. Synchronization should already be running. Go to the Update Services console. At the bottom of the left pane, click Options to show the WSUS options. View the available options.

19. In the left pane, expand Computers so that you can see All Computers.

20. Right-click All Computers and choose Add Computer Group. The Add Computer Group dialog box opens.

21. In the Name text box, type the **Group1** in the name text box. Click Add to apply your settings and to close the Add Computer Group dialog box.

End of exercise.

Exercise 2.3	Configuring Clients
Overview	For a client to get updates from a WSUS, the client has to be configured to get updates from WSUS. Therefore, during this exercise, you use group policies to configure Server02 to get updates from Server01.
Completion time	5 minutes

Mindset Question: **You have hundreds of clients that need to get Windows updates. Rather than configure each computer one-by-one, what would be the easiest way to configure all of the computers so that the computers will get the Windows updates that you specify?**

1. Log into RWDC01 as **contoso\administrator** with the password of **Password01**.

2. When the Server Manager opens, open the Tools menu and click Active Directory Users and Computers. The Active Directory Users and Computers console opens.

3. Right-click contoso.com and click New > Organizational Unit. Type **Servers** in the Name text box and click OK.

4. Navigate to and click the Computers OU.

5. Right-click Server02 and click Move.

6. Select Servers and click OK.

7. Close Active Directory Users and Computers.

8. With Server Manager, open the Tools menu and click Group Policy Management. The Group Policy Management console opens.

9. In the tree structure (left pane), navigate to and click Servers.

10. Right-click Servers and click *Create a GPO in this domain, and Link it here*.

11. When the New GPO dialog box opens, type **Server Updates** in the Name text box. Click OK.

12. Right-click Servers Update GPO and click Edit. The Group Policy Editor opens.

13. In Group Policy Object Editor, expand Computer Configuration > Policies > Administrative Templates > Windows Components and click Windows Update, as shown in Figure 2-5.

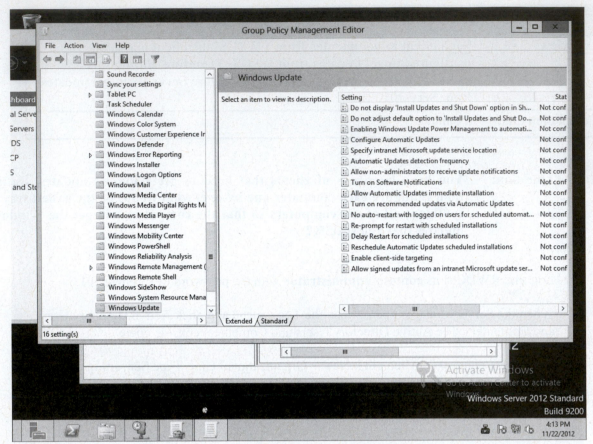

Figure 2-5
Viewing the Windows update options in a GPO

14. In the details pane, double-click *Specify Intranet Microsoft update service location*. The *Specify intranet Microsoft update service location* page displays as shown in Figure 2-6.

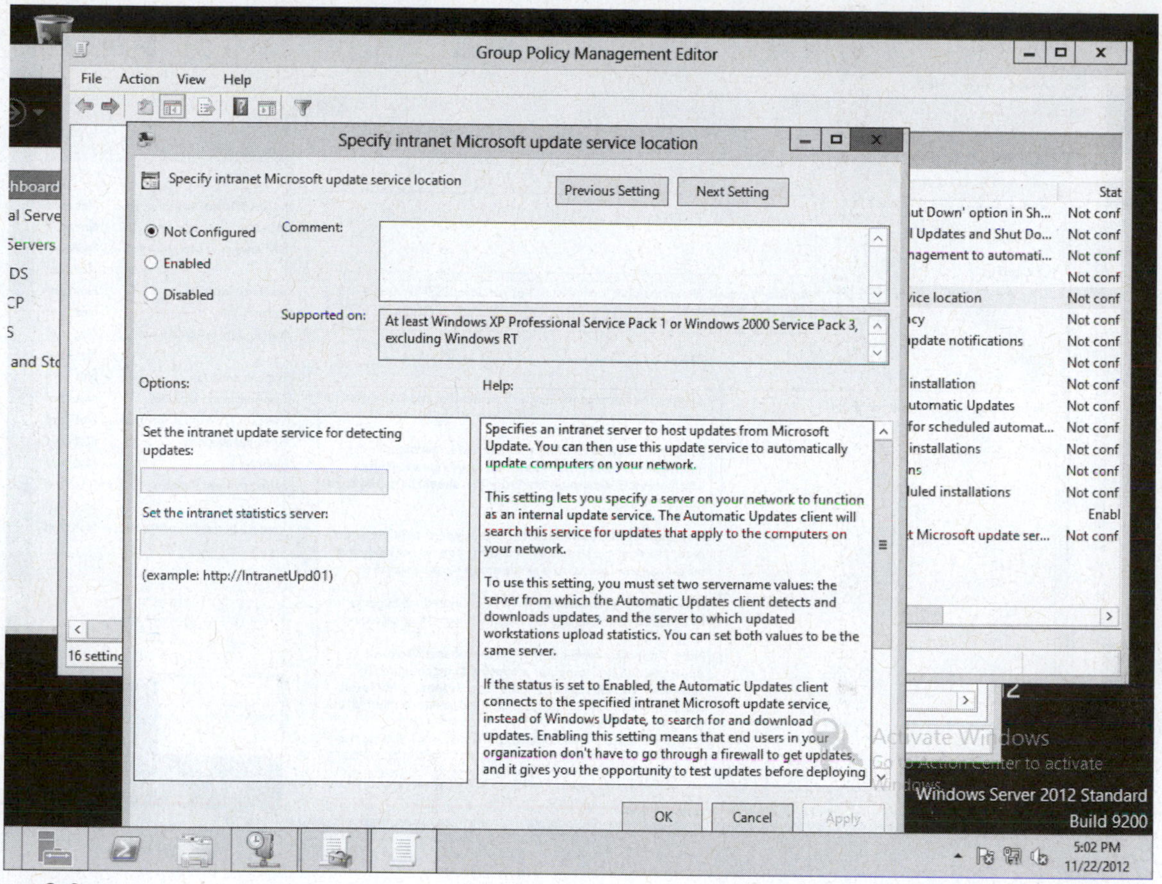

Figure 2-6
Specifying the WSUS URL

15. Select Enabled.

16. In the *Set the intranet update service for detecting updates* text box and in the *Set the intranet statistics server* text box, type **HTTP://Server01:8530**.

17. Click OK to apply your settings and to close the *Specify intranet Microsoft update service location* page.

18. In the details pane, double-click Enable client-side targeting. The Enable client-side targeting page appears (see Figure 2-7).

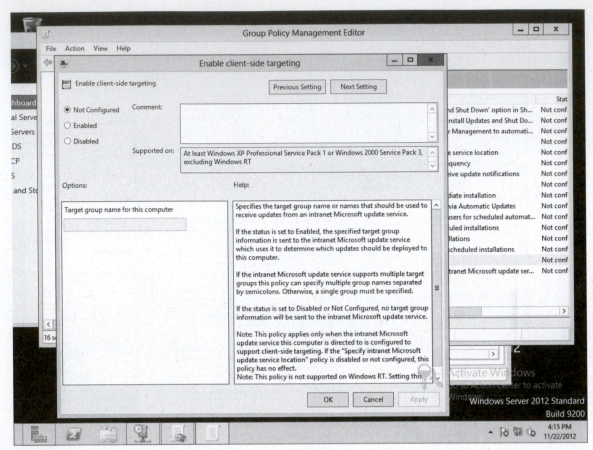

Figure 2-7
Specifying the Computer Group using GPOs

19. Select Enabled and in the *Target group name for this computer* text box, type the **Group1**.

20. Click OK to apply your settings and to close the Enable client-side targeting page.

Question 4	If you don't use group policies to configure clients to use WSUS, how would you configure the system?

End of exercise.

Exercise 2.4	Approving Updates
Overview	The WSUS server has been configured and you have a client that is ready to get updates from the WSUS server. During this exercise, you approve what updates need to be pushed..
Completion time	5 minutes

Mindset Question: **The WSUS server has been configured and the clients have been configured to get updates from the WSUS server. Before you approve updates, what should you do first?**

1. On Server01, go to the Update Services console.

2. In the left pane, expand Servers, expand Server01 and click Updates.

3. Click Updates installed/not applicable under Critical Updates.

4. On the top of the screen, on the Approval drop-down, make sure Unapproved is selected. On the top of the screen, on the Status drop-down menu, make sure Any is selected as shown in Figure 2-8.

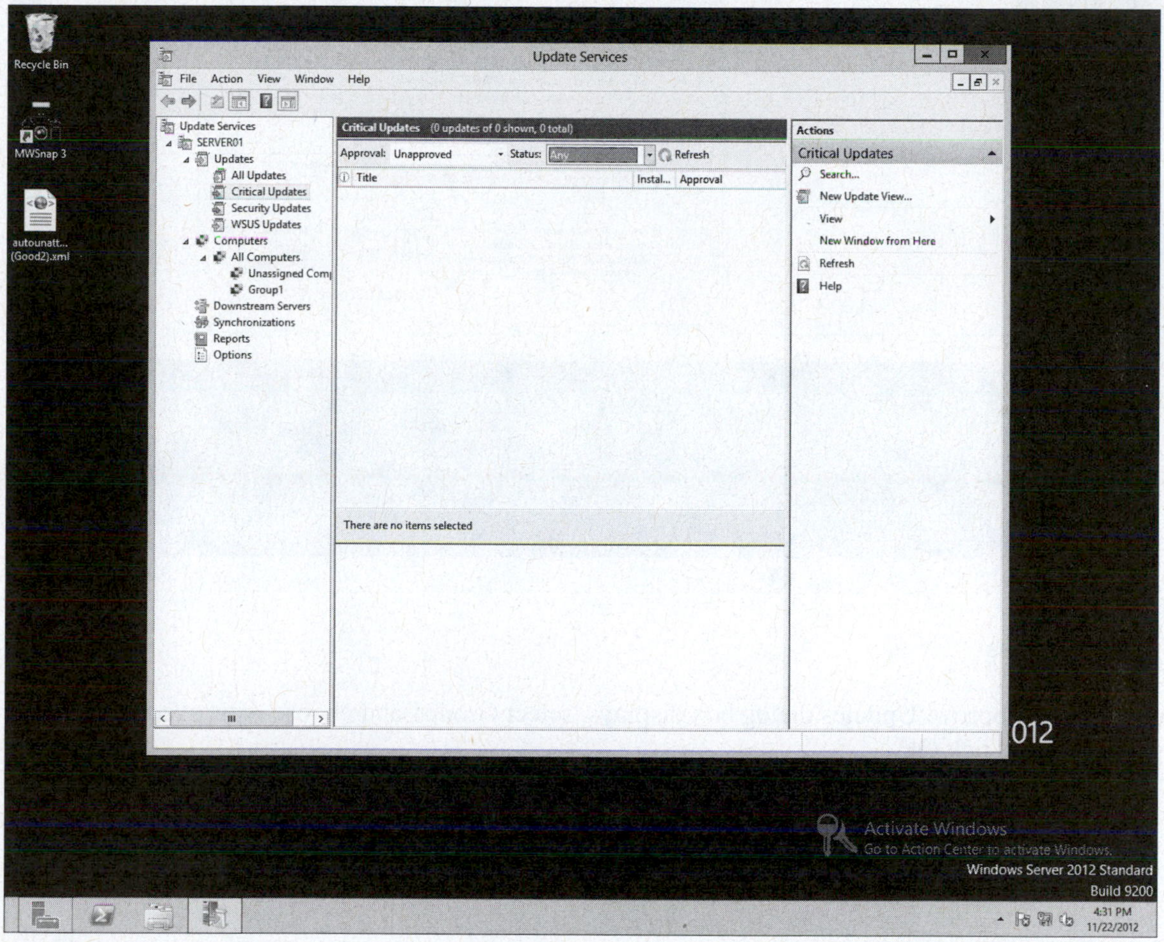

Figure 2-8
Showing unapproved updates

5. Click Refresh to display the updates.

6. To click several updates, hold the Ctrl key and click several updates. When you're finished selecting your updates, release the Ctrl key.

7. Right-click the selected update and choose Approve (see Figure 2-9).

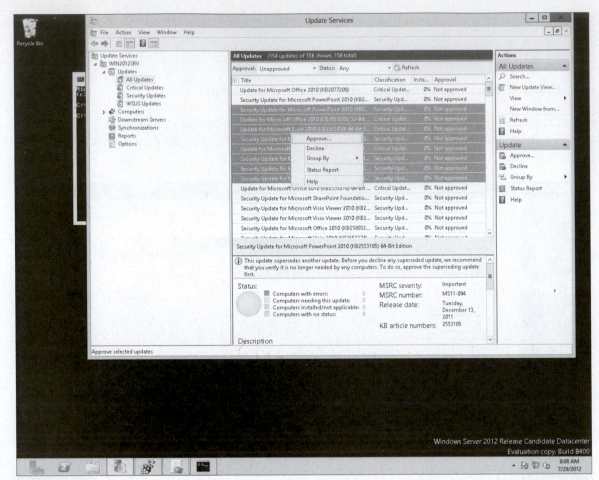

Figure 2-9
Approving updates

8. If the Approve Updates dialog box displays, select Group1 and choose Approved For Install. Click OK.

9. If a license agreement displays, prompting you for an update, click I Accept.

10. Click Close.

End of exercise.

LAB REVIEW QUESTIONS

Completion time	10 minutes

1. In Exercise 2.1, what are the two types of databaes that WSUS support?

2. In Exercise 2.2, what two sources can a WSUS server get updates from?

3. In Exercise 2.3, in WSUS, how do you specify which computers get updates?

4. In Exercise 2.3, what is the easiest way to configure the clients to use a WSUS server?

5. In Exercise 2.3, by default, what is the HTTP and what is the HTTPS URL for WSUS running on Server01. Hint: Look at the IIS Bindings for the WSUS Administration website in IIS.

Lab Challenge	Running WSUS Reports
Overview	To complete this challenge, you will describe at a high level the steps needed to run WSUS reports.
Completion time	10 minutes

You have configured WSUS and the WSUS clients. You have approved updates yesterday and you want to know how the updates are progressing. What do you need to do to view the reports?

Write out the steps you performed to complete the challenge.

End of lab.

LAB 3
MONITORING SERVERS

THIS LAB CONTAINS THE FOLLOWING EXERCISES AND ACTIVITIES:

Exercise 3.1   Using the Event Viewer

Exercise 3.2   Using the Reliability Monitor

Exercise 3.3   Using the Task Manager

Exercise 3.4   Using Resource Monitor

Exercise 3.5   Using the Performance Monitor

Exercise 3.6   Monitoring VMs

Lab Challenge   Using Network Monitor

BEFORE YOU BEGIN

The lab environment consists of student workstations connected to a local area network, along with a server that functions as the domain controller for a domain called *contoso.com*. The computers required for this lab are listed in Table 3-1.

Table 3-1
Computers Required for Lab 3

Computer	Operating System	Computer Name
Server (VM 1)	Windows Server 2012	RWDC01
Server (VM 2)	Windows Server 2012	Server01
Server (VM 3)	Windows Server 2012	Server02

In addition to the computers, you also require the software listed in Table 3-2 to complete Lab 3.

Table 3-2
Software Required for Lab 3

Software	Location
Lab 3 student worksheet	Lab03_worksheet.docx (provided by instructor)

Working with Lab Worksheets

Each lab in this manual requires that you answer questions, take screen shots, and perform other activities that you will document in a worksheet named for the lab, such as Lab03_worksheet.docx. You will find these worksheets on the book companion site. It is recommended that you use a USB flash drive to store your worksheets, so you can submit them to your instructor for review. As you perform the exercises in each lab, open the appropriate worksheet file fill in the required information, and save the file to your flash drive.

After completing this lab, you will be able to:

- Use the Event Viewer to troubleshoot and monitor servers

- Use the Reliability Monitor, to monitor the reliability of a server

- Use Task Manager and Performance Monitor to monitor the performance of a server

Estimated lab time: 120 minutes

Exercise 3.1	Using the Event Viewer
Overview	In this exercise, you use the Event Viewer to view the events stored in the Windows logs. Because there can be thousands of log entires, you learn how to filter the logs so you can concentrate on what you need to focus on, and to set up subscriptions to consolidate the logs onto one server.
Completion time	20 minutes

Mindset Question: **Traditional log files give an administrator insight on what a system or program is doing or any errors that might have occurred. What does Windows use to store Windows logs and how do the logs differ from the traditional log file?**

Looking at Events

1. Log on to the Server01 server using the **Administrator** account and the password **Password01**. The Server Manager console opens.

2. When Server Manager opens, open the Tools menu and select Event Viewer. The Event Viewer console opens.

3. Expand the Windows Logs folder and click the System log. The contents of the log appear in the detail pane.

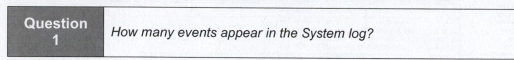

Question 1	How many events appear in the System log?

4. From the Action menu, select Filter Current Log. The Filter Current Log dialog box appears.

5. In the Event Level area, select the Critical and Warning check boxes. Then click OK.

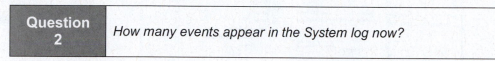

Question 2	How many events appear in the System log now?

6. From the Action menu, select Create Custom View. The Create Custom View dialog box appears.

7. In the Logged drop-down list, select Last 7 days.

8. In the Event Level area, select the Critical and Warning check boxes.

9. Leave the By log option selected and, in the Event logs drop-down list, select the Application, Security, and System check boxes, as shown in Figure 3-1.

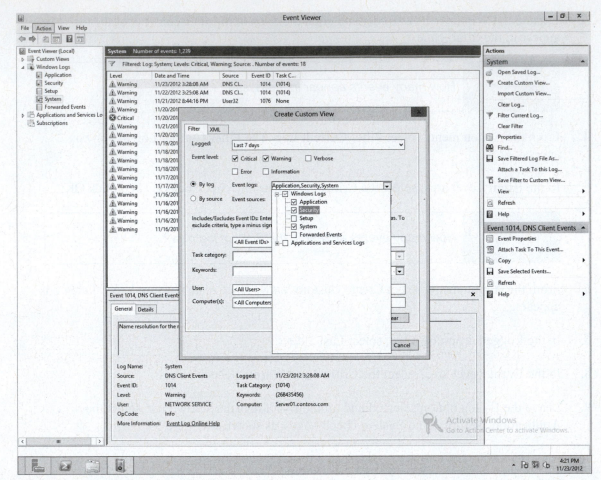

Figure 3-1
Selecting the type of logs

10. Click OK. The Save Filter to Custom View dialog box appears.

11. In the Name text box, type **Critical & Warning**. Then click OK. The Critical & Warning view you just created appears in the Custom Views folder.

Question 3	*How many events appear in the Critical & Warning custom view?*

12. Right-click System (under Windows Logs) and click Clear Filter.

13. Leave the Event Viewer console open for the next exercise.

Adding a Task to an Event

1. Using Server Manger, open the Tools menu and click Services. The Services console opens.

2. Scroll down and right-click Print Spooler and click Restart.

3. Go back to the Event Viewer. You should have two new entries in the System Logs with the Event ID of 7036. The one should say "The Print Spooler service entered the stopped state," (as shown in Figure 3-2). Right-click this event and click Attach Task to This Event.

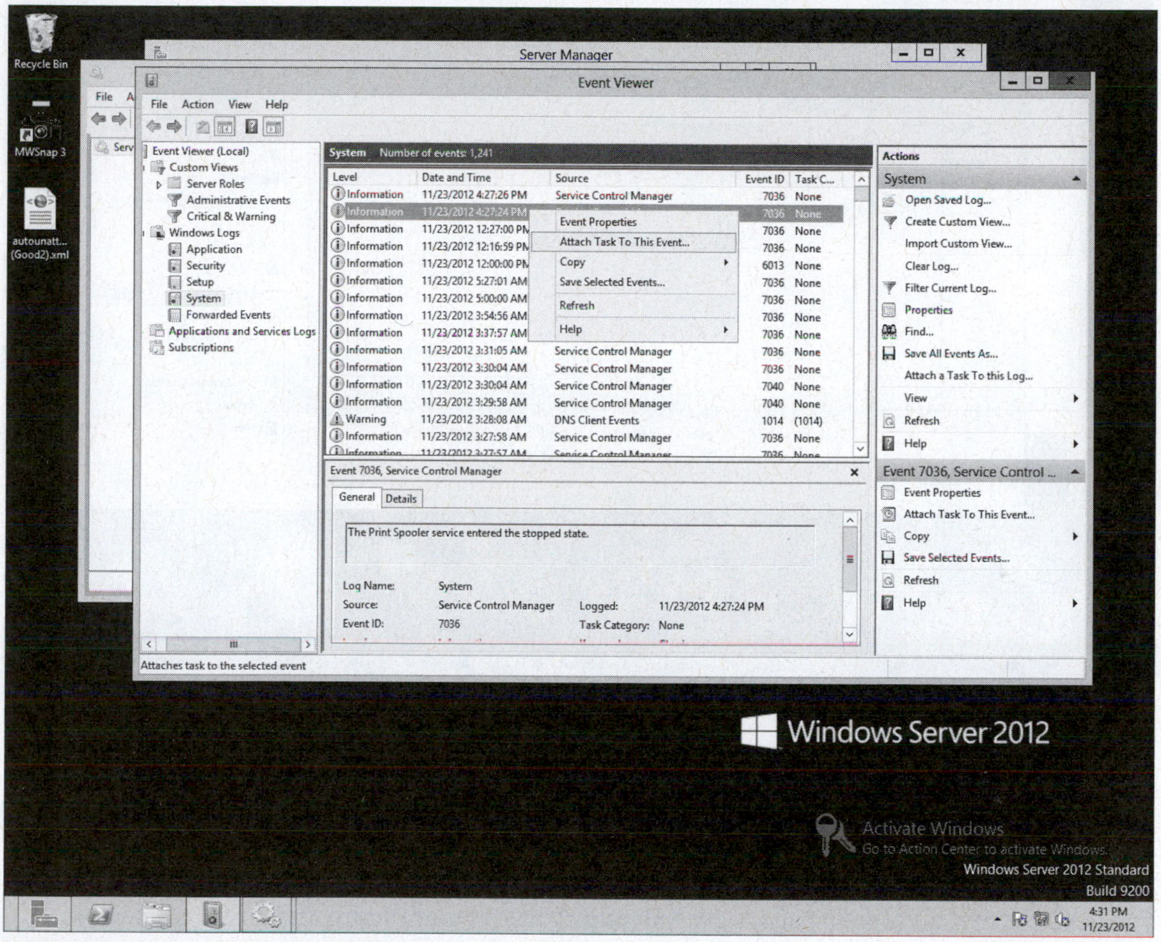

Figure 3-2
Attaching a task to an event

4. When the Create Basic Task Wizard starts, click Next.

5. When the *When a Specified Event Is Logged* page opens, click Next.

6. On the Action page (see Figure 3-3), make sure Start a program is selected and click Next.

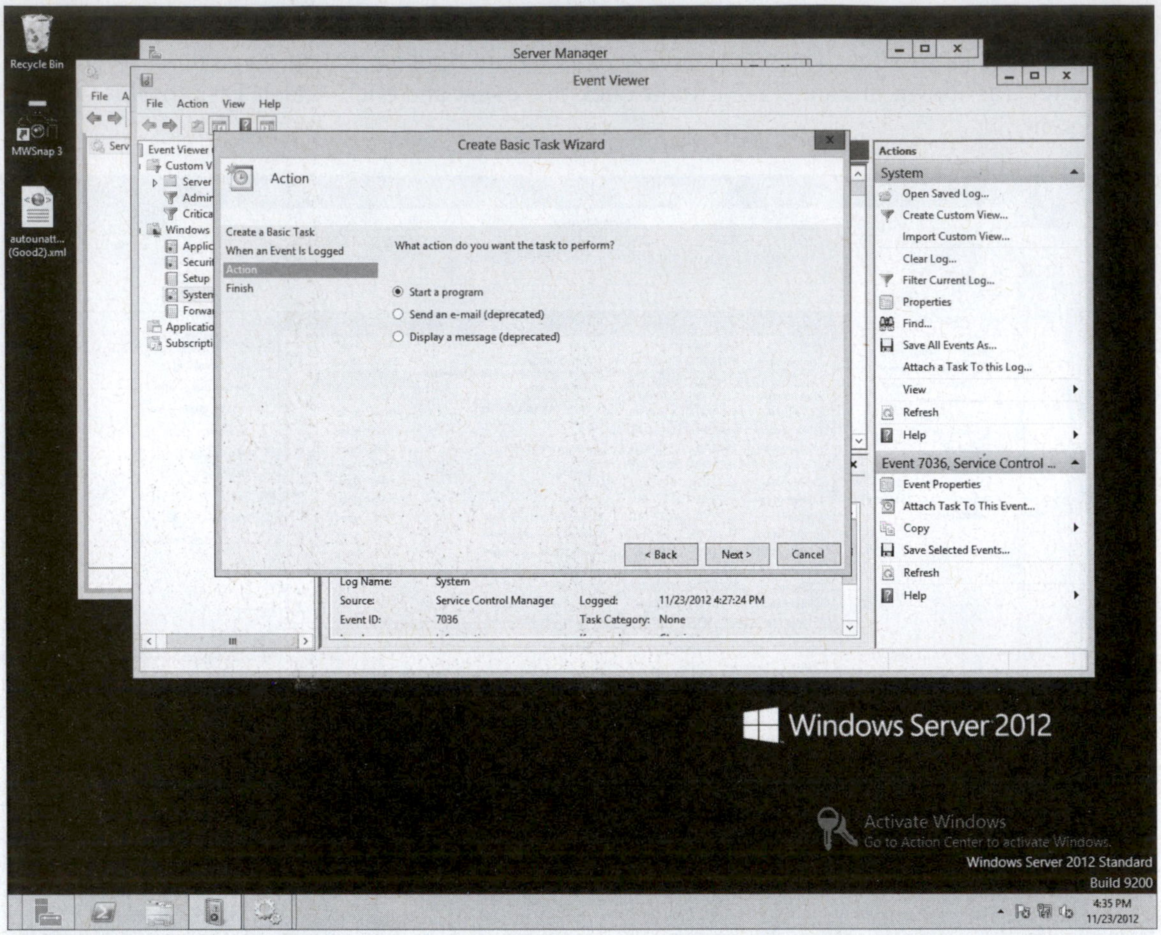

Figure 3-3
Selecting the task to perform

7. On the Start a Program page, type **Notepad** in the Program/script text box, (as shown in Figure 3-4). Click Next.

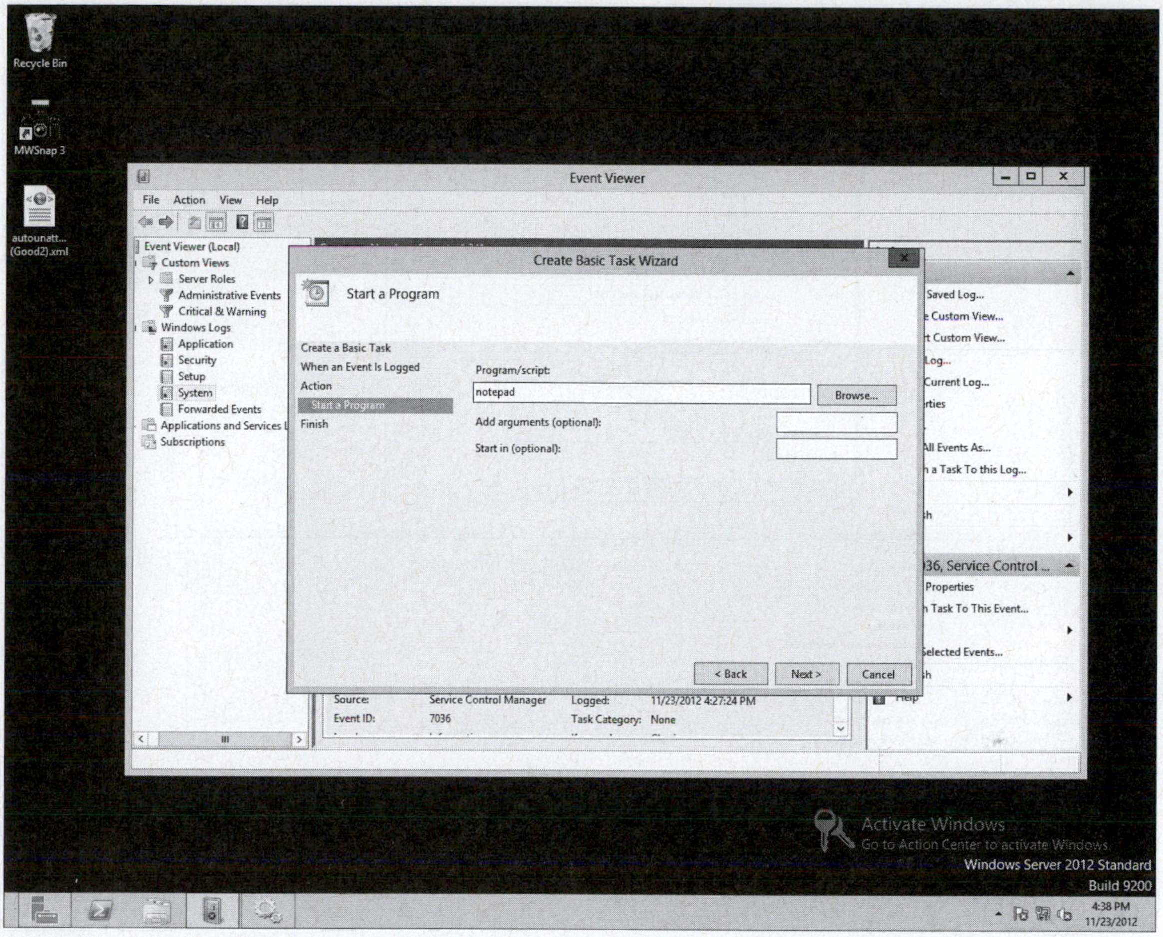

Figure 3-4
Specifying a program to start

8. On the Summary page, click Finish.

9. When an Event Viewer dialog box appears, click OK.

10. Close the Event Viewer.

11. Go back to the Services console. Right-click the Print Spooler service and click Restart. Notepad should have opened.

12. Go back to the Server Manager. Open the Tools menu and click Task Scheduler. Task Scheduler opens.

13. Expand the Task Scheduler Library and click Event Viewer Tasks.

14. Right-click the *System_Service Control Manager_7036* task and click Delete, as shown in Figure 3-5.

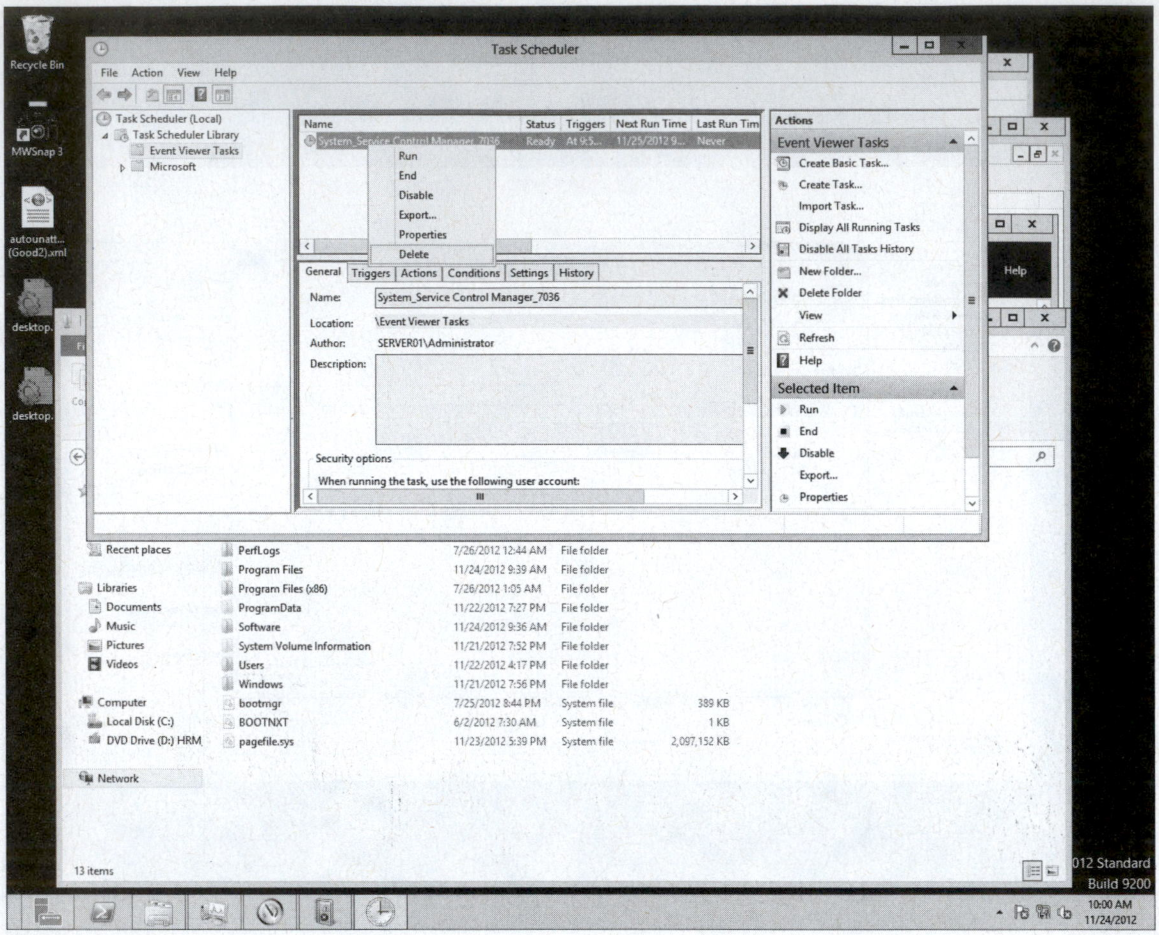

Figure 3-5
Deleting a task from Task Scheduler

15. When it asks if you want to delete this task, click Yes.

16. Close Task Scheduler, the Services console, and Notepad.

Creating a Subscription

1. Log on to the Server02 using the **contoso\Administrator** account and the password **Password01**. The Server Manager console opens.

2. On Server02, right-click Start and choose Command Prompt (Admin).

3. At the command prompt, execute the following command:

```
winrm quickconfig
```

It is fine that the service is already running.

4. To add the collecting computer name to the Administrators group, execute the following command:

```
net localgroup "Administrators" Server01$@contoso.com /add
```

5. If a message appears, indicating that changes must be made, type **Y** and then press Enter.

6. Open the Event Viewer.

7. Click Subscriptions. When it asks if you want to start the service and configure the service to automatically start, click Yes.

8. Close the Command Prompt window.

9. On Server01, right-click Start and choose Command Prompt (Admin).

10. On Server01, at the command prompt, execute the following command:

```
wecutil qc
```

11. If you are asked if you would like to proceed, type **Y** and press the Enter key.

12. Close the Command Prompt window.

13. Open Event Viewer.

14. On the Event Viewer, right-click Subscriptions and choose Create Subscription (see Figure 3-6). The Subscription Properties dialog box opens.

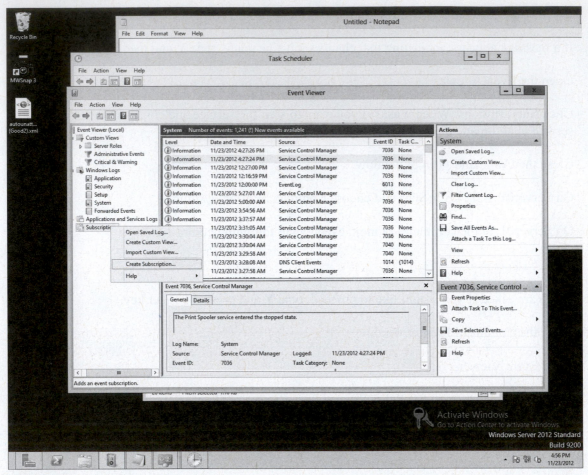

Figure 3-6
Creating a subscription

15. In the Subscription name text box (as shown in Figure 3-7), type **Server02**.

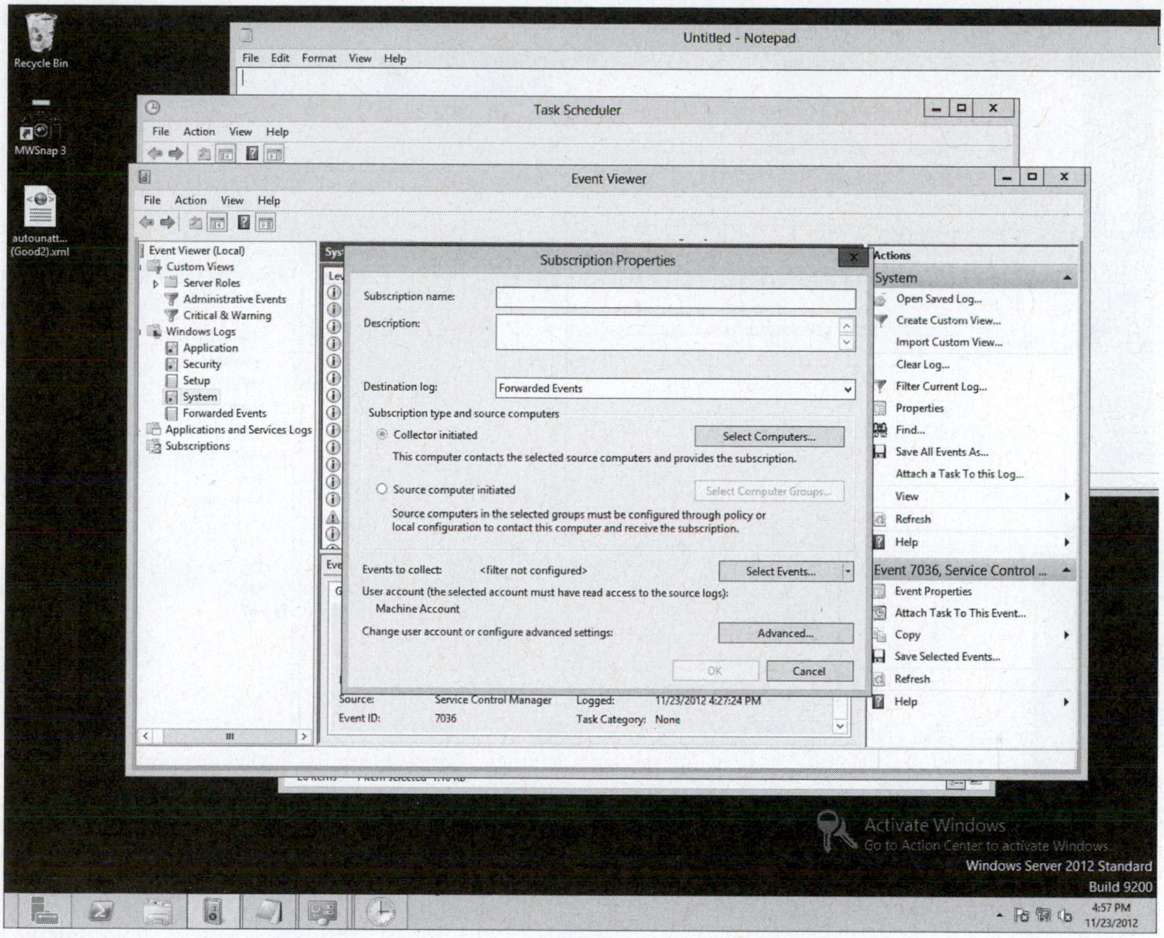

Figure 3-7
Specifying the Subscription Properties

16. Click Select Computers. The Computers dialog box opens.

17. Click Add Domain Computers. Type **Server02** in the Enter the object name to select text box and click OK.

18. If it asks you to specify a network password, use the username and password for contoso.com\administrator.

19. Click OK to close Computers dialog box.

20. Click Select Events. The Query Filter dialog box opens.

21. For Event Logs, click System logs.

22. Under Event level, type **7036** in the Includes/Excludes Event ID: text box, (as shown in Figure 3-8). Click OK to close Query Filter dialog box.

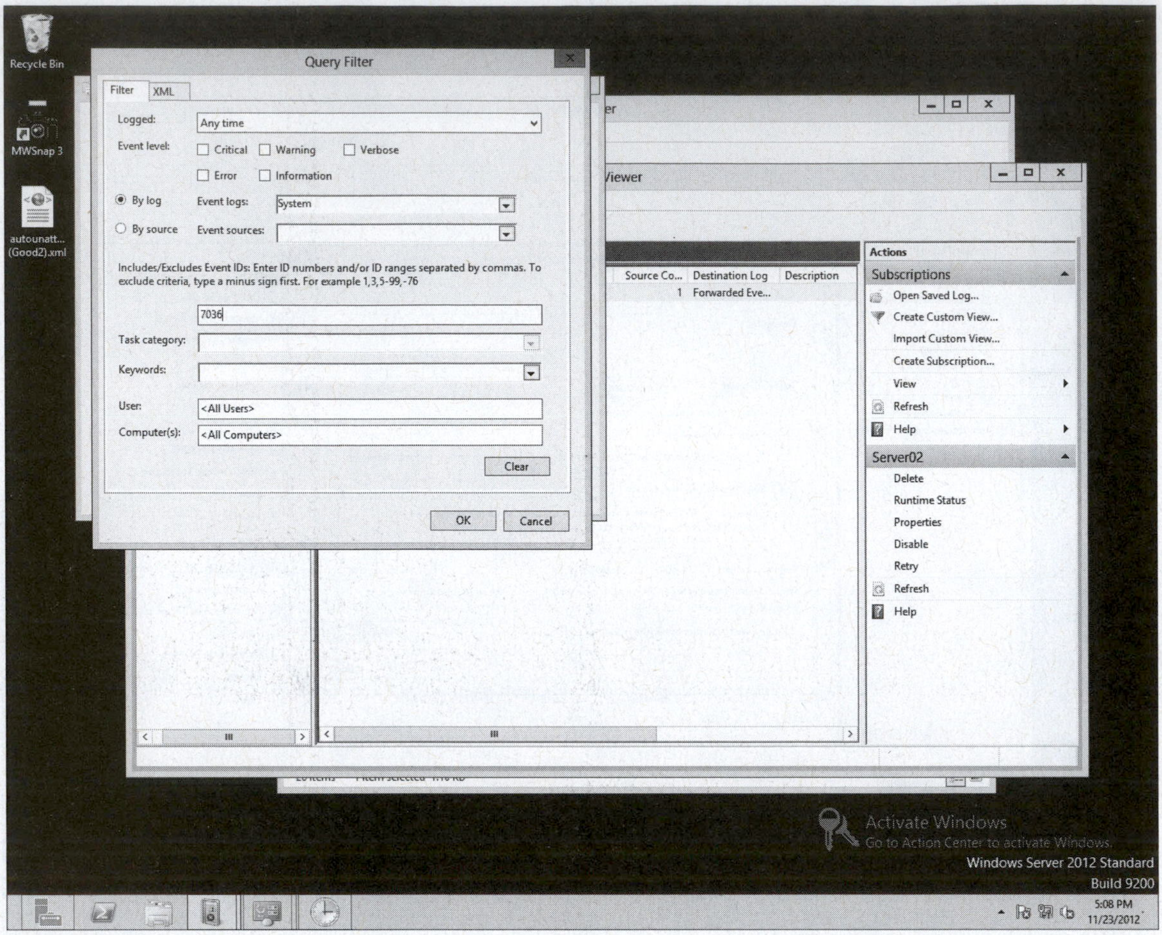

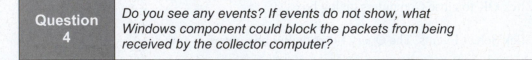

Figure 3-8
Specifying the Event to filter

23. Click OK to close the Subscription Properties dialog box.

24. On Server02, open the Services console. Right-click Print Spooler and click Restart. Close the Services console.

25. Go back to Server01. On the Event Viewer, click Forwarded Events under Windows Logs.

Question 4	*Do you see any events? If events do not show, what Windows component could block the packets from being received by the collector computer?*

Question 5	*If you check the configuration of the source computer and the collector computer and you checked the firewall, but you don't see events, what might cause you not to see the events?*

26. If events do not display immediately, check later toward the end of the lab to see if the events are displayed. If it still fails after a time, disable the Windows firewall on both servers and try again.

27. Close the Event Viewer and the Services console on Server02.

28. Close the Event Viewer on Server01.

End of exercise.

Exercise 3.2	Using the Reliability Monitor
Overview	A hidden tool that can determine the reliability of a system, including allowing you to see whether any recent changes have been made to the system itself, is the Reliability Monitor. During this exercise, you open the Reliability Monitor to check the status of the computer.
Completion time	15 minutes

1. If you are not logged into Server01, log on to the Server01 server using the **Contoso\Administrator** account and the password **Password01**. The Server Manager console opens.

2. Open the Start Menu. Type **regedit** and press the Enter key. The Registry Editor opens.

3. In the left pane, navigate to the *HKEY_LOCAL_MACHINE\SOFTWARE\Microsoft\Reliability Analysis\WMI* node.

4. In the right pane, double-click WMIEnable. In the Value data text box, type **1**, as shown in Figure 3-9. Press the OK button.

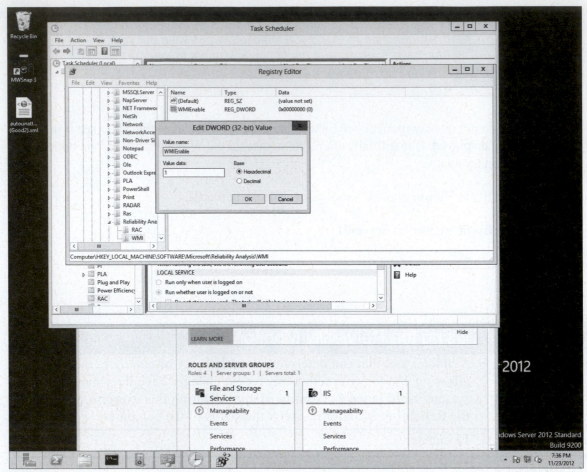

Figure 3-9
Changing the WMI Enable value

5. Close the Registry Editor.

6. On Server Manager, open the Tools menu and click Task Scheduler. The Task Scheduler opens.

7. In the left pane, navigate to the Task Scheduler > Task Scheduler Library > Microsoft > Windows > RAC.

8. Right-click RacTask and click Enable, as shown in Figure 3-10.

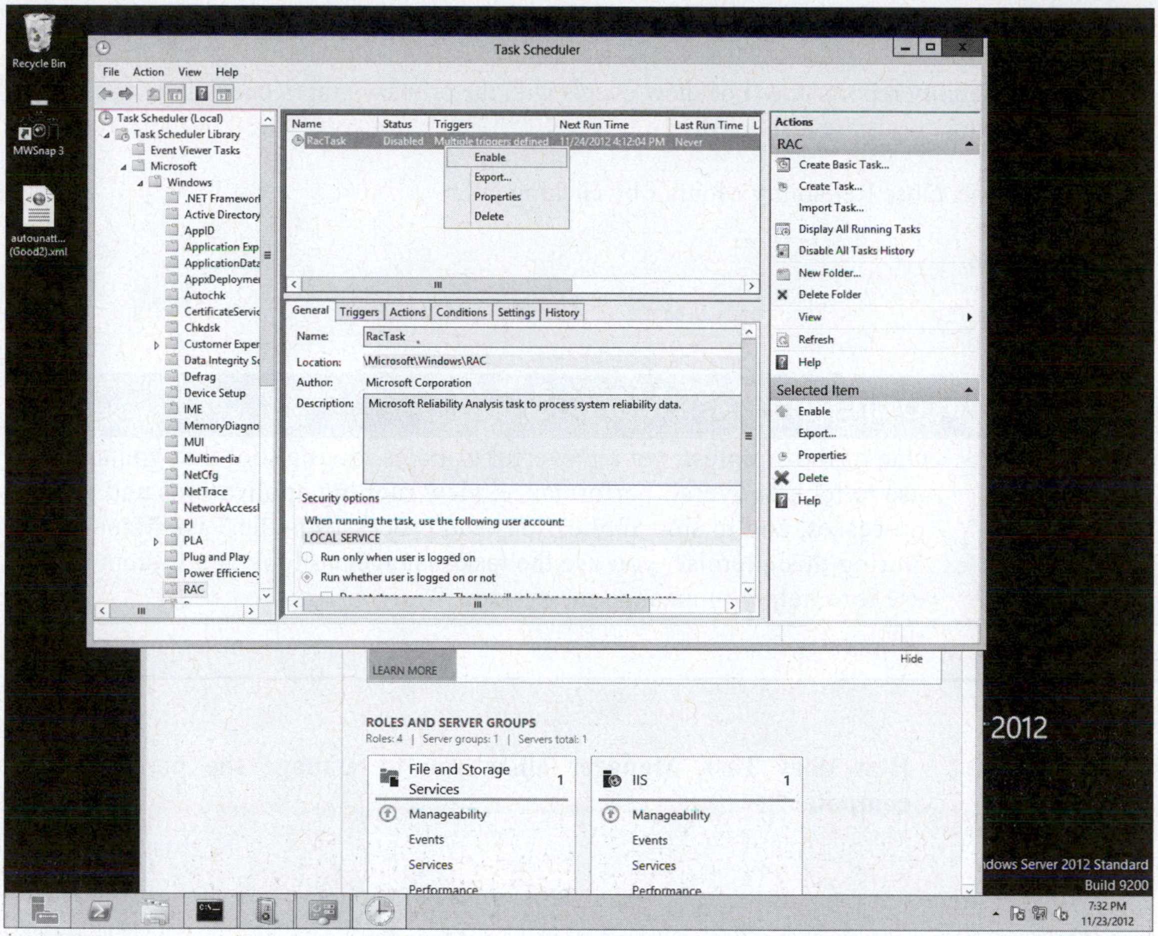

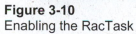

Figure 3-10
Enabling the RacTask

9. Right-click RacTask and click Run.

10. Close the Task Scheduler.

11. Open the Start Menu. Type **perfmon /rel** and press the Enter key. The Reliability Monitor opens.

Question 6	*Do you have any events? If you don't have any events, why are the events not displayed?*

12. At the bottom of the screen, click View all problem reports.

Question 7	*Were there any problems reported?*

13. Click OK to close the Problem Reports window.

14. If the reliability reports does not show events with the primary graph, check later to see whether any events are displayed.

15. When done, close Reliability Monitor by clicking OK.

End of exercise.

Exercise 3.3	Using the Task Manager
Overview	One of the simplest, yet a powerful troubleshooting tool that you can use to look at overall performance, view running applications and processes, and to stop applications and processes is the Task Manager. During this exercise, you use the task manager to look at a system and use it to help you manage the system.
Completion time	15 minutes

Mindset Question: **How does Task Manager allow you to manage the performance of a computer?**

1. On Server01, right-click the Task bar and click Task Manager.

Question 8	*What applications are running?*

Question 9	*What tabs are shown?*

2. Click the More Details.

Question 10	*What tabs are shown?*

3. If Server Manager is not open, open Server Manager.

4. Open WordPad.

Question 11	In the Apps section, what processes are used for the Server Manager and Wordpad?

5.   Click Fewer details.

6.   Right-click Windows Wordpad Application and click End Task.

7.   Click More details.

8.   Right-click Server Manager and click Open file location. The System32 folder opens.

9.   Close the System32 folder.

Question 12	How much memory is Server Manager using?

10. Right-click the Name title at the top of the first column and click Process name (as shown in Figure 3-11).

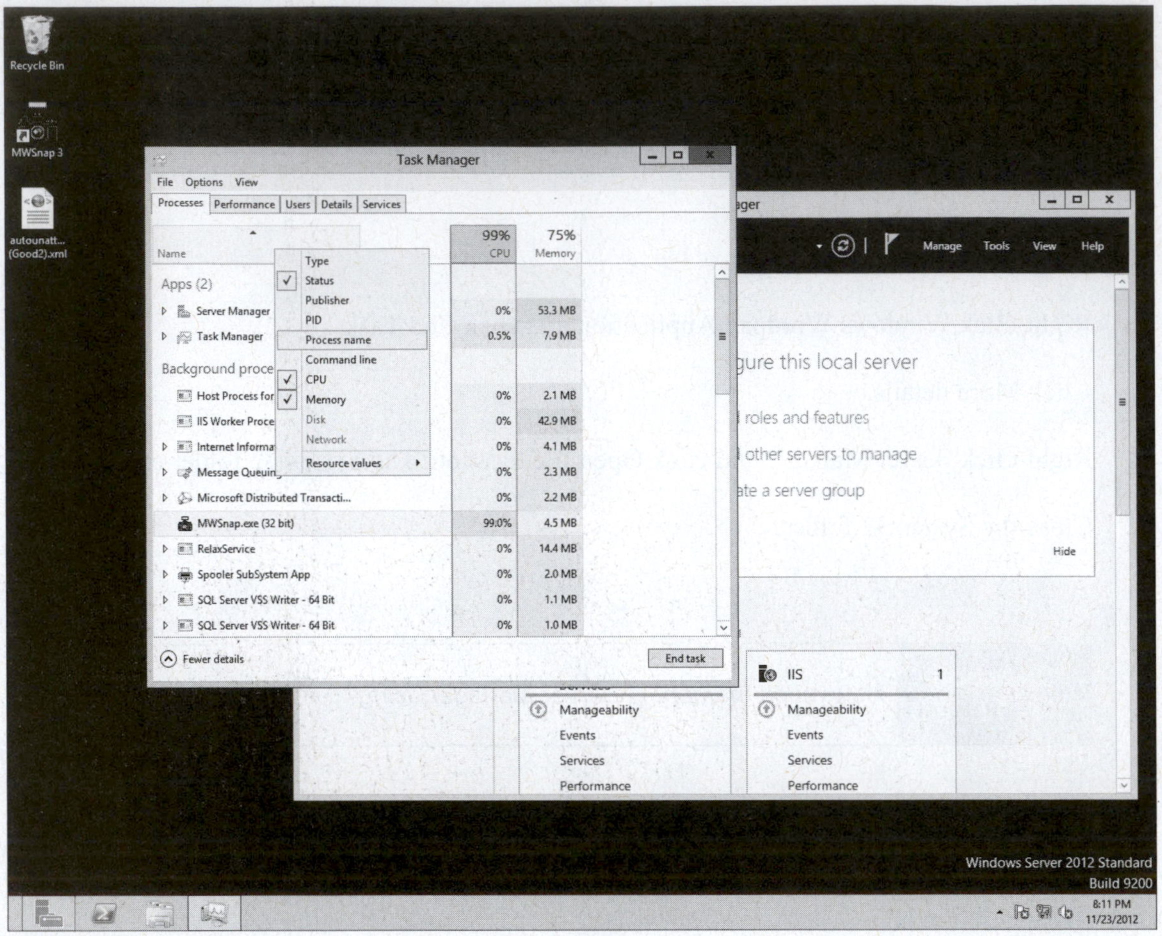

Figure 3-11
Adding the Process name so that it can also be displayed

11. Right-click Server Manager and click End Task.

12. Click the Performance tab.

Question 13	What are the primary systems that you can monitor with Task Manager?

Question 14	What system is missing in Task Manager that will greatly affect system performance?

Question 15	How many virtual processors is Server01 using?

13. Click Memory and Ethernet to view what each option has to offer.

14. Click the Users tab.

15. Expand Administrator to display the programs and processes being executed by the administrator.

16. To see a detailed list of all processes running, click the Details tab.

17. To display additional columns, right-click the Name column title and click Select columns.

18. When the Select columns dialog box opens, click to select Session ID and Threads. Click OK.

19. To sort by components that make up the most memory, click the Memory (private work set) title.

20. From time to time, a program or action might cause Windows Explorer to stop functioning. In these cases, you can use Task Manager to stop and restart Explorer. Therefore, find and right-click explorer.exe, and click End Task.

21. When it asks if you want to end explorer.exe, click End process.

22. Open the File menu and click Run new task.

23. When the Create new task, type **explorer** in the open text box and click OK.

24. To view the current services, click the Services tab.

25. Close Task Manager.

End of exercise.

Exercise 3.4	Using Resource Monitor
Overview	In this exercise, you use Resource Manager to monitor server resources.
Completion time	5 minutes

Mindset Question: **What are the four primary systems that affect overall system performance and how does one of these systems cause a bottleneck?**

1. On Server01, open the Start Menu. Type **resource monitor** and press the Enter key. The Resource Monitor opens.

Question 16	What are the primary systems that you can monitor with Resource Monitor?

2. Click the CPU tab.

3. To sort the processes alphabetically, click the Image title at the top of the first column in the Processes section.

4. Click the Memory tab.

Question 17	What process is using the most memory?

5. Click the Disk tab.

Question 18	What process is using the disk the most?

6. Click the Network tab.

Question 19	What ports is WDSServer using

7. Close the Resource Monitor.

   End of exercise.

Exercise 3.5	Using the Performance Monitor
Overview	Although the Task Manager and Resource Manager gave you a quick look at your system performance, Performance Monitor allows you to thoroughly exam the performance of a system. During this exercise, you open Performance and show various counters over a period of time.
Completion time	20 minutes

Mindset Question: **Both Performance Monitor and Task Manager can help you view the systems current performance. What are the advantages of Task Manager and what are the advantages of Performance Monitoring when looking at performance?**

Using Counters with Performance Monitor

1. On Server01, open Server Manager. Server Manager console opens.

2. Click Tools > Performance Monitor.

3. Browse to and click Monitoring Tools\Performance Monitor.

4. Click % Processor Time at the bottom of the screen. To remove the counter, click the Delete (red X) button at the top of the Window.

5. Click the Add (green plus (+) sign) button in the toolbar. The Add Counters dialog box appears.

6. Under Available counters, expand Processor, click % Processor Time, and click Show description, as shown in Figure 3-12. Read the description for % Processor Time.

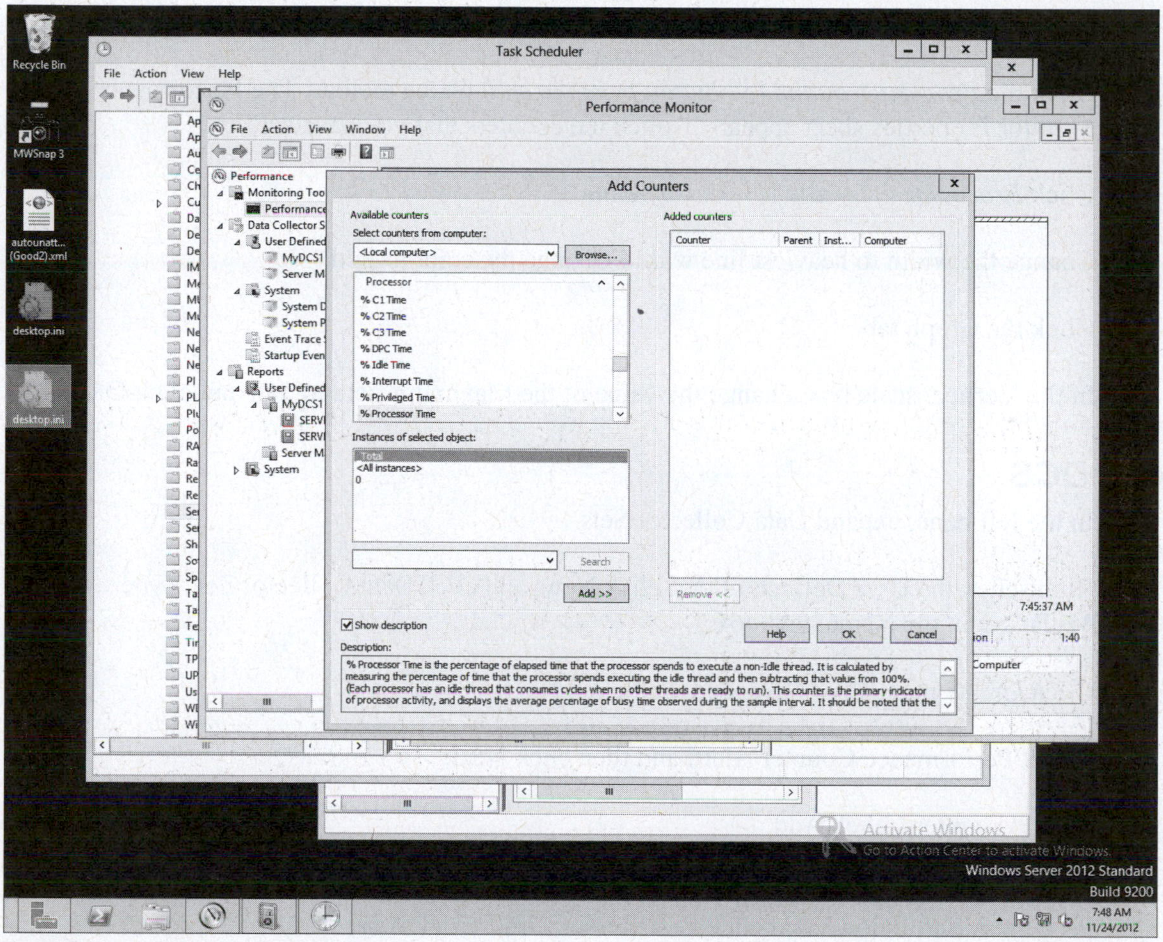

Figure 3-12
Looking at a description of a counter

7. Click Add. % Processor Time should show up in the Added counters section.

8. Under Available Counters, expand the Server Work Queues and click the Queue Length counter. Under Insces of selected objects, click 0. Then click Add.

9. Add the following counters:

   - System: Processor Queue Length
   - Memory: Page Faults/Sec
   - Memory: Pages/Sec
   - PhysicalDisk (_Total): Current Disk Queue Length

10. Click OK to close the Add Counters dialog box.

11. Open Task Manager, and close Task Manager. You should see a spike in CPU usage.

12. At the top of the graph, you see a toolbar with 13 buttons. Click the down arrow of the Change graph type (third button), and click Histogram bar.

13. Change the graph type to Report.

14. Change back to the Line graph.

15. Click the *Properties button (5th button from the end)* on the toolbar. The Performance Monitor Properties sheet appears. Notice the counters that you have selected.

16. Click *Processor (_Total)\%Processor Time*.

17. Change the width to heaviest line width. Change the color to Red.

18. Click the Graph tab.

19. In the Vertical scale box, change the value of the Maximum field to **200** and click OK.

Using DCS

1. In the left pane, expand Data Collector Sets.

2. Right-click the User Defined folder, click New, and click Data Collector Set. Type **MyDCS1** in the Name: text box.

3. Click Create manually (Advanced) and click Next.

4. Select Performance Counter Alert, and then click Next.

5. To add counters, click Add.

6. Under Available Counters, expand the Processor node by clicking the down arrow next to Processor. Scroll down and click %Processor Time. Click Add.

7. Add the following counters.

   - Server Work Queues: Queue Length counter
   - System: Processor Queue Length
   - Memory: Page Faults/Sec

- Memory: Pages/Sec
- PhysicalDisk (_Total): Current Disk Queue Length

8. Click OK, then Next.

9. Click Finish.

10. Right-click MyDCS1 and click Start.

11. Let it run for at least two minutes.

12. Right-click MyDCS1 and click Stop.

13. Open Windows Explorer and navigate to c:\PerfLogs\Admin\MyDCS1. Then open the folder that was just created.

14. Double-click DataCollector01.blg. The Performance Monitor graph opens.

Question 20	*Now that the DCS has been created, what advantages does the MyDCS1 have?*

15. Take a screen shot of the Performance Monitor window by pressing Alt+Prt Scr and then paste it into your Lab 3 worksheet file in the page provided by pressing Ctrl+V.

16. Close the Performance Monitor graph and the MyDCS1 folder.

17. Close Performance Monitor.

End of exercise.

Exercise 3.6	Monitoring VMs
Overview	If you have a physical server with multiple virtual machines, you need to ensure that one virtual machine does not consume too much assigned resources. Therefore, during this exercise, you use PowerShell commands to view resource metering.
Completion time	5 minutes

Mindset Question: **Users are complaining that a server is running slow. What tools would you use to determine whether the VM is overworked or the host is overworked.**

NOTE	*To restart this lab, you must sign off and then sign on again.*

> **NOTE**
>
> *If you do not have access to the hosting server that is running Hyper-V, you will not be able to perform this exercise.*

1. On Student01 (the Hyper-V hosting server), click the PowerShell button on the Task bar.

2. To enable Hyper-V resource metering, run the followng command:

    ```
    Get-VM -ComputerName StudentXX | Enable-VMResourceMetering
    ```

    whereas *XX* is your student number.

3. By default, the collection interval for Hyper-V metering data is one hour. To change the interval to one minute, execute the following command:

    ```
    Set-vmhost -computername StudentXX
    -ResourceMeteringSaveInterval 00:01:00
    ```

    whereas *XX* is your student number.

4. To get all VMs metering data for a host, execute the following command:

    ```
    Get-VM -ComputerName StudentXX | Measure-VM
    ```

    whereas *XX* is your student number.

5. Close PowerShell.

End of exercise.

LAB REVIEW QUESTIONS

Completion time   10 minutes

1. In Exercise 3.1, a busy server over a significant period of time will have hundreds, or even thousands, of events in the Event Viewer logs. What do you need to do when scanning through the event viewer looking for certain relevant events?

2. In Exercise 3.1, what can you use to have one server catch errors from multiple servers that are displayed in the Event Viewer?

3. In Exercise 3.2, what program allows you to see a history of recent changes?

4. In Exercise 3.3, what is a powerful tool that allows you to monitor current running programs and processes and allows you to stop those programs and processes?

5. In Exercise 3.4, what program allows you to monitor the four primary systems that affect the overall system performance?

6.   In Exercise 3.5, why did you want to create Data Collector Sets?

7.   In Exercise 3-6, what did you use to monitor the resources running VMs on Hyper-V?

Lab Challenge	Using Network Monitor
Overview	To complete this challenge, you must demonstrate to use network monitor. The NM32_x64 is located in the \\rwdc01\software folder.
Completion time	20 minutes

You want to look at what steps make a DHCP server work. Therefore, on Server02, you decide to install Microsoft Network Monitor 3.4. You want to capture the packets being sent to and from Server02 and filter the packets to only show you the DNS when using the `nslookup server01` command. The Network Monitor installation program should be on the RWDC01 server in C:\Software folder.

Write out the steps you performed to complete the challenge.

End of lab.

LAB 4
CONFIGURING DISTRIBUTED FILE SYSTEM (DFS)

THIS LAB CONTAINS THE FOLLOWING EXERCISES AND ACTIVITIES:

Exercise 4.1   Installing DFS

Exercise 4.2   Configuring DFS Namespace

Exercise 4.3   Configuring DFS Replication

Lab Challenge   Create a Fault-Tolerant Shared Folder

BEFORE YOU BEGIN

The lab environment consists of student workstations connected to a local area network, along with a server that functions as the domain controller for a domain called *contoso.com*. The computers required for this lab are listed in Table 4-1.

Table 4-1
Computers Required for Lab 4

Computer	*Operating System*	*Computer Name*
Server (VM 1)	Windows Server 2012	RWDC01
Server (VM 2)	Windows Server 2012	Server01
Server (VM 3)	Windows Server 2012	Server02

In addition to the computers, you also require the software listed in Table 4-2 to complete Lab 4.

Table 4-2
Software Required for Lab 4

Software	Location
Lab 8 student worksheet	Lab04_worksheet.docx (provided by instructor)

Working with Lab Worksheets

Each lab in this manual requires that you answer questions, take screen shots, and perform other activities that you will document in a worksheet named for the lab, such as Lab04_worksheet.docx. You will find these worksheets on the book companion site. It is recommended that you use a USB flash drive to store your worksheets, so you can submit them to your instructor for review. As you perform the exercises in each lab, open the appropriate worksheet file fill in the required information, and save the file to your flash drive.

After completing this lab, you will be able to:

- Install DFS

- Implement and configure DFS namespace

- Implement and configure DFS replication

- Use DFS for fault tolerant shared folders

Estimated lab time: 60 minutes

Exercise 4.1	Installing DFS
Overview	In this exercise, you install DFS (namespace and replication) on Server01 and Server02. In the following exercises, you configure DFS.
Completion time	10 minutes

1. Log on to the Server01 server using the **Contoso\Administrator** account and the password **Password01**. The Server Manager console opens.

2. At the top of Server Manager, select Manage and click Add Roles and Features. The Add Roles and Feature Wizard opens.

3. On the Before you begin page, click Next.

4. Select *Role-based or feature-based installation* and then click Next.

5. When asks what server to select, click Next.

6. Scroll down and expand File and Storage Services and then expand File and iSCSI Services. Select File Server (if not already installed), DFS Namespace, and DFS Replication. When asked to add features to DFS Namespace, click Add Features.

7. When you are back on the Select server roles page, click Next.

8. On the Select features page, click Next.

9. On the Confirm installation selections, click Install.

10. When the installation is complete, click the Close button.

11. Repeat the process to install File Server, DFS Namespace, and DFS replication on Server02.

End of exercise.

Exercise 4.2	Configuring DFS Namespace
Overview	During this exercise, you create several shared folders and you link them together with DFS Namespace
Completion time	25 minutes

Mindset Question: **You work for a corporation that has several file servers with multiple shared folders. You want to make it easier for users to access the shared folders. What can you do?**

1. On Server01, open Windows Explorer and create **C:\Share1** and **C:\Share2** folders.

2. Right-click Share1 and click Properties. The Properties dialog box opens.

3. Click the Sharing tab and click Advanced Sharing.

4. Click Share this folder check box.

5. Click Permissions. Click Allow Full Control for Everyone. Click OK to close the Permissions dialog box.

Question 1	Because we allow everyone full control, how do you make sure that the shared files are secure?

6. Click OK to close Advanced Sharing dialog box and click Close to close the Share1 Properties dialog box.

7. On Server01, repeat the process to share Share2.

8. On Server02, open Windows Explorer and create **C:\Share1** and **C:\Share2** folders.

9. Similar to what was done on Server01, share the Share1 and Share2 on Server02.

10. On Server01, with Server Manager, click Tools > DFS Management to open the DFS Management console.

11. In the left-pane, right-click Namespaces and select New Namespace. The New Namespace Wizard starts.

12. On the Namespace Server page, type **Server01** in the Server text box. Click Next.

13. On the Namespace Name and Settings page, type **Shares** in the Name text box.

14. Click Edit Settings. The Edit Settings dialog box opens as shown in Figure 4-1.

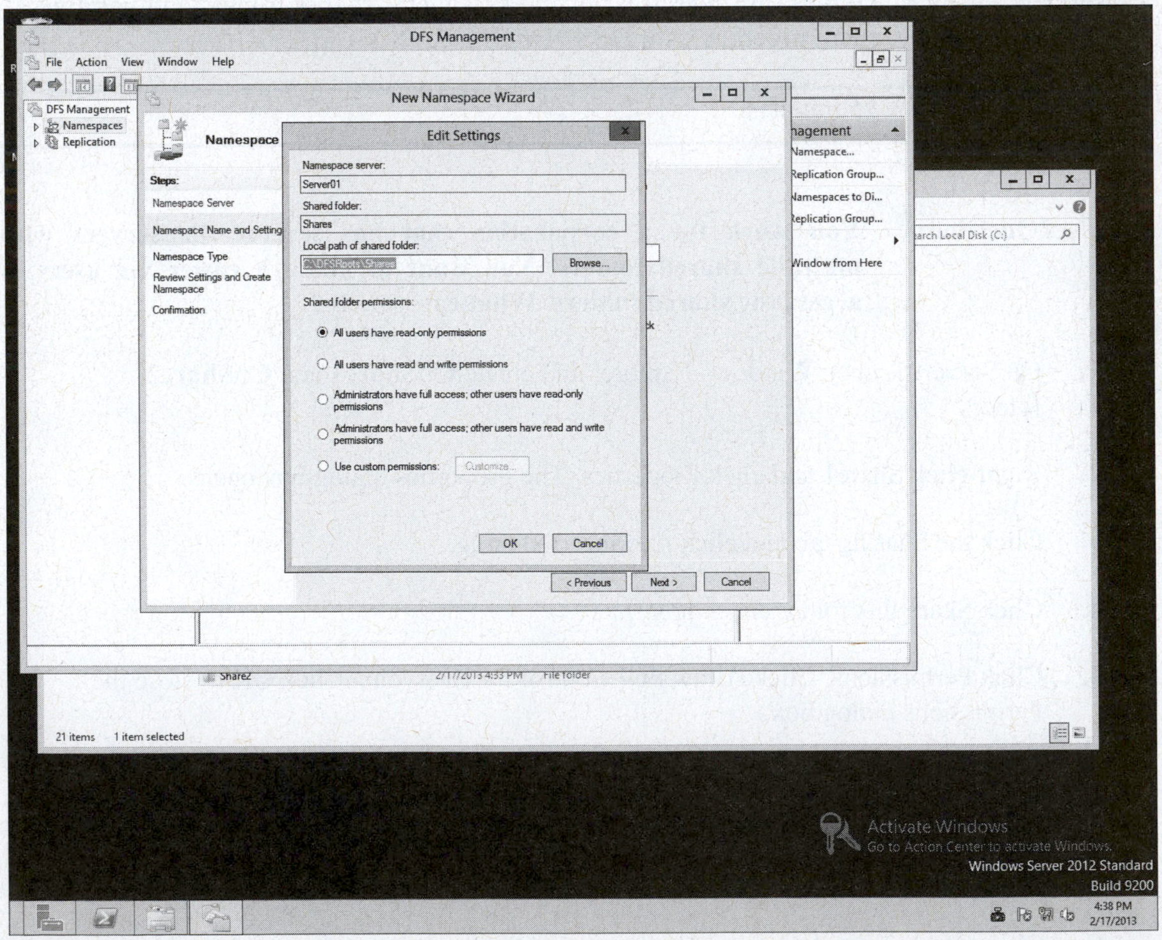

Figure 4-1
Specifying Share permissions for a DFS namespace

Question 2	What is the default location for the shares folder?

15. Click *All users have read and write permissions*. Click OK to close the Edit Settings dialog box.

16. On the Namespace Name and Settings page, click Next.

Question 3	What is the name of the domain-based namespace?

17. On the Namespace Type page, with Domain-based namespace already selected and Windows Server 2008 mode selected (as shown in Figure 4-2) click Next.

Question 4	What is the advantage of Windows Server 2008 mode?

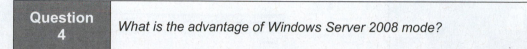

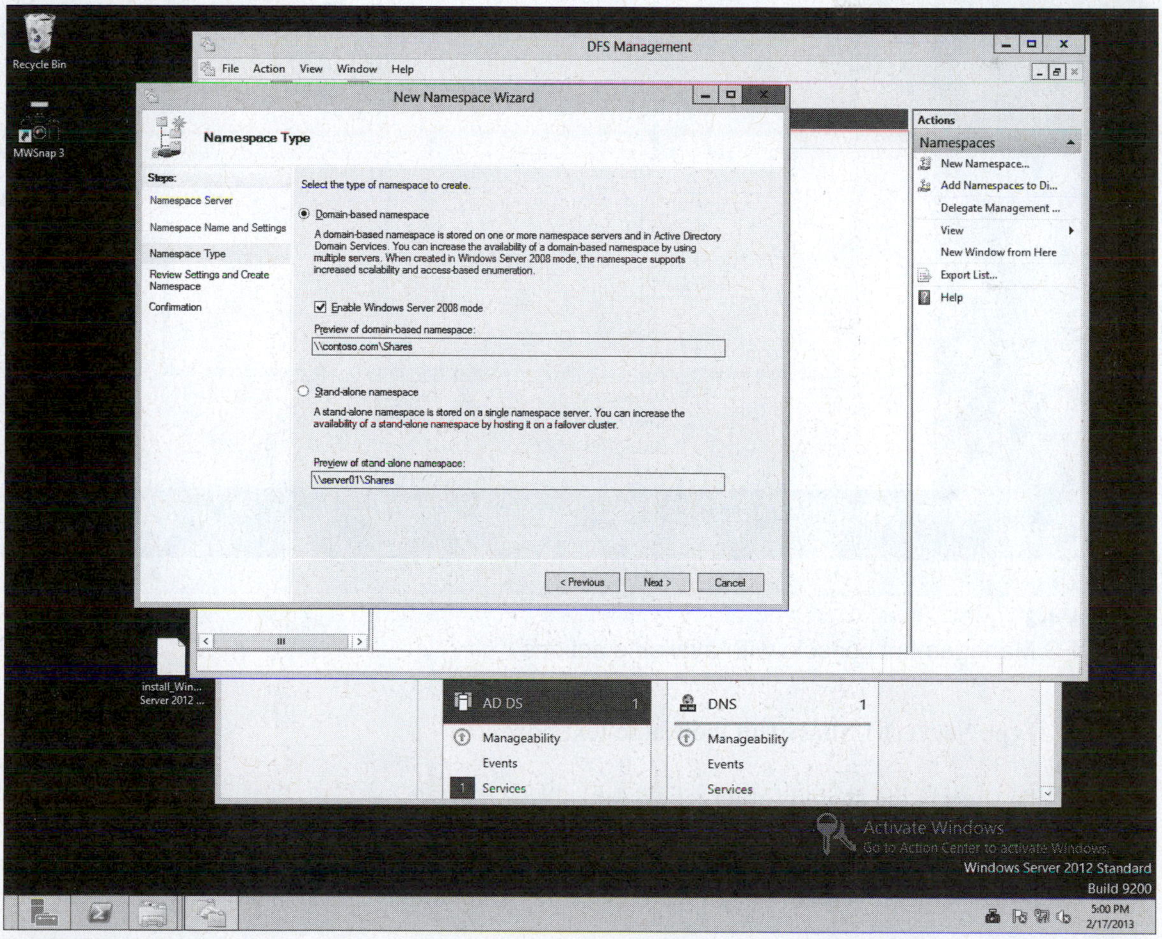

Figure 4-2
Selecting the type of namespace

18. On the Review Settings and Create Namespace page, click Create.

19. When the name space is created, click the Close button.

20. On the DFS Management console, in the left pane, expand the Namespaces node and click \\contoso.com\Shares.

21. Under Actions, click New Folder, as shown in Figure 4-3. The New Folder dialog box opens.

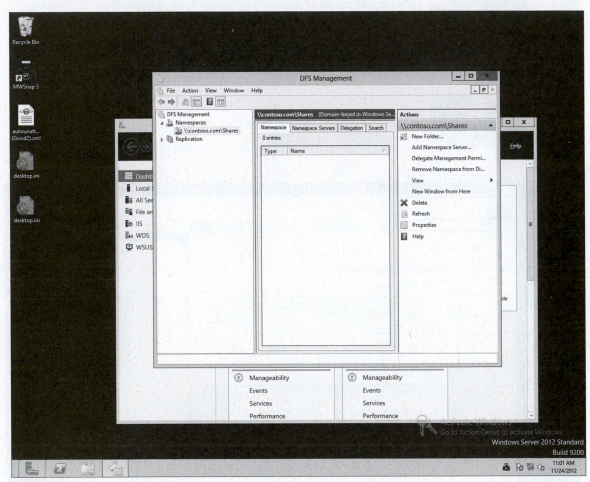

Figure 4-3
The DFS Management console with available actions

22. Type **Server01 Share1** in the Name text box.

23. To specify the shared folder, click Add.

24. In the Add Folder Target dialog box, type **\\Server01\Share1** in the Path to folder target text box. Click OK to close the Add Folder Target dialog box.

25. Click OK to close the New Folder dialog box.

26. Click New Folder. Create a new folder called **Server01 Share2** that points to \\Server01\Share2. Click OK. Click OK, again.

27. Click New Folder. Create a new folder called **Server02 Share1** that points to \\Server02\Share1. Click OK, twice

28. Click New Folder. Create a new folder called **Server02 Share2** that points to \\Server02\Share2. Click OK, twice.

29. On Server01, open a Windows Explorer window and type **contoso.com\shares** in the location text box and press Enter. See Figure 4-4.

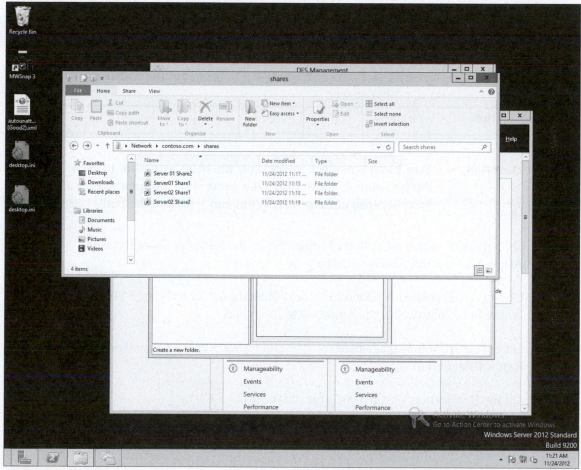

Figure 4-4
Accessing a namespace

30. Close Windows Explorer.

31. On the DFS Management console, right-click the \\Contoso.com\Shares namespace and click Properties. The Properties dialog box opens.

32. Click the Advanced tab.

33. Click to select *Enable access-based enumeration for this namespace.*

34. Click the Repl node and take a screen shot of the DFS Replication by pressing Alt+Prt Scr and then paste it into your Lab 4 worksheet file in the page provided by pressing Ctrl+V.

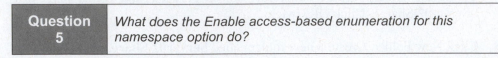

Question 5	What does the Enable access-based enumeration for this namespace option do?

35. Click OK to close the Properties dialog box.

End of exercise.

Exercise 4.3	Configuring DFS Replication
Overview	During this exercise, you configure two folders, each on a different server. You then configure DFS to replicate the content of one folder to the other server.
Completion time	10 minutes

Mindset Question: **You have a project folder that must be available in New York and Paris. Some of these files take some time to open over a slow WAN link, because of their size. What can you do to help alleviate this?**

1. On Server01, create a **C:\Share3** folder. Share the folder as Share3. Assign Allow Full Control Share permissions to Everyone.

2. On Server02, create a **C:\Share3** folder. Share the folder as Share3. Assign Allow Full Control Share permissions to Everyone.

3. On Server01 DFS Management console, right-click Replication and select New Replication Group.

4. On the Replication Group Type page, click Next.

5. On the Name and Domain page, type **Rep1** in the Name of replication group text box. Click the Next button.

6. On the Replication Group Members page, click the Add button.

7. When the Select Computers dialog box opens, type **Server01** in the Enter the object names to select text box and click OK. If it asks you to enter a network password, specify **Contoso\Administrator** and password of **Password01**.

8. Click Add and add Server02.

9. Click the Repl node and take a screen shot of the DFS Replication by pressing Alt+Prt Scr and then paste it into your Lab 4 worksheet file in the page provided by pressing Ctrl+V.

10. Back on the Replication Group Members page, click Next.

11. On the Topology Selection page (as shown in Figure 4-5), click Next.

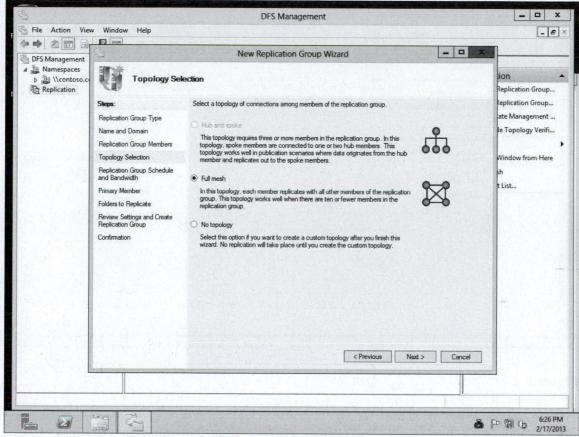

Figure 4-5
Selecting the DFS topology

12. On the *Replication Group Schedule and Bandwidth* page, click Next.

13. On the Primary Member page, select Server01 as the Primary member. Click Next.

14. On the Folders to Replicate page, click Add.

15. When the Add Folder to Replicate dialog box opens, type **C:\Share3** in the Local path of folder to replicate text box and click OK.

16. Back on the Folders to Replicate page (as shown in Figure 4-6), click Next.

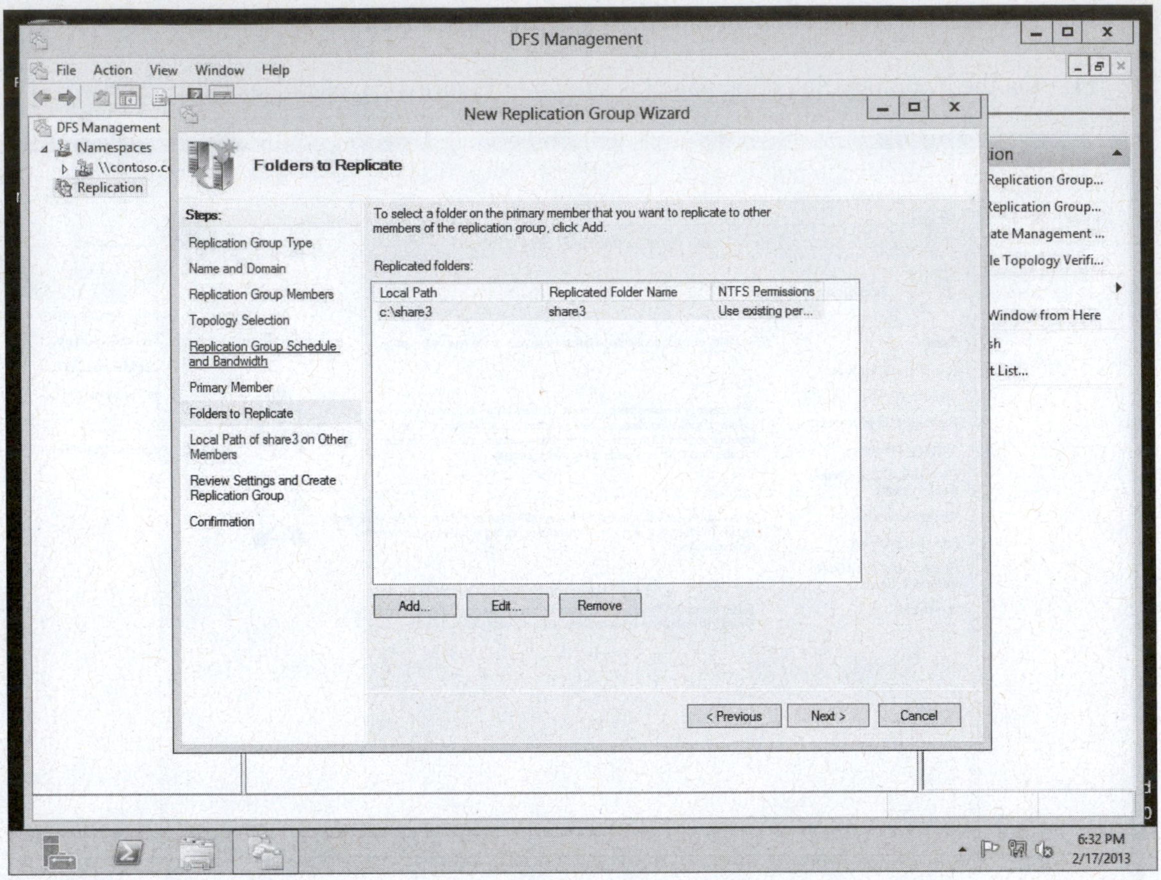

Figure 4-6
Adding folders to replicate

17. On the Local Path of Share3 on Other Members page, with Server02, click Edit.

18. Click Enabled and type **C:\Share3** in the Local path of folder text box as shown in Figure 4-7. Click OK to close the Edit dialog box.

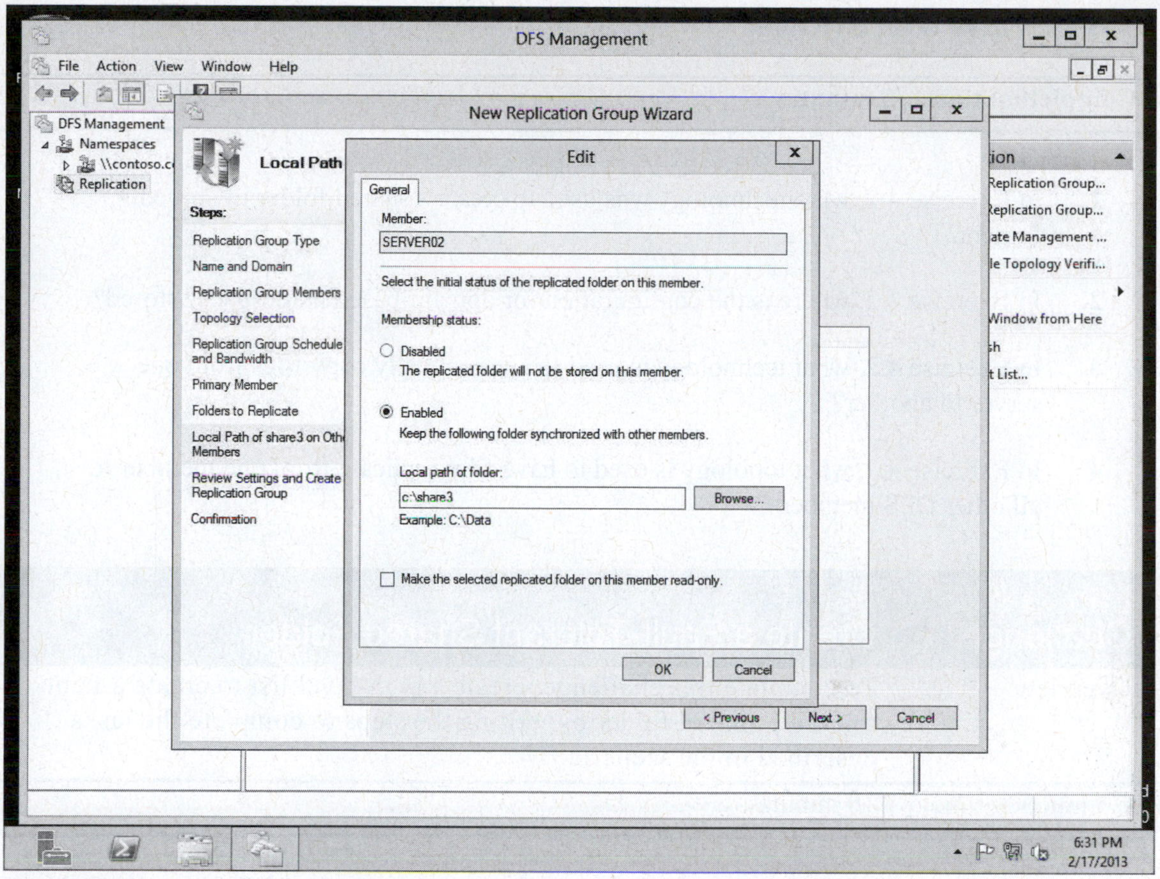

Figure 4-7
Accessing a namespace

19. Back on the Local Path of Public on Other Members page, click Next.

20. On the *Review Settings and Create Replication Group* page, click Create.

21. When the replication group has been created, click Close.

22. If you get a Replication Delay message, click OK.

23. Click the Repl node and take a screen shot of the DFS Replication by pressing Alt+Prt Scr and then paste it into your Lab 4 worksheet file in the page provided by pressing Ctrl+V.

24. On Server01, open the C:\Share3 folder.

25. Right-click the opened folder, click New and click Text Document. Name the document **Doc1.txt**.

26. Open the Doc1.txt file and type your name. Save and close the text document.

27. On Server02, open the C:\Share3 folder and verify that the Doc1 has replicated to Server02. It may take a minute or two to replicate.

End of exercise.

LAB REVIEW QUESTIONS

Completion time   5 minutes

1.   In Exercise 4.2, what technology was used to create a shared folder of shared folders?

2.   In Exercise 4.2, where is the configuration for domain-based namespaces stored?

3.   In Exercise 4.2, what technology is used to automatically copy files from one server to another?

4.   In Exercise 4.2, what topology is used to have files replicate from one member to all other DFS members?

Lab Challenge	Create a Fault-Tolerant Shared Folder
Overview	To complete this challenge, create a high-level list to create a fault-tolerante shared folder by writing the steps to complete the tasks described in the scenerio.
Completion time	10 minutes

You have content that is contained in a folder that you want to make available, even if a file server becomes unavailable. What do you need to do to accomplish this?

Write out the steps you performed to complete the challenge.

End of lab

LAB 5
CONFIGURING FILE SERVER RESOURCE MANAGER

THIS LAB CONTAINS THE FOLLOWING EXERCISES AND ACTIVITIES:

Exercise 5.1   Installing File Server Resource Manager

Exercise 5.2   Configuring Quotas

Exercise 5.3   Managing Files with File Screening

Exercise 5.4   Using Storage Reports

Lab Challenge   Enabling SMTP for FSRM

BEFORE YOU BEGIN

The lab environment consists of student workstations connected to a local area network, along with a server that functions as the domain controller for a domain called *contoso.com*. The computers required for this lab are listed in Table 5-1.

Table 5-1
Computers Required for Lab 5

Computer	Operating System	Computer Name
Server (VM 1)	Windows Server 2012	RWDC01
Server (VM 2)	Windows Server 2012	Server01

In addition to the computers, you also require the software listed in Table 5-2 to complete Lab 5.

Table 5-2
Software Required for Lab 5

Software	Location
ADMXMigrator.msi, NMI32_x64.exe, System Center Monitoring Pack for File and Storage Management.msi, and Windows8=RT-KB2769034-x64.msu	C:\Software
Lab 5 student worksheet	Lab05_worksheet.docx (provided by instructor)

Working with Lab Worksheets

Each lab in this manual requires that you answer questions, take screen shots, and perform other activities that you will document in a worksheet named for the lab, such as Lab05_worksheet.docx. You will find these worksheets on the book companion site. It is recommended that you use a USB flash drive to store your worksheets, so you can submit them to your instructor for review. As you perform the exercises in each lab, open the appropriate worksheet file fill in the required information, and save the file to your flash drive.

After completing this lab, you will be able to:

- Install and configure File Server Resource Manager

- Use Quotas to manage disk space

- Manage files with file screening

- Use Storage Reports

Estimated lab time: 60 minutes

Exercise 5.1	Installing File Server Resource Manager
Overview	During this exercise, you install File Server Resource Manager, which is used in the following exercises.
Completion time	10 minutes

1. Log in to Server01 using the **Administrator** account and the password **Password01.**

2. On Server01, at the top of Server Manager, select Manage and click Add Roles and Features to open the Add Roles and Feature Wizard.

3. On the Before you begin page, click Next.

4. Select *Role-based or feature-based installation* and then click Next.

5. When it asks for your destination server, click Next.

6. Scroll down, expand File and Storage Services, and expand File and iSCSI Services. Select File Server Resource Manager.

7. When you are asked to add additional features, click Add Features.

8. On the Select server roles page, click Next.

9. On the Select features page, click Next.

10. On the Confirm installation selections page, click Install.

11. When the installation is complete, click the Close button.

End of exercise.

Exercise 5.2	Configuring Quotas
Overview	During this exercise, you use File Server Resource Manager quotas.
Completion time	10 minutes

Mindset Question: **You can configure quotas using NTFS or using FSRM. How do the quotas differ between NTFS and FSRM?**

1. On Server01, with Server Manager, click Tools > File Server Resource Manager. The File Server Resource Manager console opens.

2. Under Quota Management, click Quota Templates. Then right-click Quota Templates and select Create Quota Template. The Create Quota Template dialog box opens.

3. In the Template name text box, type **QuotaTemplate1**.

4. In the Space limit section, in the Limit text box, type **10** and specify the unit MB.

5. Select Soft quota, as shown in Figure 5-1.

Question 1	What is the difference between a hard and soft quota?

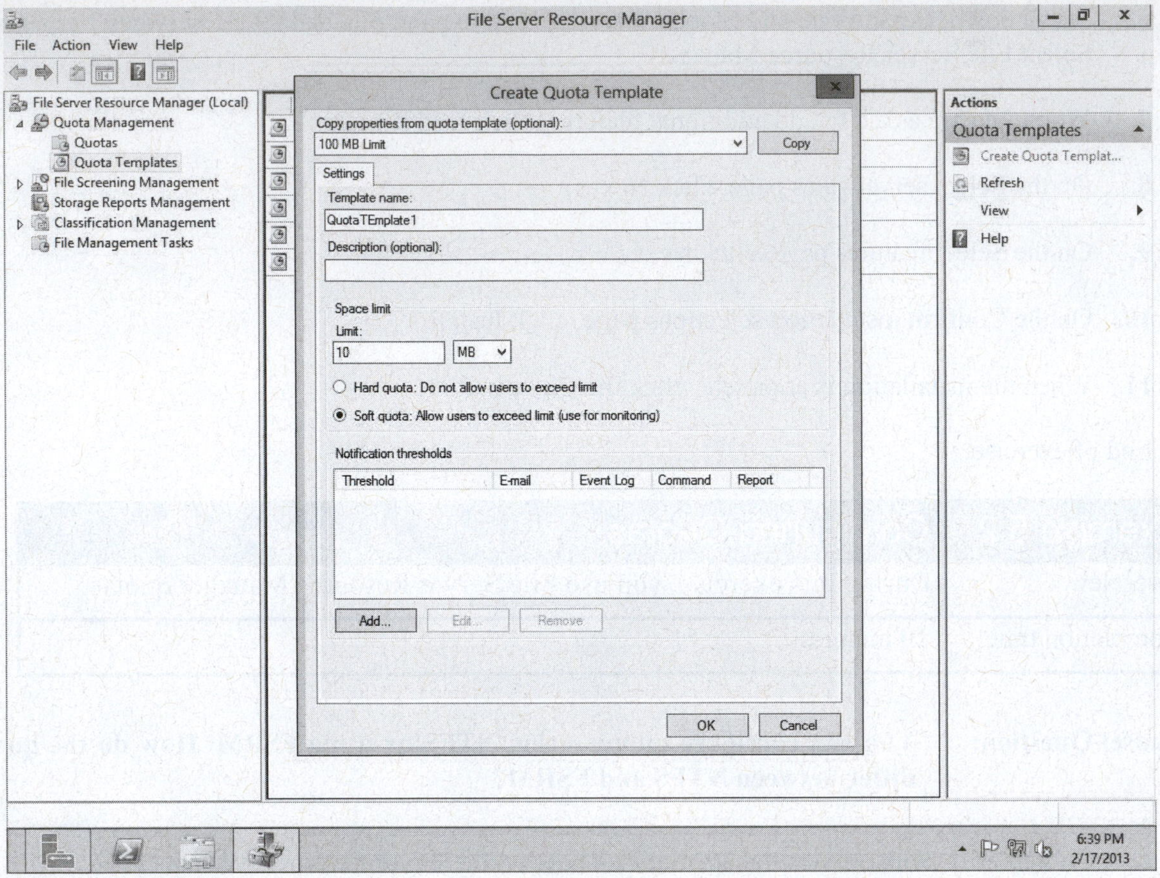

Figure 5-1
Creating a quota template

6. To add a notification, click the Add button. The Add Threshold dialog box opens.

7. Click the Event Log tab.

8. Click the Send warning to event log check box, as shown in Figure 5-2.

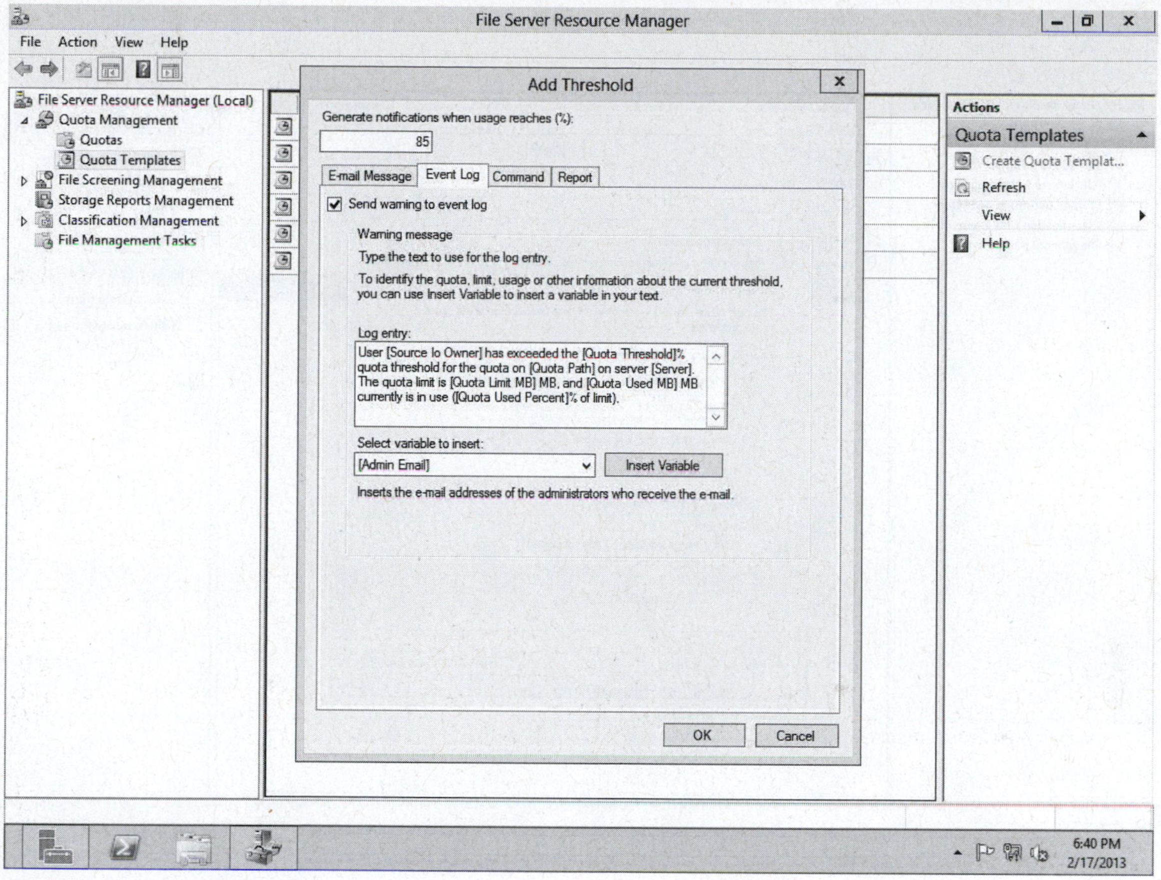

Figure 5-2
Adding an event log notification

9. Click OK to save your notification threshold and close the Add Threshold dialog box.

10. Click OK to close the Create Quota Template dialog box.

11. Click the Quota Templates node, and take a screen shot of the File Server Resource Manager window by pressing Alt+Prt Scr and then paste it into your Lab 5 worksheet file in the page provided by pressing Ctrl+V.

12. Under the Quota Management node, click the Quota Templates node.

13. Right-click the QuotaTemplate1 and click Create Quota from Template. The Create Quota dialog box opens.

14. In the Quota path, type **c:\Share1** in the Quota path text box, as shown in Figure 5-3.

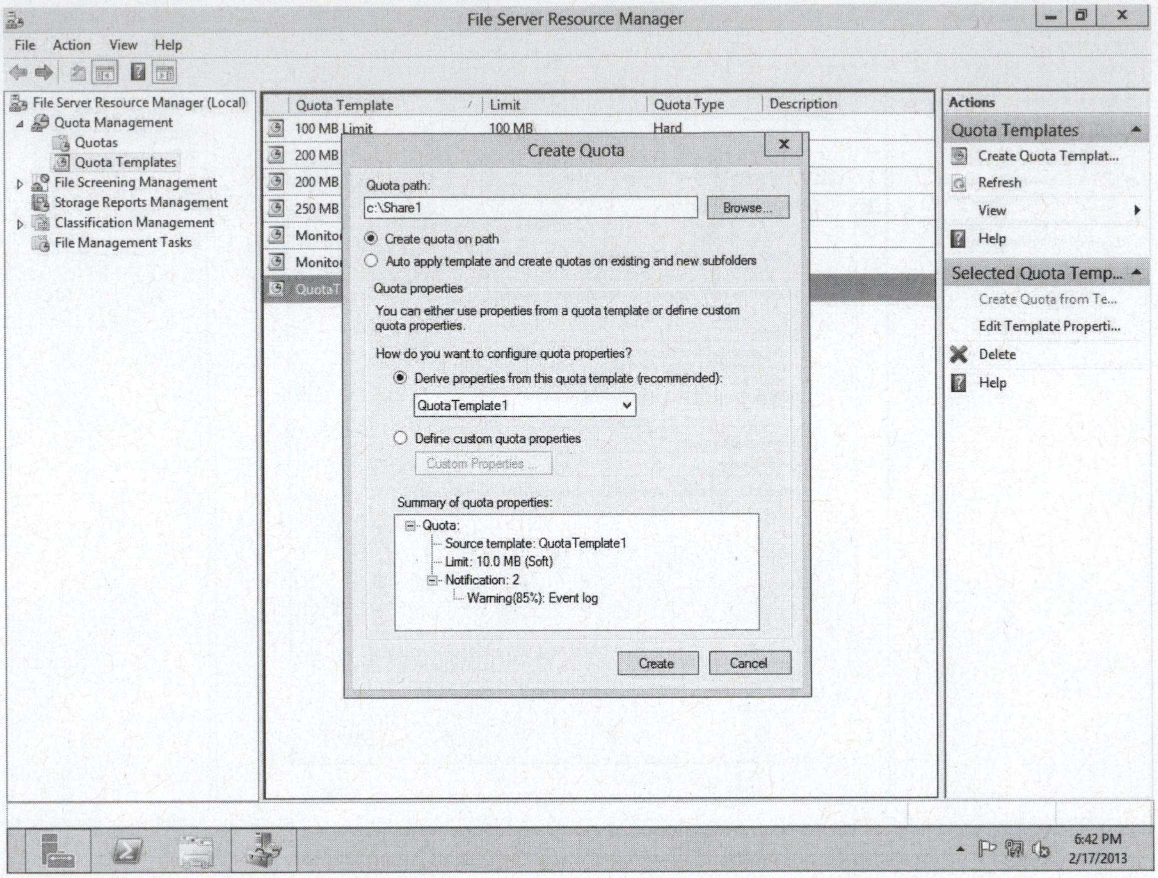

Figure 5-3
Creating a quota from a template

15. Click Create.

16. From the \\RWDC01\software folder, copy the following files to the C:\Share1 folder:

- ADMXMigrator.msi

- NM34_x64.exe

- System Center Monitoring Pack for File and Storage Management.msi

- Windows8-RT-KB2769034-x64.msu

17. On Server01, open the Event Viewer and look for an entry in the Application logs showing that the quota has been exceeded.

Question 2	*What event ID was used for the quota to be exceeded?*

18. Take a screen shot of the Event Viewer window by pressing Alt+Prt Scr and then paste it into your Lab 5 worksheet file in the page provided by pressing Ctrl+V.

19. Close Event Viewer.

End of exercise.

Exercise 5.3	Managing Files with File Screening
Overview	During this exercise, you continue to use File Server Resource Manager by using File Screening.
Completion time	10 minutes

Mindset Question: **You have a file server that ran out of disk space. Last week, there was plenty of space and this week, there is none. While looking at the files that are stored, you noticed that a couple of users have stored movie and music collections. How can you prevent this from happening in the future?**

1. On Server01, on File Server Resource Manager, click File Screening Management.

2. Click the File Groups node.

3. Right-click File Groups and select Create File Group. The Create File Group Properties dialog box opens.

4. In the File group name text box, type **FileGroup1**.

5. To include video files and add all files with the filename extension ram, type ***.ram**, and then click Add.

6. Add the following filename extensions:

*.rm

*.avi

*.wmv

*.mpg

7. To add files to exclude, type **hello.avi** in the Files to exclude text box and click Add. The Create File Group Properties dialog box should look like Figure 5-4.

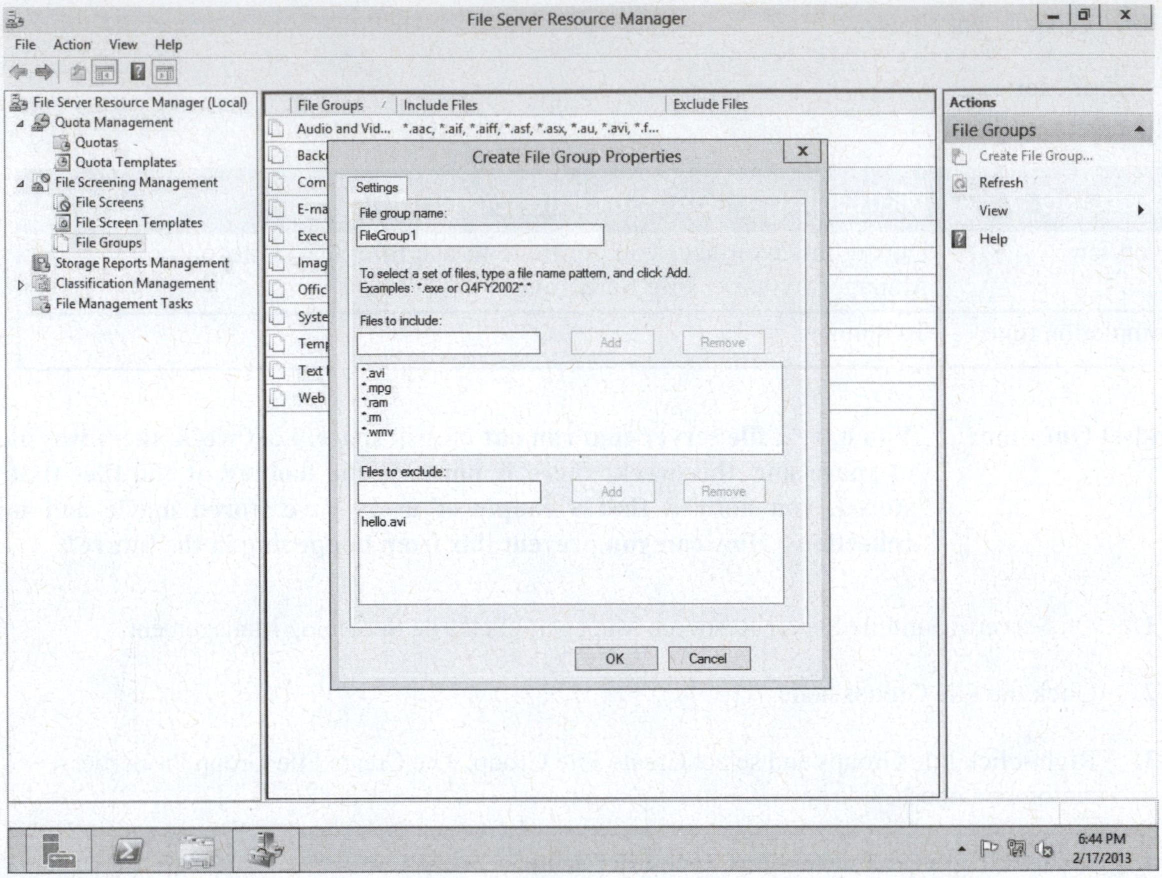

Figure 5-4
Creating file groups

8. Click OK to close the Create File Group Properties dialog box.

9. Under File Screening Management, click the File Screens node.

10. Right-click File Screens, and then click Create File Screen. The Create File Screen dialog box opens.

11. Type **C:\Share1** in the File screen path text box.

12. Click *Define custom file screen properties*, and then click Custom Properties. The File Screen Properties dialog box opens as shown in Figure 5-5.

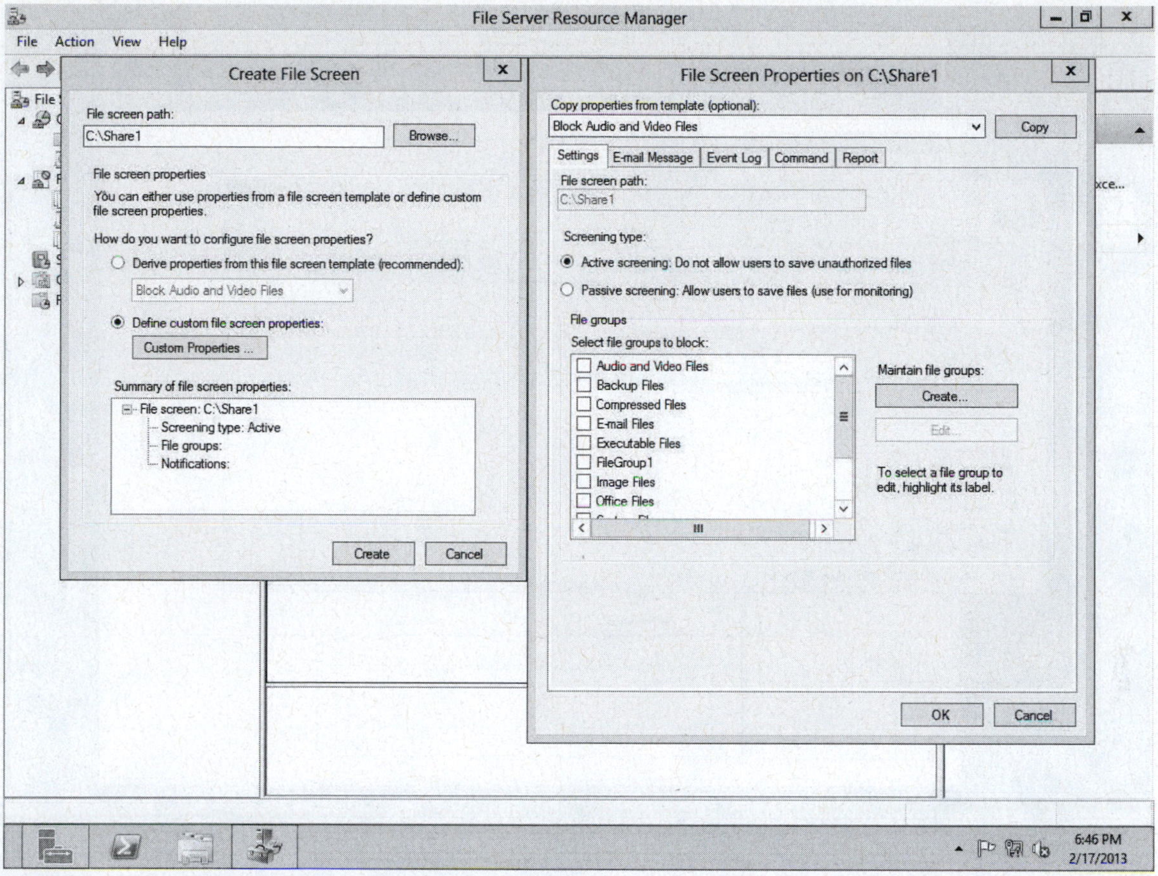

Figure 5-5
Creating a file screen

13. With Active screening already selected, click FileGroup1 in the File groups section.

14. To log an event, click the Event Log tab. Then click to select the Send warning to event log check box.

15. Click OK to close the File Screen Properties dialog box.

16. Click Create to create a new file screen

17. When it asks you to save the custom properties as a template, click *Save the custom file screen without creating a template*. Click OK.

18. With Windows Explorer, open the C:\Share1 folder.

19. In Windows Explorer, click the View tab.

20. Ensure that File name extensions is selected as shown in Figure 5-6.

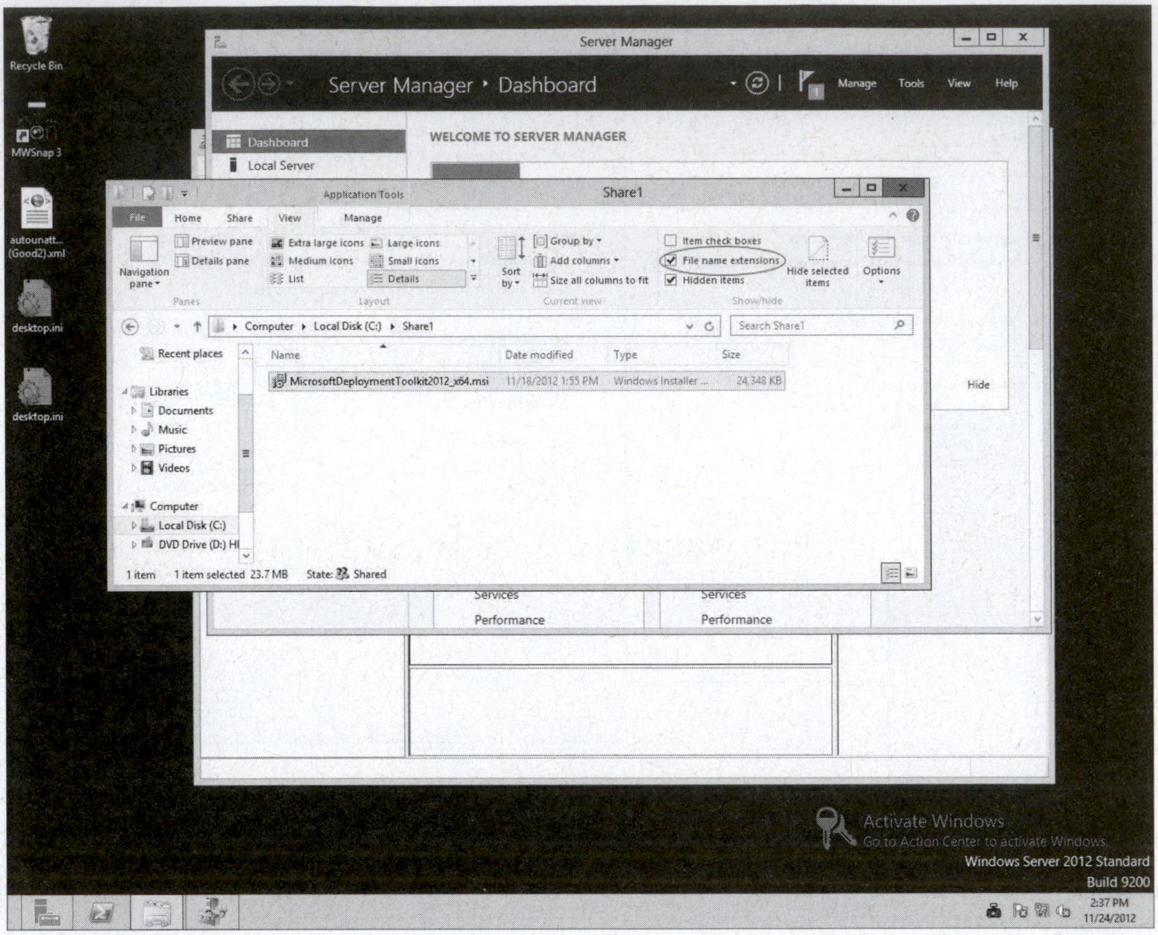

Figure 5-6
Showing File name extensions

21. On the Desktop, create a text file called **test1.avi**. Be sure that the file does not have the .txt filename extension. If it asks to change the filename extension, click OK.

> **NOTE**
>
> *Although the file has a .avi filename extension, it is really not a video file. It is just to demonstrate file screening.*

22. Copy the test1.avi file to the C:\Share1 folder.

> **Question 3**
>
> *What message did you get when you tried to copy the file?*

23. Click Cancel.

24. Rename the test1.avi file to **hello.avi**.

25. Copy the hello.avi file to the C:\Share1 folder.

26. Open the Event Viewer and access the Application logs.

Question 4	What event ID was used for files that were not permitted for file screening?

27. Close Event Viewer

28. Close the Share1 folder.

End of exercise.

Exercise 5.4	Using Storage Reports
Overview	During this exercise, you execute File Server Resource Manager storage reports.
Completion time	10 minutes

1. On Server01, on File Server Resource Manager, click Storage Reports Management.

2. Right-click Storage Reports Management, and click Generate Reports Now.

3. When the Storage Reports Task Properties dialog box opens, click Quota Usage.

4. Click the Scope tab.

5. Click the Add button. Then browse to the C:\Share1 and click OK to close the Browse For Folder dialog box.

6. Click OK to close the Storage Reports Task Properties dialog box.

7. When the Generate Storage Reports dialog box opens, click OK.

8. When a folder opens, double-click the html file. Close message box, if needed, and view the Quota Usage Report.

9. Take a screen shot of the Performance Monitor window by pressing Alt+Prt Scr and then paste it into your Lab 5 worksheet file in the page provided by pressing Ctrl+V.

10. Close Internet Explorer and File Server Resource Manager.

End of exercise.

LAB REVIEW QUESTIONS

Completion time	10 minutes

1. In Exercise 5.2, with File Server Resource Manager, what are quotas assigned to?

2. In Exercise 5.2, if you want to prevent a folder from getting too large, what type of quota should you use?

3. In Exercise 5.2, what methods can you use for notification when a quota is exceeded?

4. In Exercise 5.3, how do you prevent a user from saving unauthorized files?

5. In Exercise 5.5, what allows you to get a comprehensive report on how a disk is being used by the users?

Lab Challenge	Enabling SMTP for FSRM
Overview	To complete this challenge, you must demonstrate how to enable SMTP for FSRM by writing the steps to complete the tasks described in the scenerio.
Completion time	10 minutes

You just got quotas and file screening configured properly. You now want to be e-mailed when quotas are exceeded and when users save unauthorized files. However, the messages are not being forwarded to the e-mail server. What should you do?

Write out the steps you performed to complete the challenge.

End of lab.

LAB 6
CONFIGURING FILE SERVICES AND DISK ENCRYPTION

THIS LAB CONTAINS THE FOLLOWING EXERCISES AND ACTIVITIES:

Exercise 6.1   Encrypting Files with EFS

Exercise 6.2   Configuring the EFS Recovery Agent

Exercise 6.3   Backing Up and Restoring EFS Certificates

Exercise 6.4   Encrypting a Volume with BitLocker

Lab Challenge   Configuring Network Unlock

BEFORE YOU BEGIN

The lab environment consists of student workstations connected to a local area network, along with a server that functions as the domain controller for a domain called *contoso.com*. The computers required for this lab are listed in Table 6-1.

Table 6-1
Computers Required for Lab 6

Computer	Operating System	Computer Name
Server (VM 1)	Windows Server 2012	RWDC01
Server (VM 2)	Windows Server 2012	Server01

In addition to the computers, you also require the software listed in Table 6-2 to complete Lab 6.

Table 6-2
Software Required for Lab 6

Software	Location
Lab 6 student worksheet	Lab06_worksheet.docx (provided by instructor)

Working with Lab Worksheets

Each lab in this manual requires that you answer questions, take screen shots, and perform other activities that you will document in a worksheet named for the lab, such as Lab06_worksheet.docx. You will find these worksheets on the book companion site. It is recommended that you use a USB flash drive to store your worksheets, so you can submit them to your instructor for review. As you perform the exercises in each lab, open the appropriate worksheet file fill in the required information, and save the file to your flash drive.

After completing this lab, you will be able to:

- Encrypt files with EFS

- Configure EFS Recovery Agent

- Back up and restore EFS certificates

- Encrypt a volume with BitLocker

Estimated lab time: 70 minutes

Exercise 6.1	Encrypting Files with EFS
Overview	For files that are extremely sensitive, you can use EFS to encrypt the files.During this exercise, you encrypt a file using Encrypting File System (EFS), which is a built-in feature of NTFS.
Completion time	20 minutes

Mindset Question: You have several sales people who have sensitive material on their computer. If their laptops are stolen, the stolen information could put the company at great risk. Therefore, how can you protect the important data documents?

Encrypting Files with EFS

1. Log in to Server01 as the **Contoso\administrator** user account. The Server Manager console opens.

2. On Server01, create a **C:\Data** folder.

3. Create a text file in the C:\Data folder called **test.txt** file. Type your name in the file, close the file, then click Save to save the changes.

4. Right-click the C:\Data folder, and then click Properties. The Properties dialog box opens.

5. On the General tab, click Advanced. The Advanced Attributes dialog box appears as shown in Figure 6-1.

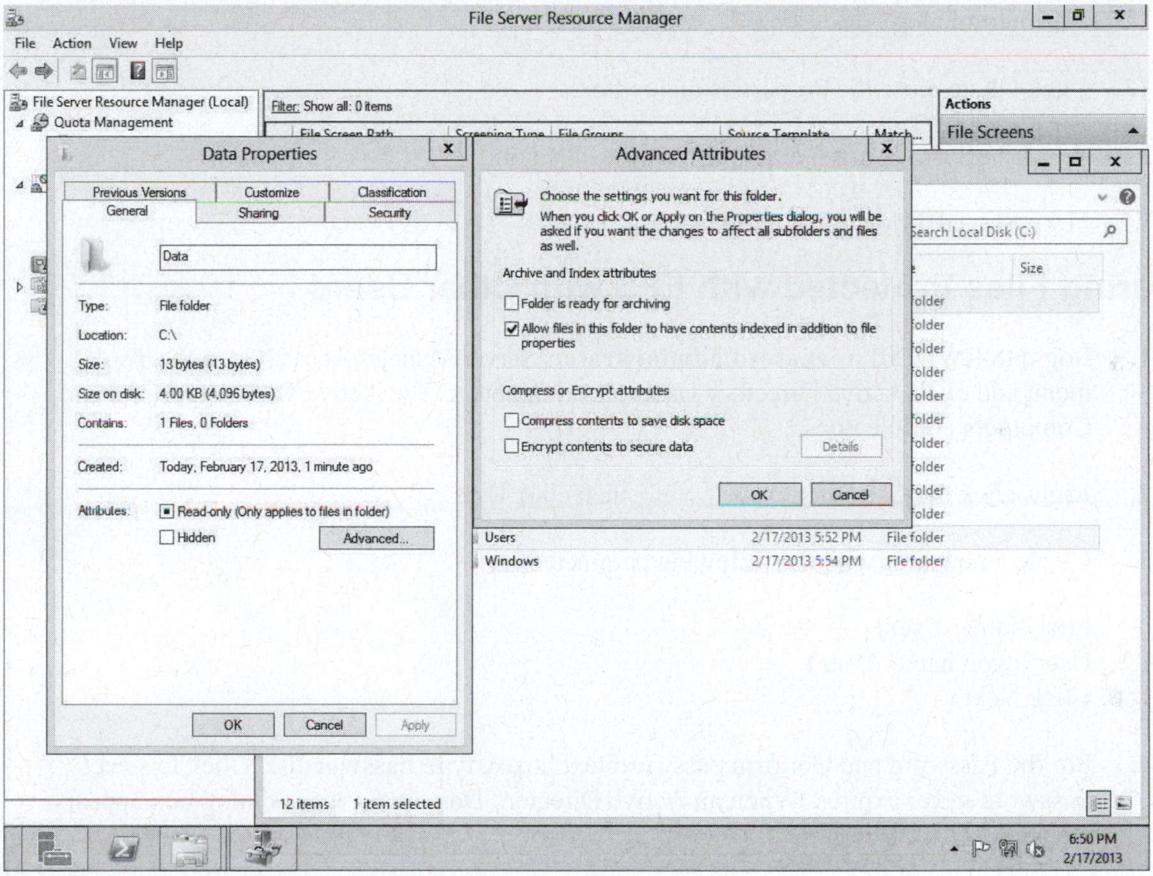

Figure 6-1
Configuring advanced attributes

6. Click to select *Encrypt contents to secure data*. Click OK to close the Advanced Attributes dialog box.

7. Click OK to close the Properties dialog box.

8. When Windows asks you to confirm the changes, click OK.

Question 1	*What color is the C:\Data folder?*

Question 2	Is the test.txt file in the C:\Data folder also encrypted?

9. Right-click the C:\Data folder and click Properties. The Properties dialog box opens.

10. Under the General tab, click Advanced. The Advanced Attributes dialog box opens.

11. Clear the *Encrypt contents to secure data* check box. Click OK to close the Advanced Attributes dialog box.

12. Click OK to close the Properties dialog box.

13. When it asks to confirm attribute changes, click OK.

14. From Server01, log off as administrator.

Sharing Files Protected with EFS with Other Users

1. Log into RWDC01 as **contoso\administrator**, Server Manager starts. Open the Tools menu and click Active Directory Users and Computers. The Active Directory Users and Computers console opens.

2. Right-click the Users node, click New, then click User.

3. Create a new user with the following parameters:

    First Name: **User1**
    User logon name: **User1**
    Click Next.

4. For the Password and Confirm password text boxes, type **Password01**. Click to select Password never expires. When an Active Directory Domain Services dialog box appears, click OK. Click Next.

5. When the user is ready to be created, click Finish.

6. Under the Users node, double-click User1. The User1 Properties dialog box opens.

7. Click the Member Of tab.

8. Click the Add button. When the Select Groups dialog box opens, type **domain admins** and click OK.

9. Click OK to close the User1 Properties dialog box.

10. On Server01, log in as **contoso\User1** with the password of **Password01**.

11. Open the C:\Data folder, right-click the test.txt file and click Properties.

12. On the General tab, click Advanced. The Advanced Attributes dialog box opens.

13.   Click *Encrypt contents to secure data*. Click OK to close the Advanced Attributes dialog box. Click OK to close the Properties dialog box.

14.   When it asks if you want to encrypt the file and its parent folder, click OK.

15.   If an Access Denied message appears, click Ignore, click Continue, click OK, and click Ignore. Click OK. If an Access Denied message appears again, click Ignore All. When you are done, the test.txt file should be green.

16.   On Server01, log out as User1 and log in as **Contoso\Administrator**.

17.   Open the C:\Data folder.

18.   Double-click to open the Test.txt file.

Question 3	What error message did you get?

19.   Click OK to close the message, and then close Notepad.

20.   Right-click the test.txt file and click Properties.

21.   Click the Security tab.

Question 4	What permissions does Administrator have?

Question 5	Why was the contoso\administrator not able to open the file?

22.   Go back to the General tab, click the Advanced button, clear the Encrypt check box, and then click OK.

Question 6	Were you able to decrypt the file?

23.   Click OK to close the Properties dialog box. After getting the Access Denied box, click Cancel to close it.

24.   On Server01, log off as Administrator and log on as **User1**.

25.   Open the C:\Data folder.

26.   Right-click the test.txt file and click Properties. The Properties dialog box opens.

27.   Click the Advanced button to open the Advanced Attributes dialog box.

28. Click to deselect the *Encrypt contents to secure data* check box, and click OK.

29. Click OK to close the Properties dialog box. When it asks you to provide administrator permission to change these attributes, click Continue.

30. Log off as User1 and log on as **contoso\administrator**.

31. Open the C:\Data folder.

32. Right-click the Test.text, and click Properties.

33. Click the Advanced button to open the Advanced Attributes dialog box.

34. Click to select the *Encrypt contents to secure data* check box. Click OK to close the Advanced Attributes dialog box.

35. Click OK to close the Properties dialog box. When it asks to apply to the folder and its contents, click OK.

36. Right-click the test.txt folder and click Properties. Click the Advanced button to open the Advanced Attributes dialog box.

37. Click the Details button. The User Access to test.txt dialog box opens as shown in Figure 6-2.

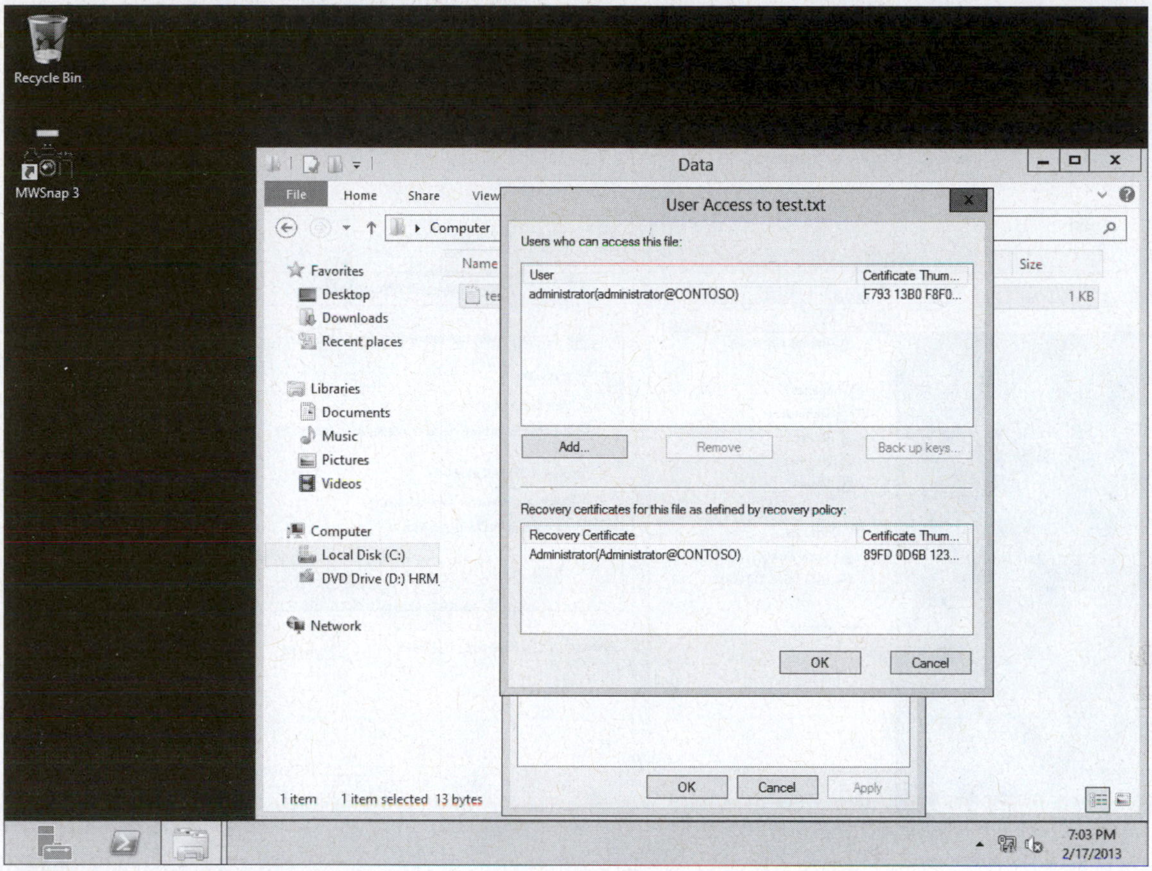

Figure 6-2
Certificate details for test.txt file

38. Click the Add button. When the Encrypting File System dialog box as shown in Figure 6-3, click User1 and click View Certificate.

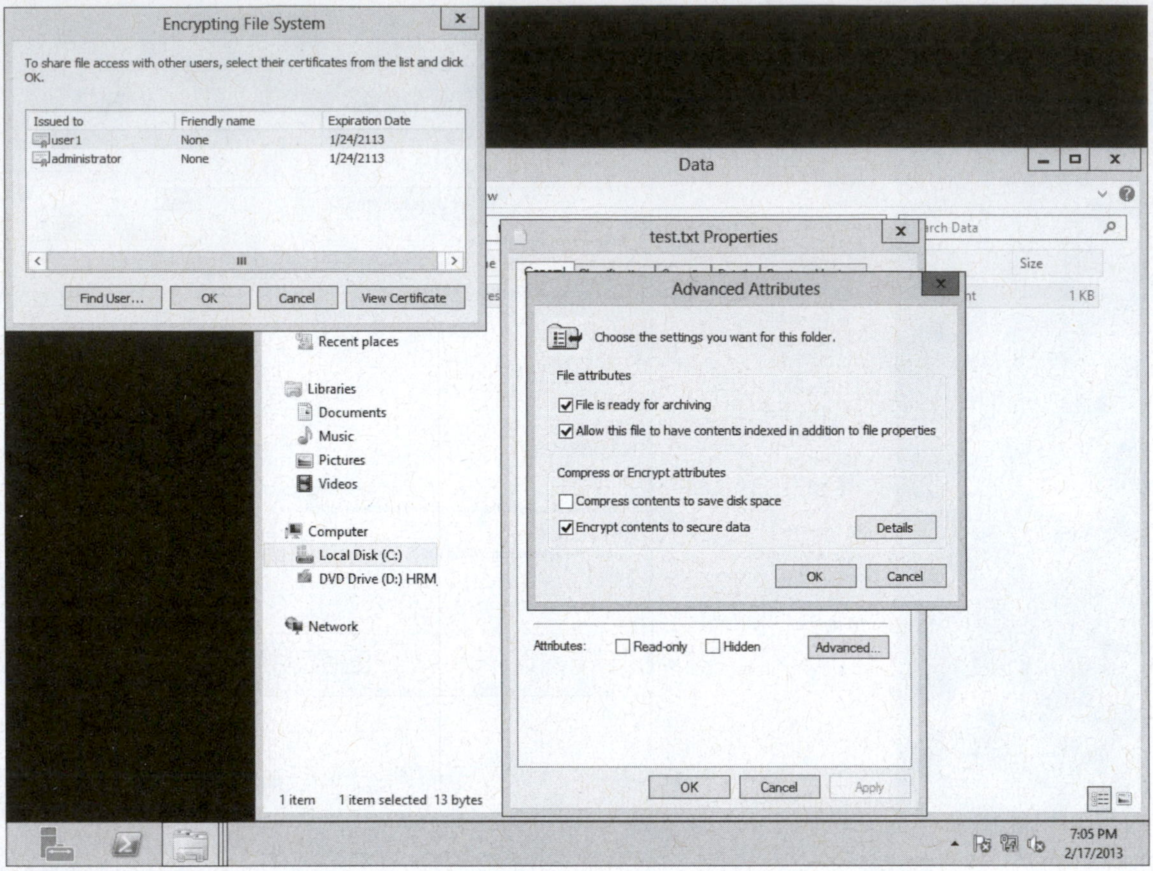

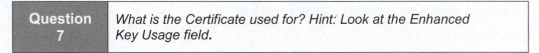

Figure 6-3
EFS certificates for test.txt

39. When the Certificate dialog box opens, click the Details tab.

Question 7	*What is the Certificate used for? Hint: Look at the Enhanced Key Usage field.*

40. Click OK to close the Certificates dialog box.

41. Click OK to close the Encrypting File System dialog box.

Question 8	*Looking at the User Access to test.txt dialog box, who has a Recovery Certificate?*

42. Take a screen shot of the User Access dialog box by pressing Alt+Prt Scr and then paste it into your Lab 8 worksheet file in the page provided by pressing Ctrl+V.

43. Click OK to close the properties windows and dialog boxes.

44. On Server01, sign out as Administrator and log in as **User1**.

45. Open the C:\Data folder and open the test.txt file.

Question 9	Were you able to open the file?

46. Close the test.txt file.

47. On Server01, sign out as User1.

End of exercise.

Exercise 6.2   Configuring the EFS Recovery Agent

Overview	During this exercise, you configure EFS Recovery Agents so that you can recover EFS encrypted files although the agent is not the owner of the file.
Completion time	15 minutes

Mindset Question: **Why do you need to have EFS Recovery Agents?**

Installing and Configuring the Certificate Authority

1.   On RWDC01, log on as **contoso\administrator**, if needed.

2.   On RWDC01, on the Server Manager, open the Manage menu and click Add Roles and Features.

3.   When the Add Roles and Features Wizard starts, click Next.

4.   On the Select installation type page, click Next.

5.   On the Select destination page, click Next.

6.   On the Select server roles page, click Active Directory Certificate Services. When you are prompted to add features, click Add Features. Then when you are back to the Select server roles page, click Next.

7.   On the Select features page, click Next.

8.   On the Active Directory Certificate Services page, click Next.

9.   On the Select role services, Certificate Authority is already selected. Click to select the following:

Certificate Enrollment Policy Web Service
Certificate Enrollment Web Service
Certification Authority Web Enrollment

When it asks you to add additional features for any of these features, click Add Features.

10. Back on the Select role services page, click Next.

11. On the Web Server Role (IIS) page, click Next.

12. On the Select role services page, click Next.

13. On the Confirm installation selections page, click Install.

14. When the Certificate Authority is installed, click Close.

15. On Server Manager, click the Exclamation Point in a yellow triangle and then click Configure Active Directory Certificate Services.

16. On the Credentials page, click Next.

17. On the Role Services page, click Certification Authority, as shown in Figure 6-4. Click Next.

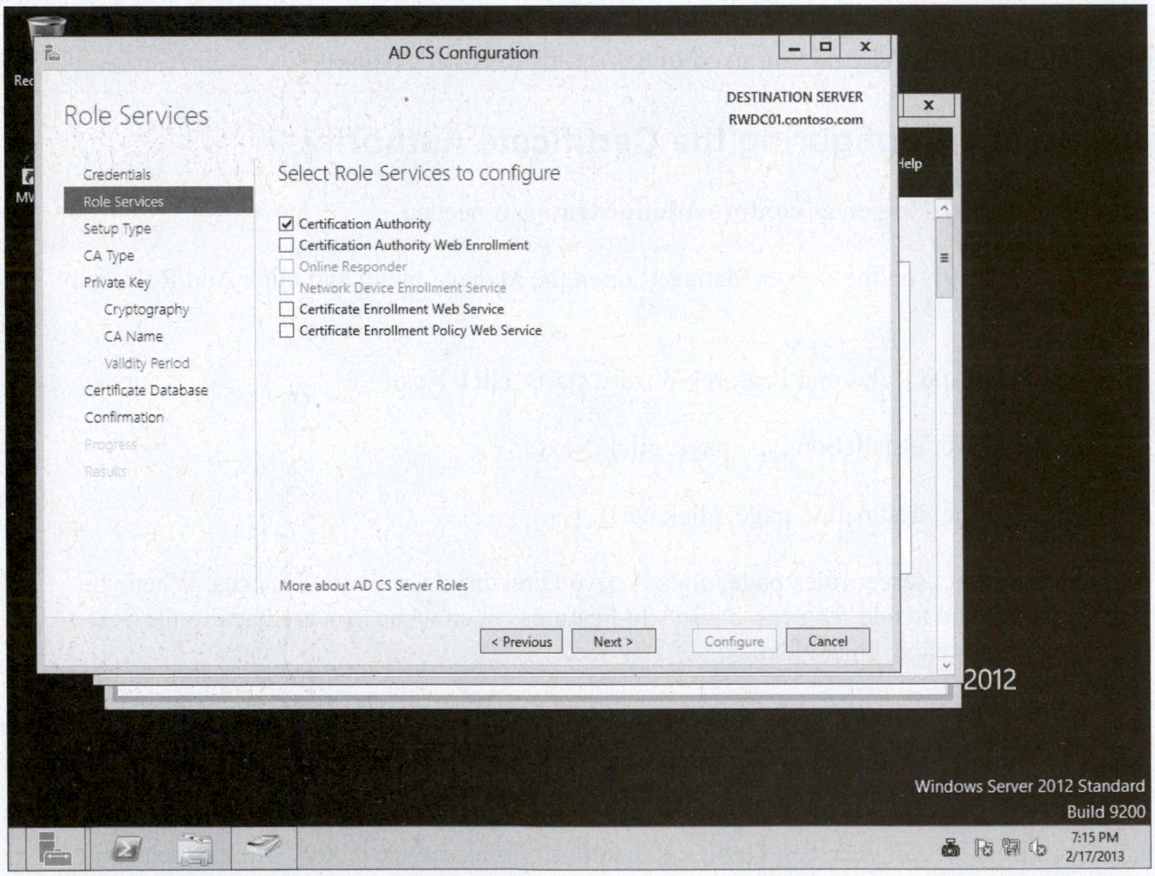

Figure 6-4
Configuring the Certification Authority

18. When it asks what setup type of CA you should install, click Next.

19. When it asks for the CA type (as shown in Figure 6-5), click Next.

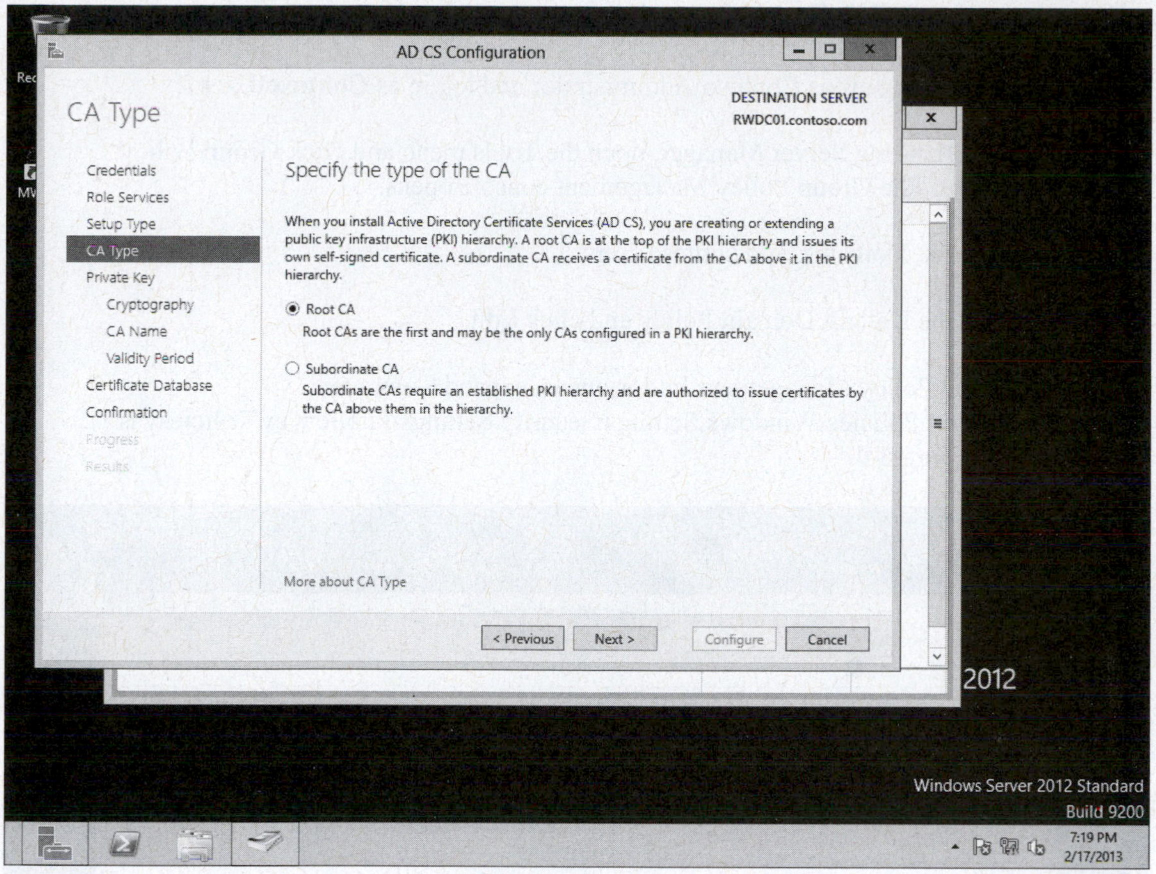

Figure 6-5
Specifying the type of CA

20. On the Specify the type of the private key page, click Next.

21. On the Specify the Cryptography for CA page, click Next.

22. On the Specify the name of the CA page, click Next.

23. For the Validity Period, click Next.

24. On the CA database page, click Next.

25. On the Confirmation page, click Configure.

26. When the CA is configured, take a screen shot of the CA is configured by pressing Alt+Prt Scr and then paste it into your Lab 6 worksheet file in the page provided by pressing Ctrl+V.

27. Click Close.

28. If it asks to configure additional role services, click No.

Configuring the EFS Recovery Agent

1. On RWDC01, log off as Contoso\Administrator and log in as **Contoso\User1**.

2. On RWDC01, using Server Manager, open the Tools menu and click Group Policy Management. The Group Policy Management console opens.

3. Expand Forest, Domains, and contoso.com.

4. Right-click the Default Domain Policy and click Edit.

5. When Group Policy Management Editor opens, expand Computer Configuration\Policies\Windows Settings\Security Settings\Public Key Policies\ as shown in Figure 6-6.

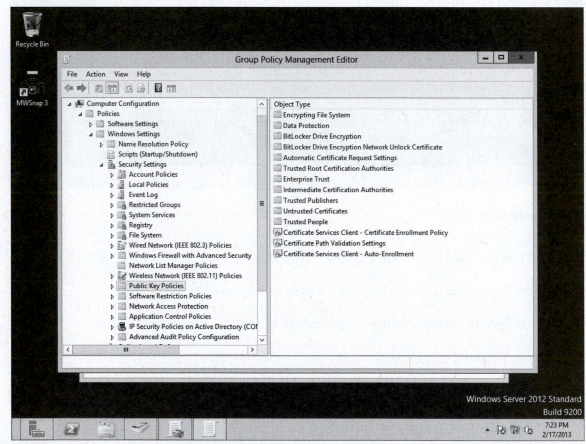

Figure 6-6
Opening the GPO public key policies

6. Right-click Encrypting File System, and select Create Data Recovery Agent. If you double-click Encrypting File System, you will see the Administrator listed in the right pane as shown in Figure 6-7.

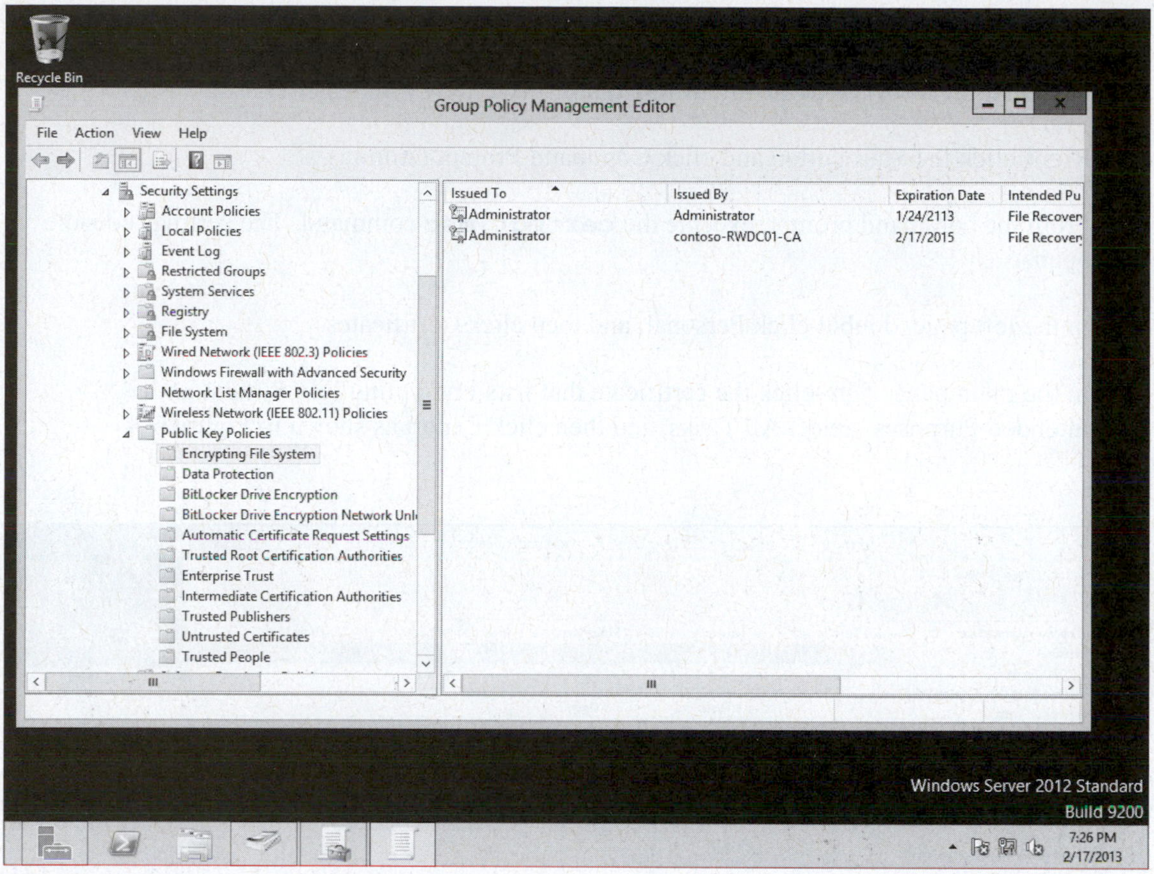

Figure 6-7
Viewing the current EFS recovery agents

7.   On RWDC01, log off as Contoso\User1 and log in as **Contoso\Administrator**.

Question 10	What is needed for a user to become a data recovery agent?

End of exercise.

Exercise 6.3	Backing Up and Restoring EFS Certificates
Overview	During this exercise, you back up an EFS certificate and later restore after you delete the certificate.
Completion time	10 minutes

Mindset Question: **You had a standalone computer that failed and had to be rebuilt. On the computer, you had some files that were encrypted with EFS. Fortunately, you backed up the files from time to time to a removable drive. After you rebuilt the computer, you decide to copy the files from the removable drive. Although you are using the same username and password that you used before, you cannot open the files because they are encrypted. What can you do?**

Backing Up the EFS Certificates

1. Log on to Server01 as **contoso\administrator**. The Server Manager console opens.

2. Right-click the Start button and click Command Prompt (Admin).

3. From the command prompt, execute the `certmgr.msc` command. The certmgr console opens.

4. In the left pane, double-click Personal, and then click Certificates.

5. In the main pane, right-click the certificate that lists Encrypting File System under Intended Purposes. Select All Tasks, and then click Export as shown in Figure 6-8.

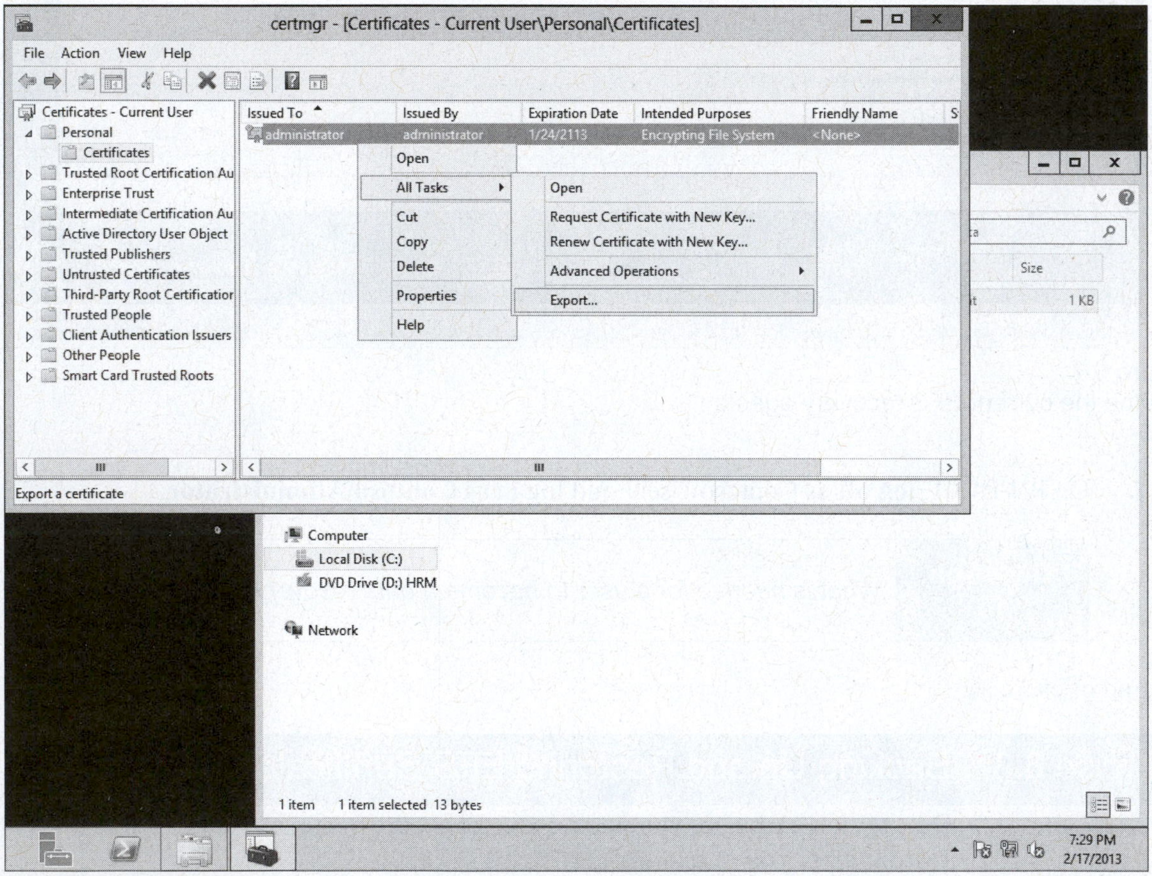

Figure 6-8
Exporting a certificate

6. When the Certificate Export Wizard starts, click Next.

7. On the Export Private Key page, click Yes, export the private key, and then click Next.

8. On the Export File Format page as shown in Figure 6-9, click Next.

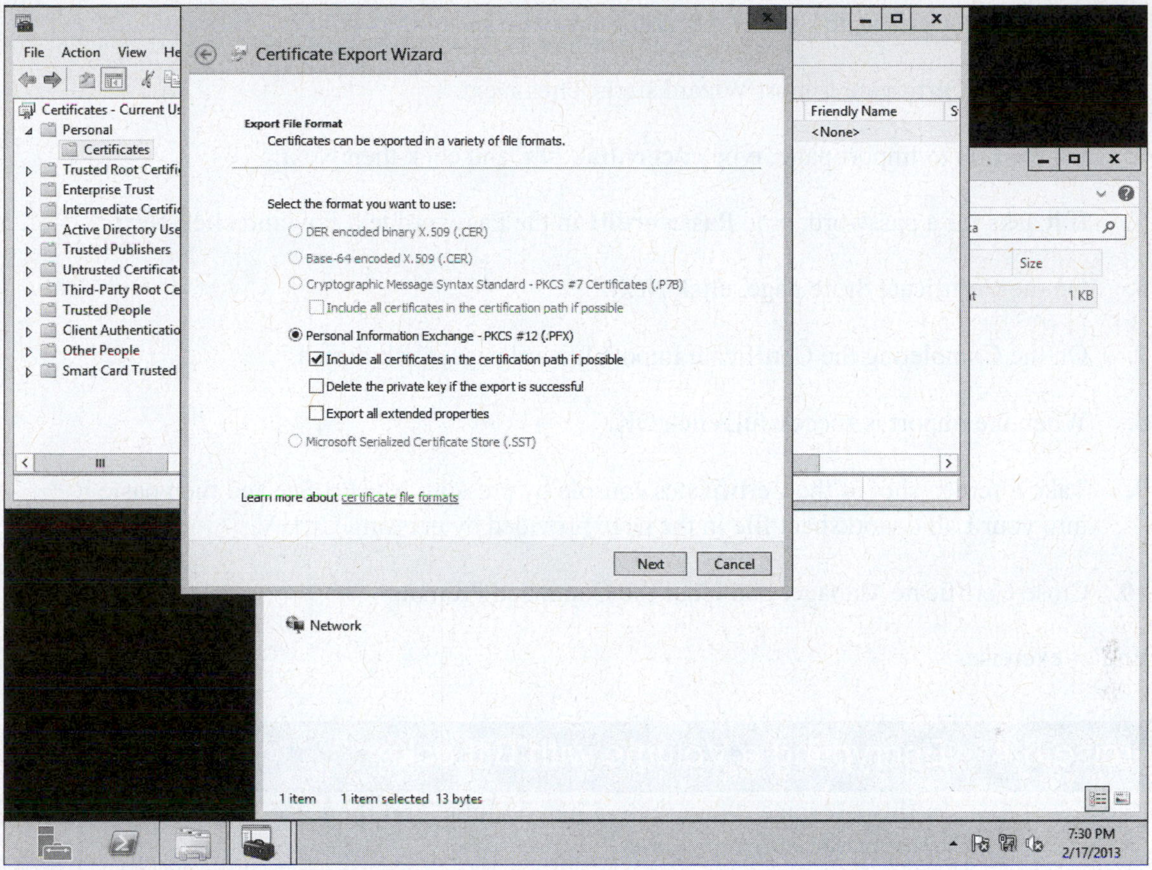

Figure 6-9
Specifying the exported format

9. On the Security page, select the Password check box, and type in the password of **Password01** in the Password and Confirm password text boxes. Click Next.

Question 11	What is the difference between the cer and the pfx format when backing up digital certificates?

10. On the File to Export page, type **C:\Cert.bak** in the File name text box, Click Next.

11. Take a screen shot of the Certificate Export wizard by pressing Alt+Prt Scr and then paste it into your Lab 6 worksheet file in the page provided by pressing Ctrl+V.

12. When the wizard is complete, click Finish.

13. When the export is successful, click OK.

Restoring the EFS Certificate

1. Right-click the Administrator certificate and click Delete. When it asks if you want to delete the certificate, read the warning and click Yes.

2. Right-click Certificates, select All Tasks, and then select Import.

3. When the Certificate Import Wizard starts, click Next.

4. On the File to Import page, type **c:\cert.bak.pfx**, and click then Next.

5. If it asks for a password, type **Password01** in the Password text box and click Next.

6. On the Certificate Store page, click Next.

7. On the Completing the Certificate Import Wizard page, click Finish.

8. When the import is successful, click OK.

9. Take a screen shot of the Certificates console by pressing Alt+Prt Scr and then paste it into your Lab 6 worksheet file in the page provided by pressing Ctrl+V.

10. Close Certificate Manager and close the Command Prompt.

End of exercise.

Exercise 6.4	Encrypting a Volume with BitLocker
Overview	In this exercise, you create a new volume and then use BitLocker to encrypt the entire volume.
Completion time	10 minutes

Mindset Question: **How does EFS and BitLocker differ?**

1. Log in to Server02 as the **Contoso\Administrator** user account. The Server Manager console opens.

2. On Server02, on Server Manager, click Manage and click Add Roles and Features. The Add Roles and Feature Wizard opens.

3. On the Before you begin page, click Next.

4. Select Role-based or feature-based installation and then click Next.

5. On the Select destination server page, click Next.

6. On the Select server roles page, click Next.

7. On the Select features page, select BitLocker Drive Encryption.

8. When the Add Roles and Features Wizard dialog box displays, click Add Features.

9. On the Select Features page, click Next.

10. On the Confirm installation selections page, click Install.

11. When BitLocker is installed, click Close.

12. Reboot the Server02.

13. Log in to Server02 as the **Contoso\Administrator**. The Server Manager console opens.

14. Using Server Manager, open the Tools menu and click Computer Management. The Computer Management console opens.

15. Expand the Storage node and click Disk Management.

16. Right-click the C drive and click Shrink Volume.

17. In the *Enter the amount of space to shrink in MB* text box, type **3000** and click Shrink.

18. Under Disk 0, right-click the unused space and click New Simple Volume.

19. When the Welcome to the New Simple Volume Wizard starts, click Next.

20. On the Specify Volume Size page, click Next.

21. On the Assign Drive Letter or Path page, click Next.

22. On the Format Partition page, click Next.

23. When the wizard is complete, click Finish.

24. Close Computer Management.

25. Click the Start button, and then click the Control Panel.

26. Click BitLocker Drive Encryption. The BitLocker Drive Encryption window opens as shown in Figure 6-10.

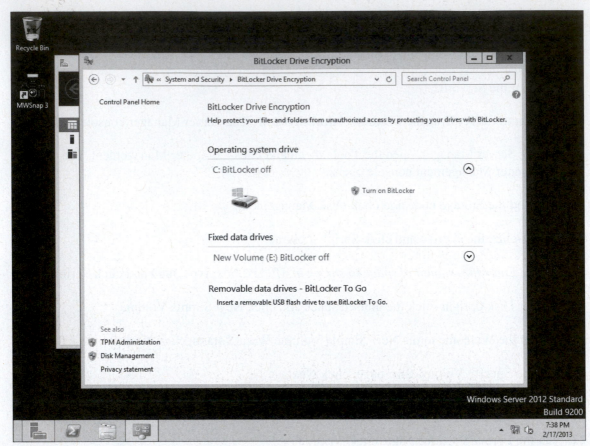

Figure 6-10
Opening the BitLocker settings

27. Click the down arrow next to the E drive. Then click Turn on BitLocker. A BitLocker Drive Encryption (E:) window opens.

28. On the *Choose how you want to unlock this drive* page, click to select the *Use a password to unlock the drive*. Type a password of **Password01** in the *Enter your password and Reenter your password* text boxes, and then click Next.

29. On the *How do you want to back up your recovery key?* page, click Save to a file option.

30. When the *Save BitLocker recovery key as dialog box* opens, type **\\rwdc01\Software** before BitLocker Recovery Key <GUID>.txt and click Save. Click Next.

31. On the BitLocker Drive Encryption (E:) page, select Encrypt entire drive radio button, and click Next.

32. On the *Are you ready to encrypt this drive?* page, click Start encrypting.

33. When the drive is encrypted, close the BitLocker Drive Encryption window.

34. Take a screen shot of the BitLocker window by pressing Alt+Prt Scr and then paste it into your Lab 6 worksheet file in the page provided by pressing Ctrl+V.

End of exercise.

LAB REVIEW QUESTIONS

Completion time	10 minutes

1. In Exercise 6.1, how do you enable EFS?

2. In Exercise 6.1, how do you allow other users to view an EFS file that you

3. In Exercise 6.2, how does a user get to be an EFS Recovery Agent?

4. In Exercise 6.3, what format did you use when backing up the certificates, so that it can also store the private and public keys?

5. In Exercise 6.4, what did you use to encrypt an entire volume?

6. In Exercise 6.4, from where do you control BitLocker?

Lab Challenge	Configuring Network Unlock
Overview	To complete this challenge, you will demonstrate how to enable Network Unlock.
Completion time	10 minutes

Starting with Windows Server 2012, Windows supports a Network Unlock feature, whereas when a computer connects to an organization domain, volumes that are encrypted with BitLocker will automatically be decrypted. What are the hardware and software components for Network Unlock and where is the Unlock key stored?

End of lab.

LAB 7
CONFIGURING ADVANCED AUDIT POLICIES

THIS LAB CONTAINS THE FOLLOWING EXERCISES AND ACTIVITIES:

Exercise 7.1   Implementing Auditing

Exercise 7.2   Implementing Advanced Auditing

Exercise 7.3   Using AuditPol.exe

Lab Challenge   Auditing Removable Devices

BEFORE YOU BEGIN

The lab environment consists of student workstations connected to a local area network, along with a server that functions as the domain controller for a domain called *contoso.com*. The computers required for this lab are listed in Table 7-1.

Table 7-1
Computers Required for Lab 7

Computer	Operating System	Computer Name
Server (VM 1)	Windows Server 2012	RWDC01
Server (VM 2)	Windows Server 2012	Server01

In addition to the computers, you also require the software listed in Table 7-2 to complete Lab 7.

Table 7-2
Software Required for Lab 7

Software	Location
Lab 7 student worksheet	Lab07_worksheet.docx (provided by instructor)

Working with Lab Worksheets

Each lab in this manual requires that you answer questions, take screen shots, and perform other activities that you will document in a worksheet named for the lab, such as Lab07_worksheet.docx. You will find these worksheets on the book companion site. It is recommended that you use a USB flash drive to store your worksheets, so you can submit them to your instructor for review. As you perform the exercises in each lab, open the appropriate worksheet file fill in the required information, and save the file to your flash drive.

After completing this lab, you will be able to:

- Configure standard audit policies

- Configure advanced audit policies

- Using AuditPol.exe to manage audit policies

- Audit removable devices

Estimated lab time: 60 minutes

Exercise 7.1	Implementing Auditing
Overview	During this exercise, you use standard Advanced Audit Policies to help keep track of who uses and attempts to use your network resources.
Completion time	15 minutes

Mindset Question: **Why is auditing important on today's network?**

1. Log in to Server01 as **Contoso\Administrator** with the password of **Password01**.

2. On Server01, when the Server Manager opens, open the Tools menu and click Event Viewer. The Event Viewer console opens.

3. Expand Windows Logs and click Security.

Question 1	*By looking at the current logs, what security events are being captured?*

4. Log in to RWDC01 as **Contoso\Administrator** with the password of **Password01**.

5. When Server Manger opens, click Local Server.

6. In the Properties pane, click On for *IE Enhanced Experience Improvement Program*.

7. When the *Internet Explorer Enhanced Security Configuration* dialog box opens, click Off for the Administrators group.

8. Click OK to close the Enhanced Security Configuration dialog box.

9. Using Server Manager, open the Tools menu and click Group Policy Management. The Group Policy Management console opens.

10. Expand Forest:contoso.com > Domains > contoso.com and click Default Domain Policy. If a Group Policy Management Console dialog box opens, read the message and then click to select *Do not show this message again*, then click OK.

11. In the right-pane, click the Settings tab.

Question 2	*Are there any audit policy settings configured for the Default Domain Policy?*

12. Expand the Domain Controllers node and click Default Domain Controllers Policy.

13. In the right-pane, click the Settings tab.

Question 3	*Are there any audit policy settings configured for the Default Domain Controllers Policy?*

14. Right-click the contoso.com node and click *Create a GPO in this domain, and Link it here*. The New GPO dialog box opens.

15. For the name, type **Audit Policy** and click OK to close the New GPO dialog box.

16. Right-click the Audit Policy and click Edit. The Group Policy Management Editor opens.

17. Expand Computer Configuration>Policies>Windows Settings>Security Settings>Local Policies, and click Audit Policy. The Policy settings show as shown in Figure 7-1.

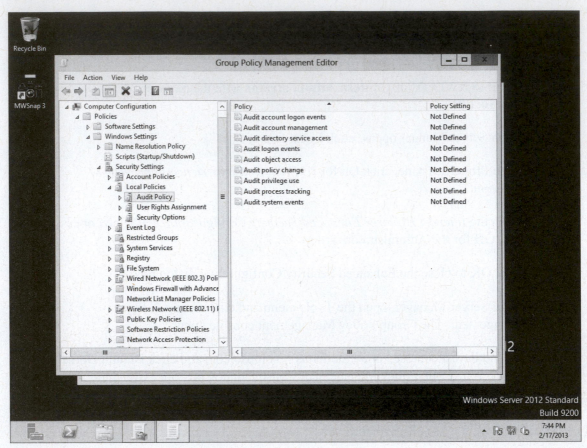

Figure 7-1
Configuring basic audit policies

18. Double-click Audit account logon events. The Audit account logon events Properties dialog box opens, as shown in Figure 7-2.

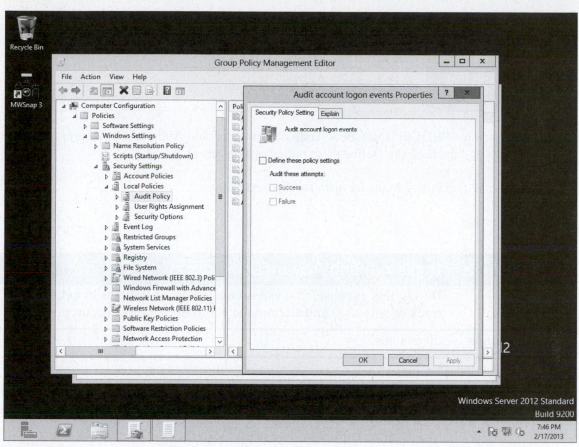

Figure 7-2
Enabling auditing of logon events

19. Click to select Define these policy settings and click to select both Success and Failure. Click OK to close the Audit account logon events Properties dialog box.

20. Double-click Audit Object access. The Audit object access Properties dialog box opens.

21. Click to select Define these policy settings and click to select both Success and Failure. Click OK to close the Audit object access Properties dialog box.

22. Go to Server01. With the Event Viewer open and Security highlighted, press F5 to refresh the Security logs.

23. Right-click the Start button and click Command Prompt (Admin). The Command Prompt opens.

24. Execute the following command:

```
gpupdate /force
```

25. Go back to the Event Viewer and refresh the Security logs again.

26. Take a screen shot of the Event Viewer window by pressing Alt+Prt Scr and then paste it into your Lab 7 worksheet file in the page provided by pressing Ctrl+V.

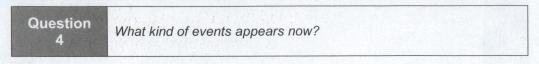

Question 4	What kind of events appears now?

27. Go back to RWDC01. Open both Audit object access and Audit account logon events and uncheck the Define these policy settings check boxes.

28. Leave Group Policy Manager open for the next exercise.

End of exercise.

Exercise 7.2	Implementing Advanced Auditing
Overview	During this exercise, you use Advanced Audit Policies to help keep track of who uses and attempts to use your network resources.
Completion time	20 minutes

Mindset Question: **What advantage does advanced auditing have over standard auditing?**

1. On the RWDC01 server, if the Group Policy Management Editor is not open for the Audit Policy policy, right-click the Audit Policy and click Edit.

2. In the Group Policy Management Editor on RWDC01, navigate to Computer Configuration\Policies\Windows Settings\Security Settings\Advanced Audit Policy Configuration and click Audit Policies, as shown in Figure 7-3.

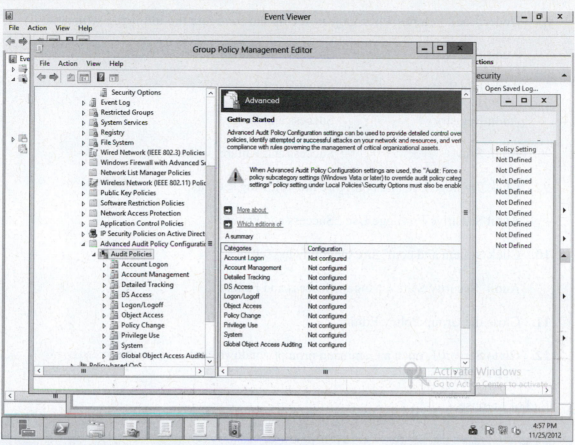

Figure 7-3
Configuring Advanced Audit Policy configuration settings

3. Under Audit Policies, double-click Logon/Logoff.

4. Double-click Audit Account Lockout. When the Audit Account Lockout Properties dialog box opens, click to select Configure the following audit events, and then select Success. Click OK to close Audit Lockout Properties.

5. Configure the following settings:

   Audit Logoff   Success

   Audit Logon   Success and Failure

6. Take a screen shot of the Group Policy Management Editor window by pressing Alt+Prt Scr and then paste it into your Lab 7 worksheet file in the page provided by pressing Ctrl+V.

7. Under Account Policies, click Account Management and configure the following settings:

   Audit Computer Account Management   Success and Failure

   Audit Security Group Management   Success and Failure

   Audit User Account Management   Success and Failure

8. Under Audit Policies, click Object Access and configure the following settings:

    Audit File Share   Success and Failure

    Audit File System   Success and Failure

    Audit Registry   .   Success and Failure

    Audit SAM   Success and Failure

9. Click Privilege Use and configure the following settings:

    Audit Sensitive Privilege Use   Success and Failure

10. Click System and configure the following settings:

    Audit Security State Change   Success and Failure

11. Close the Group Policy Editor.

12. Go to Server01, open a Command prompt windows, and execute the `gpupdate /force` command.

End of exercise.

Exercise 7.3	Using AuditPol.exe
Overview	During this exercise, you use AuditPol.exe to manage auditing.
Completion time	10 minutes

Mindset Question: **What advantage does auditpol.exe have over standard and advanced audit policies?**

1. On the RWDC01 server, open a Command Prompt, and execute the following command to get a list of all Audit settings:

    ```
    auditpol /get /category:*
    ```

2. To see the audit policy set for Contoso\User1, execute the following command:

    ```
    auditpol.exe /get /user:contoso\user1 /category:*
    ```

3. Observe that there is no audit policy defined for Contoso\User1. To set the audit policy for User1 so that account management is audited for User1, execute the following command:

    ```
    auditpol.exe /set /user:contoso\user1 /subcategory:"user account management" /success:enable /failure:enable
    ```

4. To display the settings for everyone again, run the following command:

    ```
    auditpol /get /category:*
    ```

5. To get the settings for user1, execute the following settings:

    ```
    auditpol.exe /get /category:* /user:user1
    ```

Question 5	Are the audit policies configured with Group Policies displayed when you specified a single user?

6. Take a screen shot of the Command Prompt window by pressing Alt+Prt Scr and then paste it into your Lab 7 worksheet file in the page provided by pressing Ctrl+V.

7. To reset the settings for user1, execute the following settings:

    ```
    auditpol /remove /user:contoso\user1
    ```

8. Verify that the per-user setting was removed by running the following command:

    ```
    auditpol.exe /get /user:contoso\user1 /category:*
    ```

End of exercise.

LAB REVIEW QUESTIONS

Completion time	10 minutes

1. In Exercise 7.1, what is the location where you would find the standard auditing settings?

2. In Exercise 7.2, what is the location where you would find the advanced auditing settings?

3. In Exercise 7.2, which category would you use to enable auditing of the Registry?

4. In Exercise 7.3, what command did you use to configure a user-based audit policy?

Lab Challenge	Auditing Removable Devices
Overview	To complete this challenge, you must demonstrate how to add audit removable devices by writing the steps to complete the tasks described in the scenerio.
Completion time	5 minutes

You need to determine when someone inserts a USB flash drive into a system in case it is being used to copy sensitive material. What can you do?

Write out the steps you performed to complete the challenge.

End of lab.

LAB 8
CONFIGURING DNS ZONES

THIS LAB CONTAINS THE FOLLOWING EXERCISES AND ACTIVITIES:

Exercise 8.1	Installing DNS
Exercise 8.2	Creating Primary and Secondary Zones
Exercise 8.3	Creating an Active Directory Integrated Zone
Exercise 8.4	Configuring Zone Delegation
Exercise 8.5	Configuring a Stub Zone
Exercise 8.6	Configuring Forwarding and Conditional Forwarding Zones
Exercise 8.7	Configuring Zone Transfers
Lab Challenge	Using the DNSCMD Command To Manage Zones

BEFORE YOU BEGIN

The lab environment consists of student workstations connected to a local area network, along with a server that functions as the domain controller for a domain called *contoso.com*. The computers required for this lab are listed in Table 8-1.

Table 8-1
Computers Required for Lab 8

Computer	Operating System	Computer Name
Server (VM 1)	Windows Server 2012	RWDC01
Server (VM 2)	Windows Server 2012	Server01

In addition to the computers, you also require the software listed in Table 8-2 to complete Lab 8.

Table 8-2
Software Required for Lab 8

Software	Location
Lab 8 student worksheet	Lab08_worksheet.docx (provided by instructor)

Working with Lab Worksheets

Each lab in this manual requires that you answer questions, take screen shots, and perform other activities that you will document in a worksheet named for the lab, such as Lab08_worksheet.docx. You will find these worksheets on the book companion site. It is recommended that you use a USB flash drive to store your worksheets, so you can submit them to your instructor for review. As you perform the exercises in each lab, open the appropriate worksheet file fill in the required information, and save the file to your flash drive.

After completing this lab, you will be able to:

- Configure DNS zones including primary zones, secondary zones, and Active Directory Integrated zones.

- Configure Zone delegation

- Configure a Stub Zone

- Configure Forwarding and Conditional Forwarding zones

- Configure Zone Transfers

- Use DNSCMD command to manage zones

Estimated lab time: 80 minutes

Exercise 8.1	Installing DNS
Overview	In Lesson 1, you already installed DNS on RWDC01. However, we need a second DNS server for future exercises. Therefore, during this exercise, you install a second DNS server on Server01.
Completion time	10 minutes

1. Log in to Server01 as the **Contoso\administrator** user account. The Server Manager console opens.

2. When Server Manager opens, select Manage and click Add Roles and Features.

3. On the Before you begin page, click Next.

4. Select *Role-based or feature-based installation*, and then click Next.

5. Click *Select a server from the server pool*, click Server01.contoso.com, and then click Next.

6. On the Select server roles page, click DNS Server.

7. When the Add Roles and Features Wizard dialog box appears, select Add Features, and then click Next.

8. When the Select features page opens, click Next.

9. On the DNS Server page, click Next.

10. On the Confirm installation selections page, click the Install button.

11. When the installation is done, click the Close button.

End of exercise.

Exercise 8.2	Creating Primary and Secondary Zones
Overview	During this exercise, you create primary and secondary zones on RWDC01 and Server01.
Completion time	15 minutes

Mindset Question: **For the Contoso Corporation, you are building a new network. Therefore, you need to install DNS to support your network. You have three primary sites. So how many primary zones and how many secondary zones would you create to support the primary site?**

Creating a Standard Forward Lookup Primary Zone

1. Log in to RWDC01 as the **Contoso\administrator** user account. The Server Manager console opens.

2. On Server Manager, click Tools > DNS to open the DNS Manager console. If necessary, expand the DNS Manager console to a full-screen view.

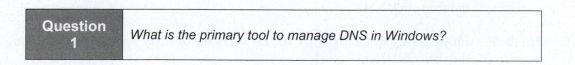

Question 1	*What is the primary tool to manage DNS in Windows?*

3. Expand the server so that you can see the Forward Lookup Zones and Reverse Lookup Zones folders, if needed.

4. Click, then right-click Forward Lookup Zones, and then click New Zone.

5. When the Welcome to the New Zone Wizard page opens, click Next.

6. On the Zone Type page (as shown in Figure 8-1), with the Primary zone radio button already selected, click to deselect the Store the zone in Active Directory option. Click Next.

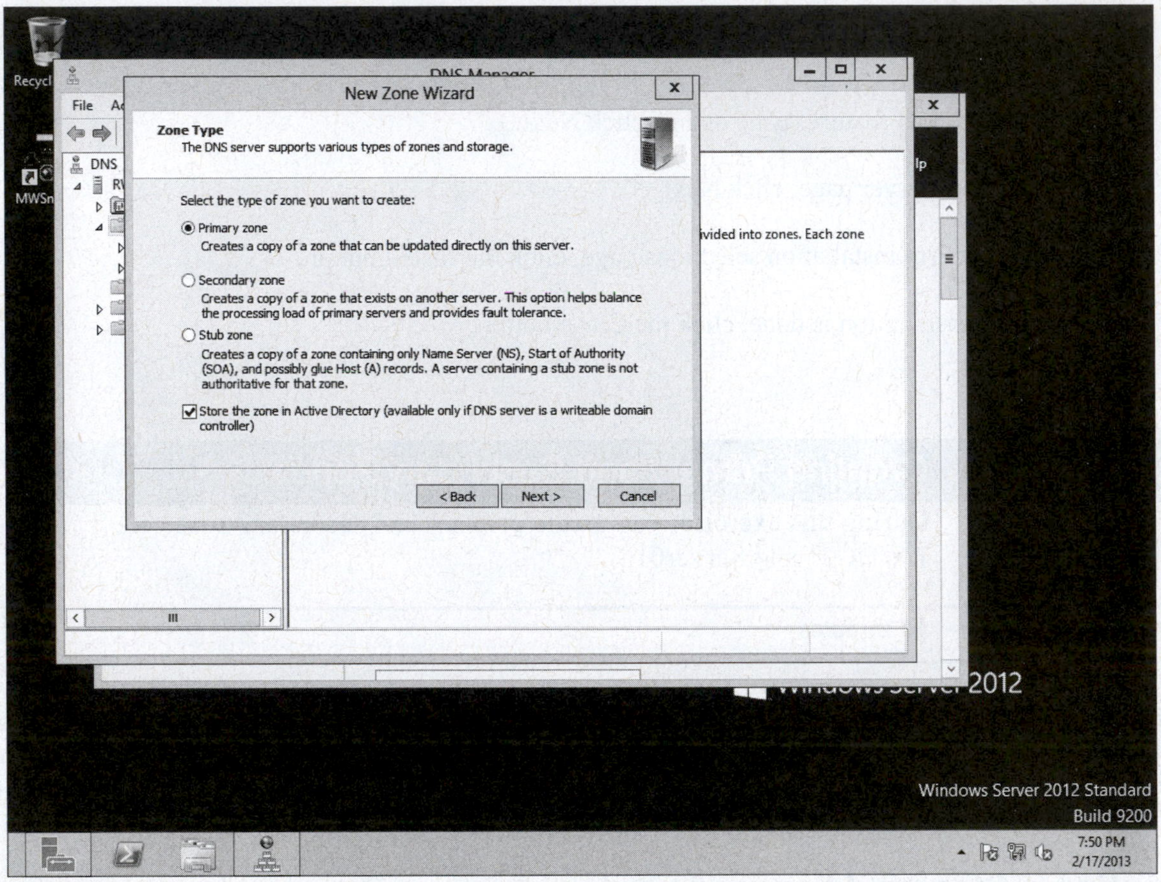

Figure 8-1
Creating a new zone

7. The Zone Name page opens. In the Zone name text box, type **adatum.com**, and then click Next.

8. On the Zone File page, ensure that the *Create a new file with this file name* radio button is selected, and then click Next.

9. On the Dynamic Update page, ensure that the *Do not allow dynamic updates radio button* is selected, and then click Next.

10. When the Completing the New Zone Wizard page displays, click Finish.

Creating a Standard Forward Lookup Secondary Zone

1. On Server01, click Tools > DNS to open the DNS Manager console. If necessary, expand the DNS Manager console to a full-screen view.

2. Expand the server so that you can see the Forward Lookup Zones and Reverse Lookup Zones folders, if needed.

3. Click, then right-click Forward Lookup Zones, and then click New Zone.

4. When the Welcome to the New Zone Wizard page opens, click Next.

5. On the Zone Type page, select the Secondary zone radio button and click Next. The Zone Name page appears.

6. In the Zone name text box, type **adatum.com**, and then click Next.

7. On the Master DNS Servers page, type **192.168.1.50** as shown in Figure 8-2 and then press the Enter key. Click Next.

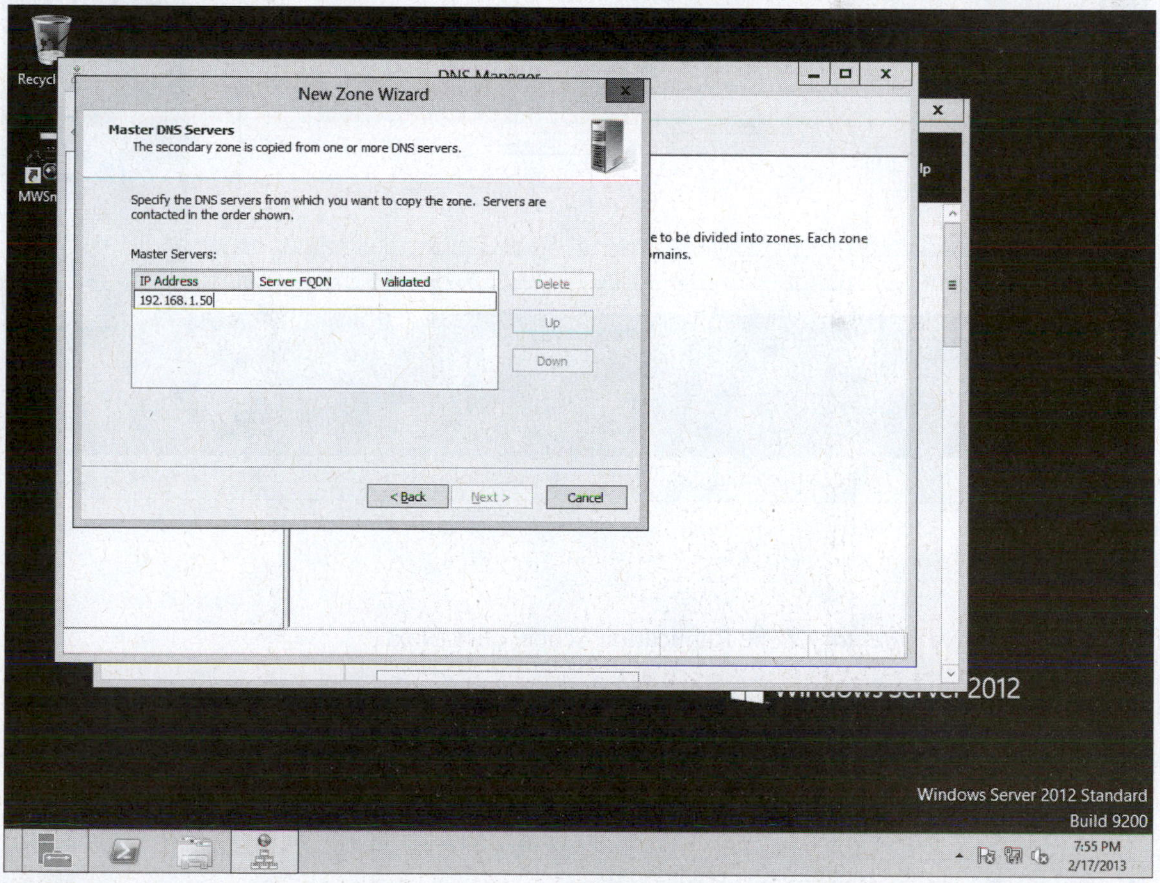

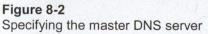

Figure 8-2
Specifying the master DNS server

8. When the Completing the New Zone Wizard page opens, click Finish.

Creating a Standard Reverse Lookup Primary Zone

1. On RWDC01, go to the DNS Manager console. Right-click Reverse Lookup Zones, and then click New Zone.

2. When the Welcome to the New Zone Wizard page opens, click Next.

3. On the Zone Type page (as shown in Figure 8-3), click Next.

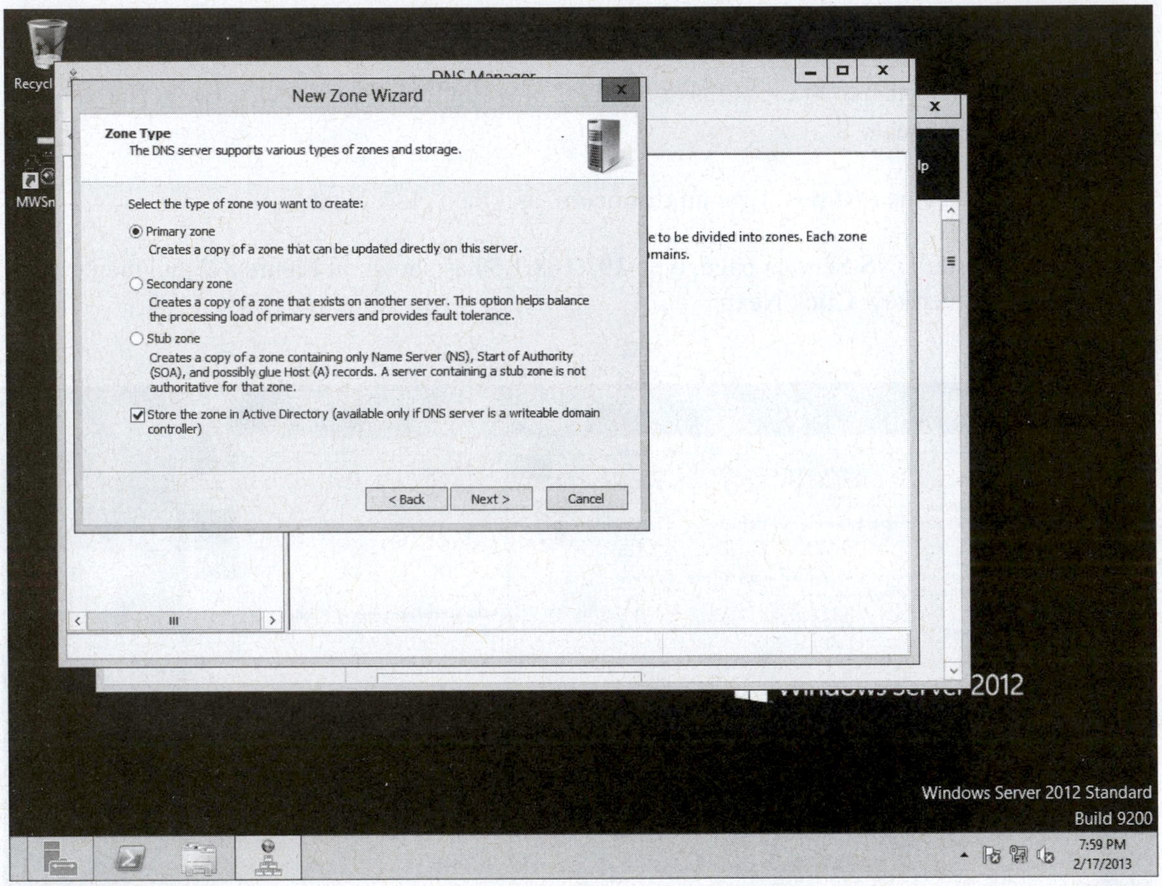

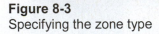

Figure 8-3
Specifying the zone type

4. On the Active Directory Zone Replication Scope, click Next.

5. On the Reverse Lookup Zone Name page, with IPv4 Reverse Lookup Zone already selected, click Next.

6. Type in the network address of **172.24.1**. Click Next.

7. On the Dynamic Update page, click Next.

8. When the Completing the New Zone Wizard page opens, click Finish.

End of exercise.

Exercise 8.3	Creating an Active Directory Integrated Zone
Overview	During this exercise, you create an Active Directory Integrated zone.
Completion time	5 minutes

Mindset Question: **You decide that you want to improve the DNS system for your company and you are thinking of switching to Active Directory-Integrated zones. What are the advantages of Active Directory-Integrated zones?**

1.   On RWDC01, go to the DNS Manager console.

2.   Right-click the Forward Lookup Zones and click New Zone.

3.   When the New Zone Wizard starts, click Next.

4.   With Primary zone and Store the zone in Active Directory options are already selected, click Next.

5.   On the Active Directory Zone Replication Scope dialog box, click Next.

6.   On the Zone Name page, type **fabrikam.com** and click Next.

7.   On the Dynamic Update page, with the *Allow only secure dynamic updates* selected, click Next.

Question 2	What is needed to perform secure dynamic updates?

8.   Click Finish. The fabrikam.com domain is created.

End of exercise.

Exercise 8.4	Configuring Zone Delegation
Overview	In this exercise, you delegate a subdomain called *support under fabrikam.com* on a different DNS server.
Completion time	5 minutes

Mindset Question: **You are working for the Contoso Corporation. Why would you want to use zone delegation and conditional forwarding?**

1.   On RWDC01, go to the DNS Manager console. Under Forward Lookup Zones, click and right-click Fabrikam.com and click New Delegation.

2. When the Welcome to the New Delegation Wizard starts, click Next.

3. In the Delegated domain text box, type **support** (as shown in Figure 8-4) and then click Next.

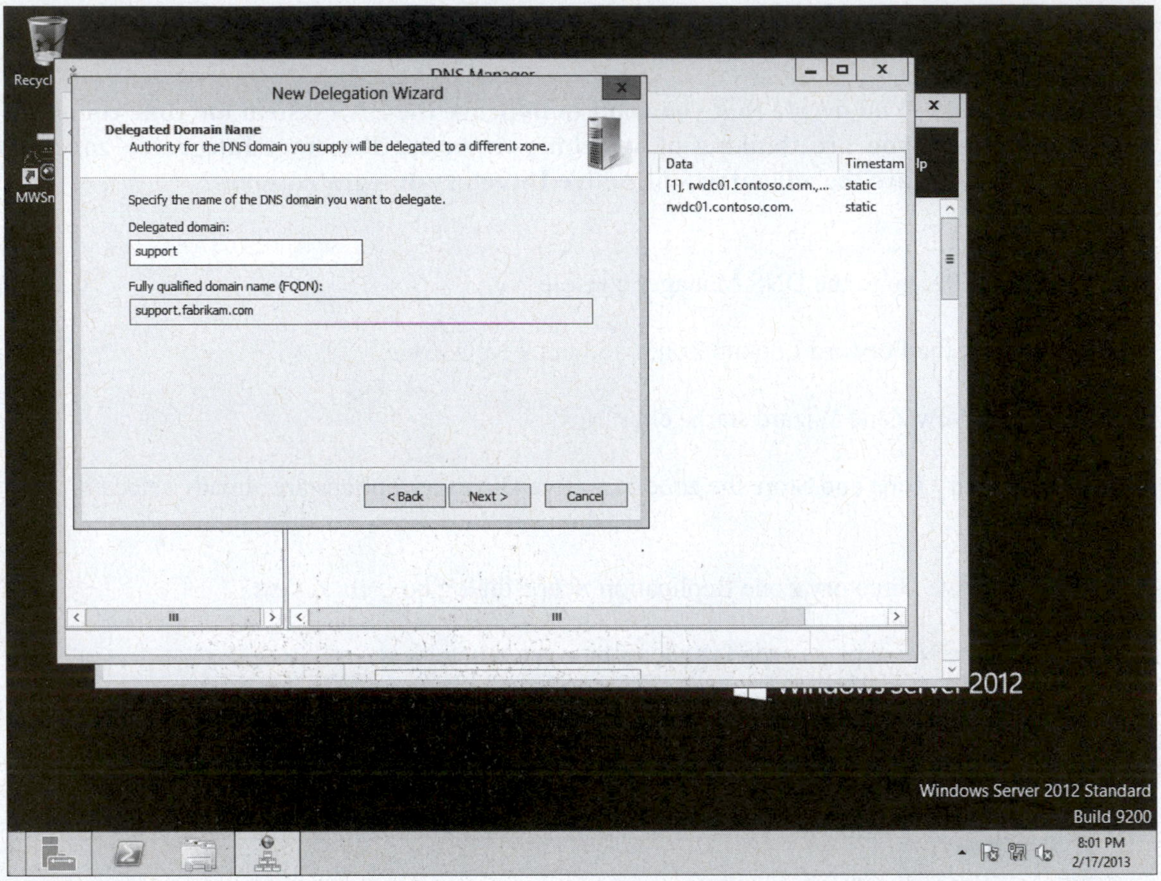

Figure 8-4
Delegating a domain

4. On the New Name Servers page, click the Add button, type **Server01** in the *Server fully qualified domain name (FQDN)* text box, and click Resolve. Don't worry about the red circle with the white X; the zone in Server01 still needs to be created. Click the OK button to close the New Name Server record dialog box. Click Next.

5. When the wizard is complete, click the Finish button.

6. On Server01, go to the DNS Manager console. Right-click Forward Lookup Zones, and click New Zone.

7. When the New Zone Wizard starts, click Next.

8. On the Zone type, with the Primary zone already selected, click Next.

9. On the Zone Name page, type **support.fabrikam.com** in the Zone name text box and click Next.

10. On the Zone File page, click Next.

11. On the Dynamic Update page, click Next.

12. When the wizard is complete, click Finish.

End of exercise.

Exercise 8.5	Creating a Stub Zone
Overview	In this exercise, you create a stub zone that points directly to another DNS server.
Completion time	10 minutes

Mindset Questions: **What resource records are found in the stub zone?**

1. On RWDC01, go to the DNS Manager console. Right-click Forward Lookup Zones, and click New Zone.

2. When the New Zone Wizard begins, cick Next.

3. When the Zone Type page opens, select the Stub zone radio button and click Next.

4. On the Active Directory Zone Replication Scope page, click Next.

5. On the Zone Name page, type **litware.com** in the Zone name text box, and then click Next.

6. On the Master DNS Servers page, type **192.168.1.60** and press the Enter key. Click Next.

7. When the Completing the New Zone Wizard displays, click Finish.

8. On Server01, go to the DNS Manager console. Right-click Forward Lookup Zones and click New Zone.

9. When the New Zone Wizard, click Next.

10. On the Zone Type page, click Next.

11. On the Zone Name page, type **litware.com** and click Next.

12. On the Zone File page, click Next.

13. On the Dynamic Update page, click Next.

14. When the wizard is complete, click Finish.

15. Take a screen shot of the DNS Manager window by pressing Alt+Prt Scr and then paste it into your Lab 8 worksheet file in the page provided by pressing Ctrl+V.

End of exercise.

Exercise 8.6	Configuring Forwarding and Conditional Forwarding Zones
Overview	To improve performance, you can control which DNS servers requests are forwarded to when performing naming resolution by configuring forwarding and creating conditional forwarding zones. Therefore, during this exercise, you configure forwarding and create a conditional forwarding zone.
Completion time	10 minutes

Configuring Forwarders

1. On Server01, go to the DNS Manager console. Right-click Server01 and select Properties. The Server Properties dialog box opens.

2. Select the Forwarders tab.

3. Click the Edit button. The Edit Forwarders dialog box opens as shown in Figure 8-5.

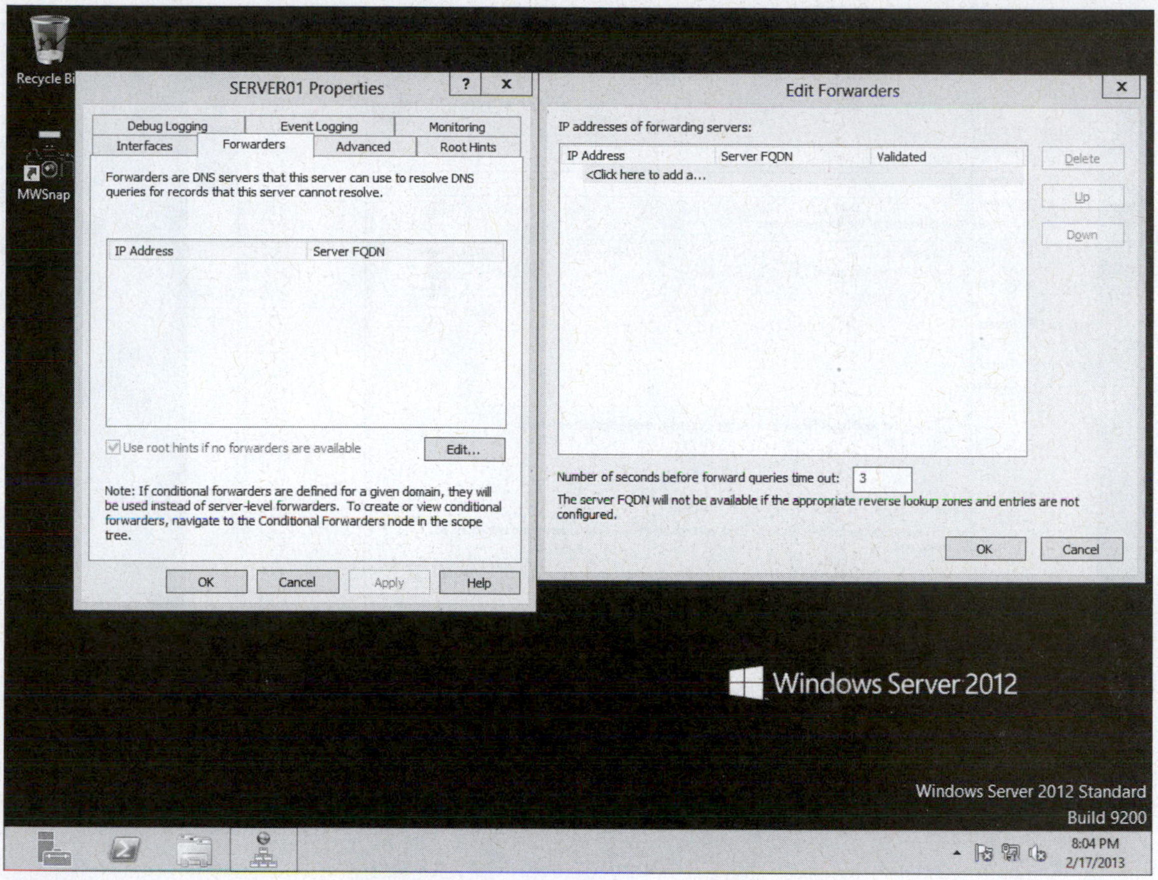

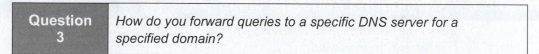

Figure 8-5
Specifying DNS servers to forward request to

4. In the IP address column, type **192.168.1.50** and press the Enter key. Click the OK button to close the Forwarders dialog box.

5. Click the OK button to close the server Properties dialog box.

Configuring Conditional Forwarders

1. On Server01, use the DNS Manager console to create a primary lookup zone called **lucernepublishing.com**.

Question 3	How do you forward queries to a specific DNS server for a specified domain?

2. On RWDC01, go to the DNS Manager console. Click Conditional Forwarders Zones. Right-click Conditional Forwarders Zones and click New Conditional Forwarder. The New Conditional Forwarder dialog box appears as shown in Figure 8-6.

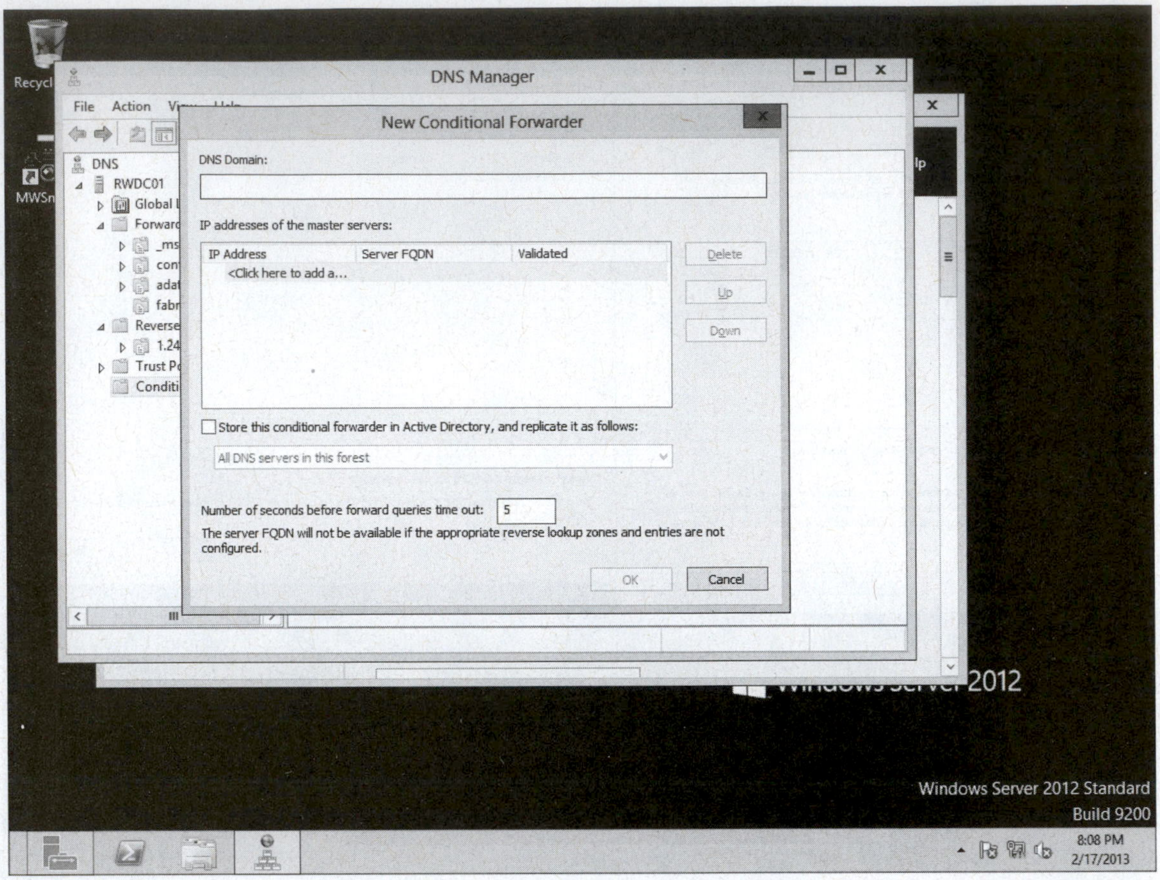

Figure 8-6
Creating a new conditional forwarder

3. Type **lucernepublishing.com** in the DNS Domain text box.

4. In the IP Address column, type **192.168.1.60** in the IP addresses column and press the Enter key.

5. Click **OK** to close the New Conditional Forwarder dialog box.

End of exercise.

Exercise 8.7	Configuring Zone Transfers
Overview	By configuring zone transfers, you can control which servers DNS information is copied.
Completion time	10 minutes

Mindset Questions: You need to configure zone transfers between multiple DNS servers. What are the three types of zone transfer available?

1. On RWDC01, using the DNS Manager console, click adatum.com and then right-click the adatum.com zone and click Properties. The Properties dialog box opens.

2. Click the Zone Transfers tab.

3. With the Allow zone transfers option already selected (as shown in Figure 8-7), you can choose Only to the following Servers.

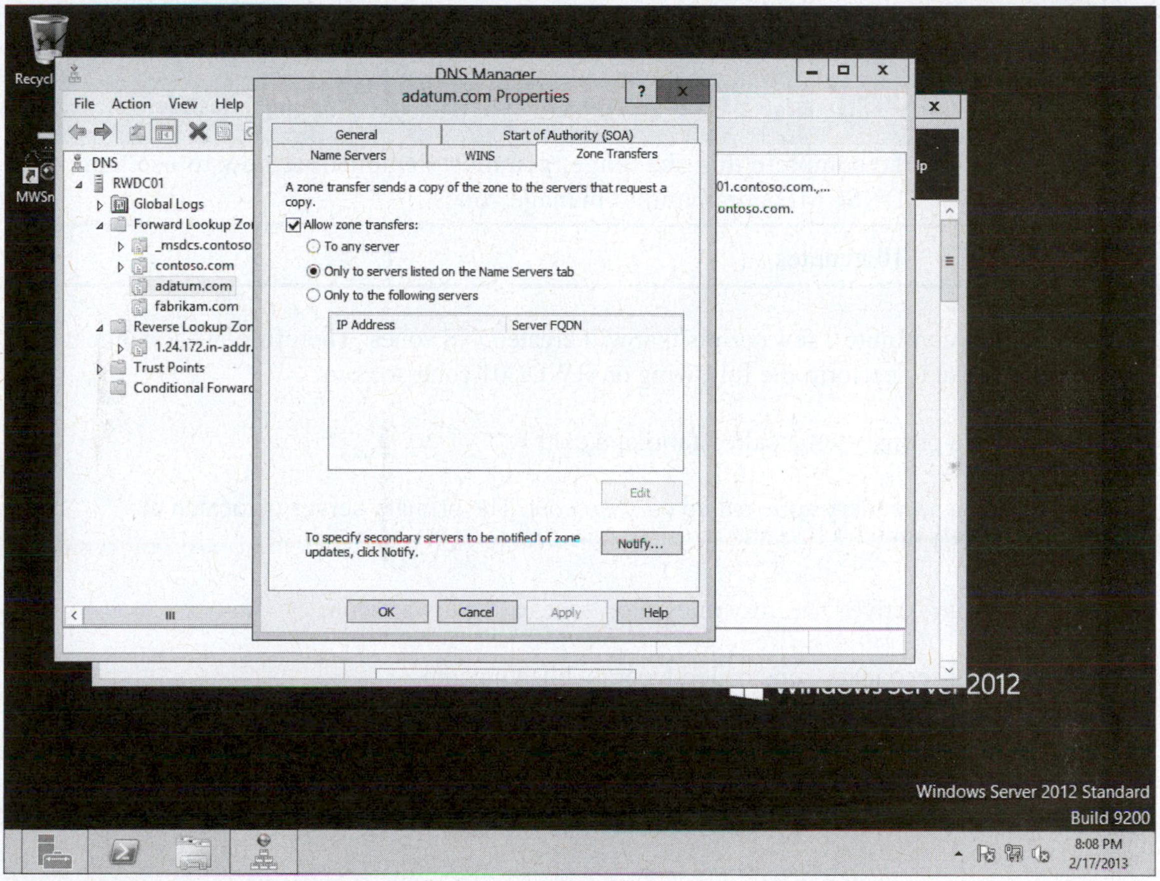

Figure 8-7
Configuring zone transfers

4. Click Notify, click The following servers, type **192.168.1.60** in the IP Address columna, and press the Enter key. Then click OK.

5. Click OK to close the Properties dialog box.

End of exercise.

LAB REVIEW QUESTIONS

Completion time   10 minutes

1. In Exercise 8.2, what must you create before creating the secondary zone?

2. In Exercise 8.3, what is the prerequisite to have Active Directory-Integrated zones?

3. In Exercise 8.6, how do you configure all queries that a DNS server cannot directly resolve be forwarded to your ISP's DNS server?

4. In Exercise 8.6, where did you configure forwarding?

5. In Exercise 8.7, how did you configure zone transfers?

Lab Challenge	Using the DNSCMD Command to Manage Zones
Overview	To complete this challenge, you must demonstrate how to use the DNSCMD command to manage zones.
Completion time	10 minutes

You need to configure a few scripts that will create DNS zones. Therefore, what commands would you use to perform the following on RWDC01.contoso.com:

Create a primary zone called fabrikam.com

Create a secondary zone called *contoso.com*. The primary server is located at 192.168.1.60

Create an Active Directory integrated zone called litware.com

Delete a secondary zone called lucernpublishing.com.

Force a zone replication for the lucernpublishing.com zone.

End of lab.

LAB 9
CONFIGURING DNS RECORDS

THIS LAB CONTAINS THE FOLLOWING EXERCISES AND ACTIVITIES:

Exercise 9.1   Managing DNS Resource Records

Exercise 9.2   Configuring Round Robin

Exercise 9.3   Configuring Zone Scavenging

Exercise 9.4   Troubleshooting DNS

Lab Challenge   Using the DNSCMD Command to Manage Resource Records

BEFORE YOU BEGIN

The lab environment consists of student workstations connected to a local area network, along with a server that functions as the domain controller for a domain called *contoso.com*. The computers required for this lab are listed in Table 9-1.

Table 9-1
Computers Required for Lab 9

Computer	Operating System	Computer Name
Server (VM 1)	Windows Server 2012	RWDC01

In addition to the computers, you also require the software listed in Table 9-2 to complete Lab 9.

Table 9-2
Software Required for Lab 9

Software	Location
Lab 9 student worksheet	Lab09_worksheet.docx (provided by instructor)

Working with Lab Worksheets

Each lab in this manual requires that you answer questions, take screen shots, and perform other activities that you will document in a worksheet named for the lab, such as Lab09_worksheet.docx. You will find these worksheets on the book companion site. It is recommended that you use a USB flash drive to store your worksheets, so you can submit them to your instructor for review. As you perform the exercises in each lab, open the appropriate worksheet file fill in the required information, and save the file to your flash drive.

After completing this lab, you will be able to:

- Manage DNS Resource Records

- Configure round robin

- Configure Zone Scavenging

- Troubleshoot DNS

- Using DNSCMD command to manage Resource Records

Estimated lab time: 60 minutes

Exercise 9.1	Managing DNS Resource Records
Overview	In the previous lab, you created several zones. With the exception of default resource records that are created when you create a zone, you need to add resource records. Therefore, during this exercise, you create resource records.
Completion time	15 minutes

Mindset Question: **In this lab, you create DNS resource records. Which resource record is the most common resource record?**

1. Log in to RWDC01 as the **Contoso\administrator** user account. The Server Manager console opens.

2. On Server Manager, click Tools > DNS to open the DNS Manager console. If necessary, expand the DNS Manager console to a full-screen view.

3. Under RWDC01, expand Forward Lookup Zones.

Question 1	What records will you find in a forward lookup zone?

4. Right-click adatum.com and click Properties. The Properties dialog box opens.

Question 2	What records can you configure in the Properties dialog box?

Question 3	What is the default minimum TTL for SOA records?

5. Click OK to close the Properties dialog box.

6. Right-click adatum.com and click New Host (A or AAAA). The New Host dialog box opens as shown in Figure 9-1.

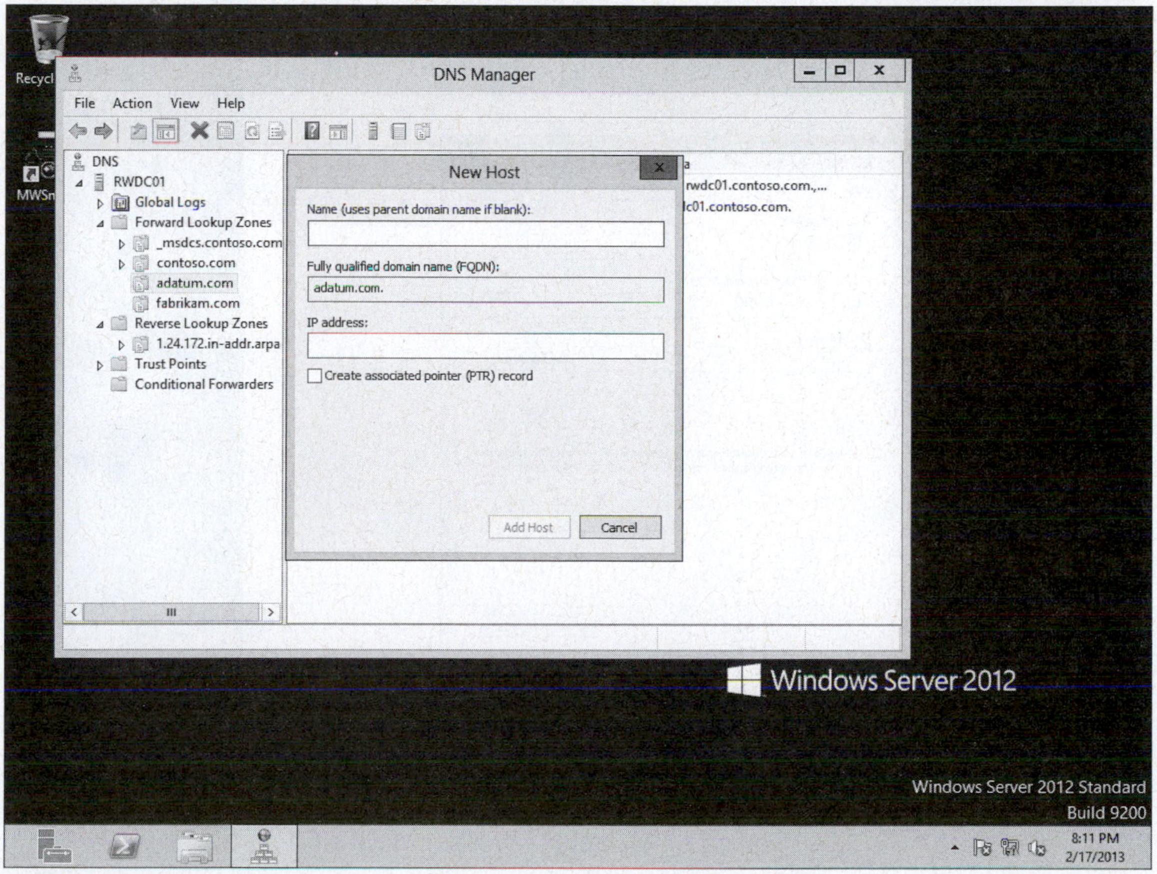

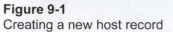

Figure 9-1
Creating a new host record

7. In the Name text box, type **PC1**. For the IP address text box, type **192.168.1.201**. click Add Host.

8. When the record has been created, click OK, then click Done.

9. Right-click adatum.com and click New Host (A or AAAA). In the Name text box, type **PC2**. For the IP address text box, type **192.168.1.202**. Select the *Create associated pointer (PTR) record*. Click Add Host. When the record has been created, click OK, then click Done.

10. Take a screen shot of the DNS Manager window by pressing Alt+Prt Scr and then paste it into your Lab 9 worksheet file in the page provided by pressing Ctrl+V.

11. Expand the Reverse Lookup Zones and click 1.168.192.in-addr.arpa zone. Notice that the 192.168.1.202 record is there, but not the 192.168.1.201. You might need to refresh the zone if 192.168.1.202 has not yet appeared. To refresh the zone, press the F5 key.

Question 4	*What records are kept in the reverse-lookup zones?*

12. Right-click 1.168.192.in-addr.arpa and click New Pointer (PTR). The New Resource Record dialog box opens as shown in Figure 9-2.

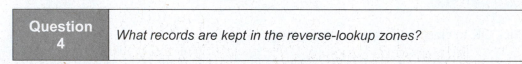

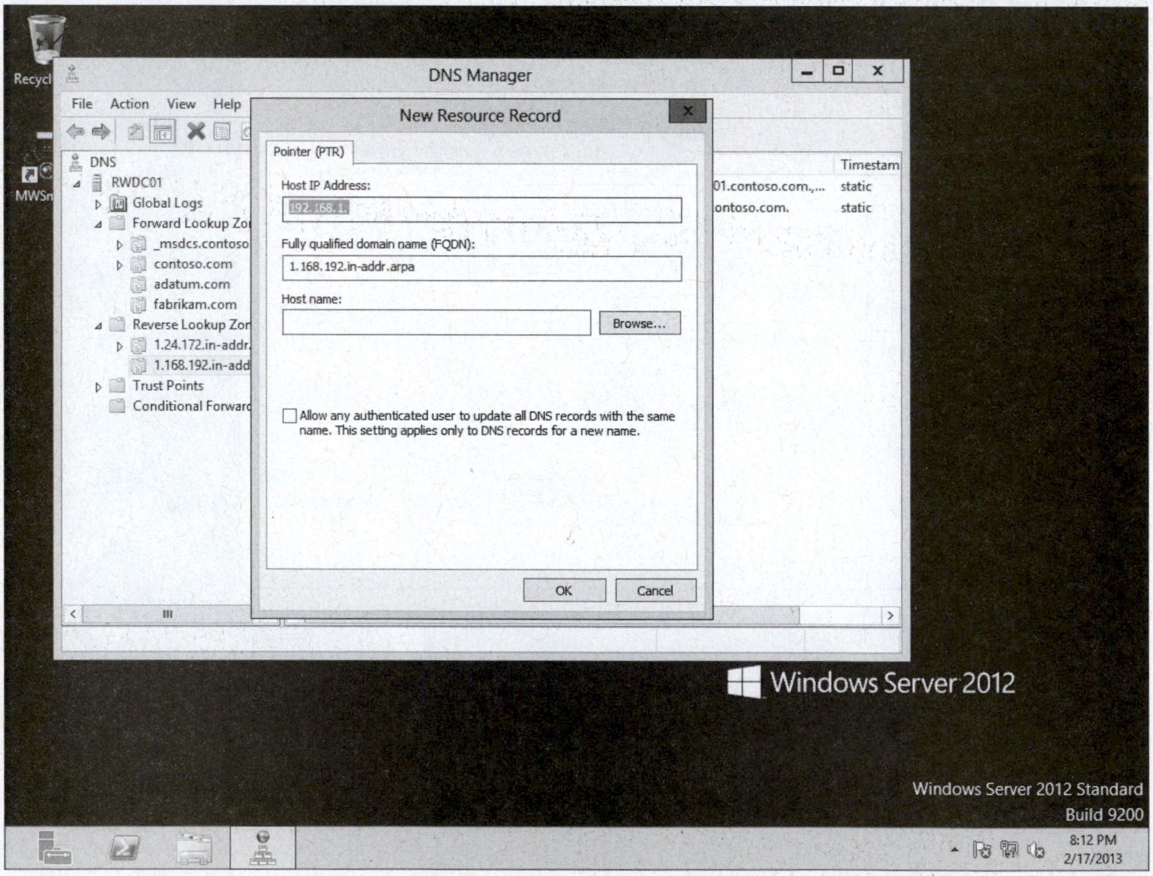

Figure 9-2
Creating a new PTR record

13. On the Host IP Address text box, change the text to **192.168.1.201**. In the Host name text box, type **PC1**. Click OK.

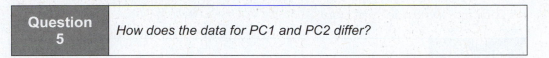

Question 5	How does the data for PC1 and PC2 differ?

14. Double-click 192.168.1.201. Change the Host name from PC1 to **PC1.contoso.com.** (with a period at the end). Click OK

Question 6	What does the period at the end signify?

15. Take a screen shot of the DNS Manager window by pressing Alt+Prt Scr and then paste it into your Lab 9 worksheet file in the page provided by pressing Ctrl+V.

16. Right-click adatum.com and click New Host (A or AAAA). In the Name text box, type **PC3**. For the IP address text box, type **192.168.1.203**. Select the Create associated pointer (PTR) record. Click Add Host. When the record has been created, click OK, and then click Done.

17. Right-click adatum.com and click New Alias (CNAME). In the Alias name, type **www**. In the Fully qualified domain name (FQDN) for target host text box, type **PC3.adatum.com**.

Question 7	What is the fully qualified domain name?

18. Click OK.

19. Right-click the Start button and click Command Prompt (Admin). The Administrator: Command Prompt opens.

20. To see the name PC1 resolved to its IP address, execute the following command:

```
nslookup PC3.adatum.com
```

Question 8	What address was returned?

21. To see the IP resolution of 192.168.1.203 to its name, execute the following command:

```
nslookup 192.168.1.203
```

Question 9	What name was returned?

22. To see the resolution of the alias www.adatum.com to its name and IP address, execute the following command:

```
nslookup www.adatum.com
```

Question 10	What name and IP address was returned?

23. Right-click adatum.com and click New Mail Exchange (MX). In the Host or child domain text box, type **PC2**. In the Fully Qualified domain name (FQDN) of mail server, type **adatum.com**.

Question 11	What is the default Mail server priority?

24. Click OK.

25. Right-click the PC1 Host (A) record under adatum.com, and click Properties.

Question 12	What fields are displayed?

26. Click OK to close the Properties dialog box.

27. Open the View menu and click Advanced.

28. Right-click the PC1 Host (A) record and click Properties.

Question 13	What new field is now available with the Advanced view?

29. Change the Time to live to **15** minutes. Click OK to close the Properties dialog box.

End of exercise.

Exercise 9.2	Configuring Round Robin
Overview	By default, DNS Round Robin is enabled. Round robin operates by providing one DNS server IP address to a given query, then provides a different IP address for the next query, and so on, until a configured list of DNS server IP addresses runs out. The last query causes a loop-around to the first IP address and begins the sequence over again. In this exercise, you create two resource records to demonstate round robin switching between two separate DNS IP addresses
Completion time	10 minutes

1. On RWDC01, with DNS Manager console, create a host record for web.adatum.com that points to 192.168.1.205.

2. Create a second host record for web.adatum.com that points to 192.168.1.206.

3. At the command prompt, execute the following command:

    `nslookup web.adatum.com`

Question 14	What addresses were returned?

4. Re-execute the `nslookup web.adatum.com` command.

Question 15	What addresses were returned?

5. Execute the following command:

    `ping web.adatum.com`

    Don't worry that the ping fails; focus on the address that is returned.

6. Execute the `ping web.adatum.com` command, and then execute the command a couple more times. Observe that the return address toggles back and forth between 192.168.1.205 and 192.168.1.206, in effect, balancing the query load between two IP addresses.

End of exercise.

Exercise 9.3	Configuring Zone Scavenging
Overview	With dynamic addresses, often resource records will be added to a DNS zone, and will remain there unless they are manually deleted or scavanged. During this exercise, you configure zone scavenging.
Completion time	10 minutes

Mindset Question: If you want DNS zone scavenging, where do you have to enable zone scavenging?

1. On RWDC01, with DNS Manager console, right-click the RWDC01 and click *Set Aging/Scavenging for all Zones*. The Server Aging/Scavenging Properties dialog box opens as shown in Figure 9-3.

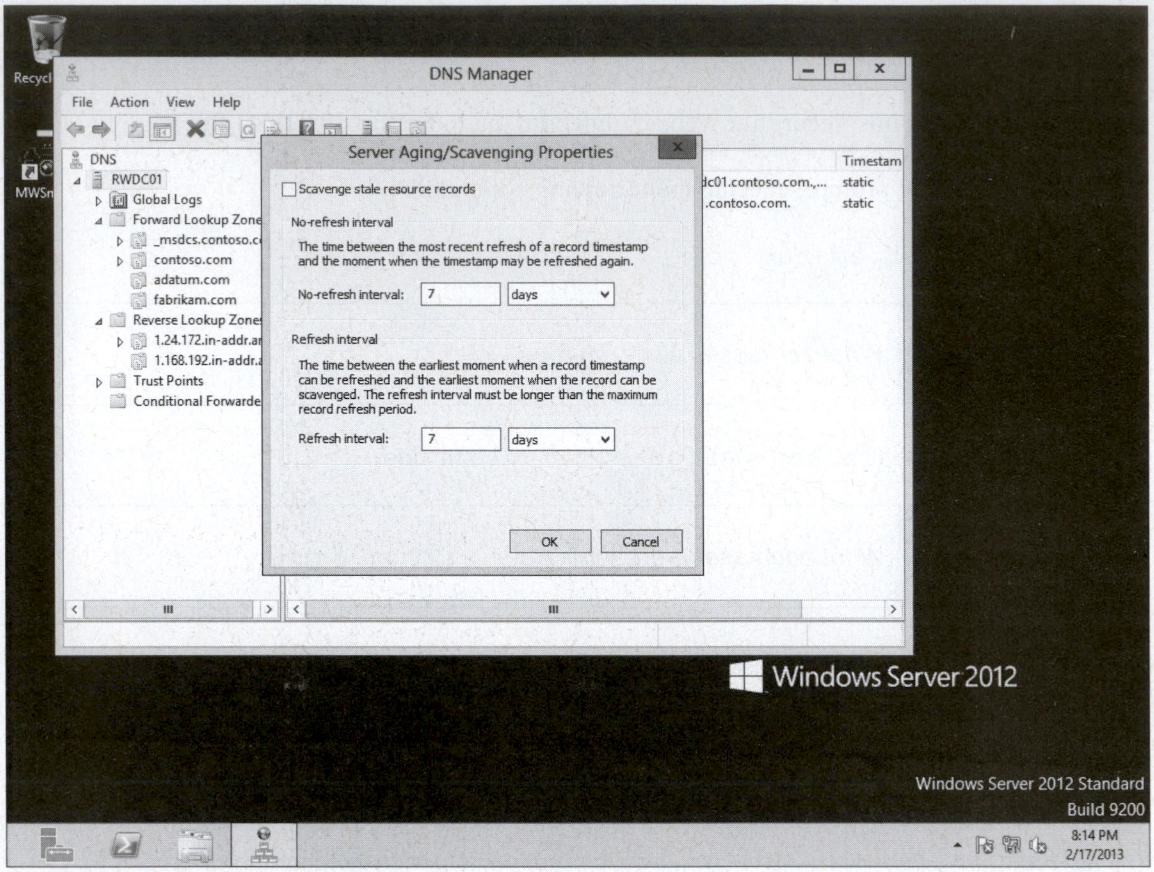

Figure 9-3
Configuring aging and scavenging settings

2.   Click the *Scavenge stale resource records* option.

3.   Click the OK button to close the *Server Aging/Scavenging Properties* dialog box.

4.   Click to enable the *Apply these settings to the existing Active Directory-integrated zones* option. Click OK to close the Server Aging/Scavenging Confirmation dialog box.

5.   Right-click the adatum.com zone and click Properties.

6.   On the General tab, click the Aging button. The Zone Aging/Scavenging Properties dialog box opens.

7.   Click to enable the *Scavenge stale resource records* option.

8.   Take a screen shot of the DNS Manager window by pressing Alt+Prt Scr and then paste it into your Lab 9 worksheet file in the page provided by pressing Ctrl+V.

9.   Click the OK button to close the *Server Aging/Scavenging Properties* dialog box.

10. When you are prompted to apply aging/scavenging settings to the Standard Primary zone, click Yes.

11. Click the OK button to close the Properties dialog box.

End of exercise.

Exercise 9.4	Troubleshooting DNS
Overview	In Exercise 9.2, you used nslookup to show name/IP resolution. However, during this exercise, you use nslookup in other ways to test DNS. You also use the DNS built-in tools to test DNS.
Completion time	10 minutes

1. On RWDC01, at the command prompt, execute the following command:

```
nslookup PC1.adatum.com
```

2. To start nslookup in interactive mode, execute the following command:

```
nslookup
```

3. To display the SOA record for adatum.com domain, execute the following commands:

```
set type=soa
```

```
adatum.com
```

4. To display the MX record for the adatum.com domain, execute the following commands:

```
set type=mx
```

```
adatum.com
```

5. Take a screen shot of the Command Prompt window by pressing Alt+Prt Scr and then paste it into your Lab 9 worksheet file in the page provided by pressing Ctrl+V.

6. Close the Command Prompt.

7. On RWDC01, with DNS Manager console, right-click the RWDC01 and click Properties. The properties dialog box opens.

8. Click the Monitoring tab. Figure 9-4 shows the Monitoring tab.

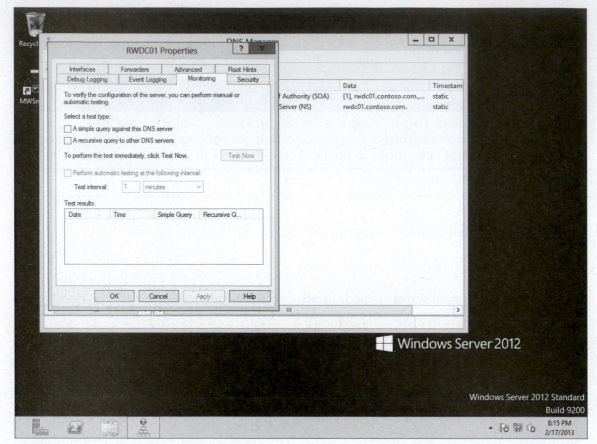

Figure 9-4
Monitoring the DNS server

9. Select to enable the following settings:

    A simple query against this DNS server

    A recursive query to other DNS servers

10. Click Test Now.

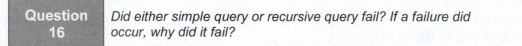

| Question 16 | Did either simple query or recursive query fail? If a failure did occur, why did it fail? |

11. Close DNS Manager.

End of exercise.

LAB REVIEW QUESTIONS

Completion time	10 minutes

1. In Exercise 9.1, what is the most commonly used DNS resource record?

2. In Exercise 9.1, where is the default TTL stored?

3. In Exercise 9.1, where are PTR records stored?

4. In Exercise 9.1, what view do you need to be in to modify the TTL for an individual record?

5. In Exercise 9.2, how did you enable round robin?

6. In Exercise 9.3, to enable zone scavenging, what two places did you have to configure?

7. In Exercise 9.4, what tool is used to test DNS queries?

Lab Challenge	Using the DNSCMD Command to Manage Resource Records
Overview	To complete this challenge, you must demonstrate how to use the DNSCMD command.
Completion time	5 minutes

You need to configure a few scripts that will create DNS zones. What commands would you use to perform the following on RWDC01.contoso.com for the contoso.com domain:

Add a host record for Test01 with an IPv4 address of 192.168.1.221 on the RWDC01 server.

Delete the Test01 record that you just created in the previous step.

End of lab.

LAB 10
CONFIGURING VPN AND ROUTING

THIS LAB CONTAINS THE FOLLOWING EXERCISES AND ACTIVITIES:

Exercise 10.1   Installing and Configuring RRAS

Exercise 10.2   Configuring a VPN Server

Exercise 10.3   Configuring a VPN Client

Exercise 10.4   Configuring Split Tunneling

Exercise 10.5   Configuring Routing

Exercise 10.6   Resetting Servers

Lab Challenge   Using the Route Command

BEFORE YOU BEGIN

The lab environment consists of student workstations connected to a local area network, along with a server that functions as the domain controller for a domain called *contoso.com*. The computers required for this lab are listed in Table 10-1.

Table 10-1
Computers Required for Lab 10

Computer	Operating System	Computer Name
Server (VM 1)	Windows Server 2012	RWDC01
Server (VM 2)	Windows Server 2012	Server01
Server (VM 3)	Windows Server 2012	Server02

In addition to the computers, you also require the software listed in Table 10-2 to complete Lab 10.

Table 10-2
Software Required for Lab 10

Software	Location
Lab 10 student worksheet	Lab10_worksheet.docx (provided by instructor)

Working with Lab Worksheets

Each lab in this manual requires that you answer questions, take screen shots, and perform other activities that you will document in a worksheet named for the lab, such as Lab10_worksheet.docx. You will find these worksheets on the book companion site. It is recommended that you use a USB flash drive to store your worksheets, so you can submit them to your instructor for review. As you perform the exercises in each lab, open the appropriate worksheet file fill in the required information, and save the file to your flash drive.

After completing this lab, you will be able to:

- Install and configure Remote Access Role

- Configure VPN settings

- Configure routing

Estimated lab time: 125 minutes

Exercise 10.1	Installing and Configuring RRAS
Overview	To configure standard VPN connections, you use Routing and Remote Access Server. You install Routing and Remote Access Server on Server01.
Completion time	15 minutes

Mindset Question: **During this lab, you install and configure Routing and Remote Access Server. What are all of the functions that the Routing and Remote Access Server can perform?**

1. Log in to Server01 as the **Contoso\administrator** user account. The Server Manager console opens.

2. On Server Manager, click Manage and click Add Roles and Features. The Add Roles and Feature Wizard opens.

3. On the Before you begin page, click Next.

4. Select *Role-based or feature-based installation* and then click Next.

5. On the Select destination server page, click Next.

6. Scroll down and select Remote Access.

7. When the Add Roles and Features Wizard dialog box opens, click Add Features.

8. Back on the Select server roles page, click Next. On the Select features page, click Next.

9. On the Remote Access page, click Next. On the Select role services page, keep DirectAccess and VPN (RAS) selected and select Routing. Click Next.

10. On the Confirm installation selections page, click Install.

11. When the installation is complete, click Close.

End of exercise.

Exercise 10.2	Configuring a VPN Server
Overview	Server01 will be the primary application server, which will be used for most applications.
Completion time	30 minutes

Mindset Question: **Routing and Remote Access Server supports VPN connections. What are the types of VPN connections that are supported by Routing and Remote Access Server?**

1. On Server01, on the Task bar, right-click the Network and Sharing Center icon and click Open Network and Sharing Center.

2. Click Change adapter settings.

3. Right-click Ethernet and click Rename. Change the name to Internal and press the Enter key.

4. Right-click Ethernet 2 and click Rename. Change the name to External and press the Enter key. When done, the Network Connections should look similar to Figure 10-1.

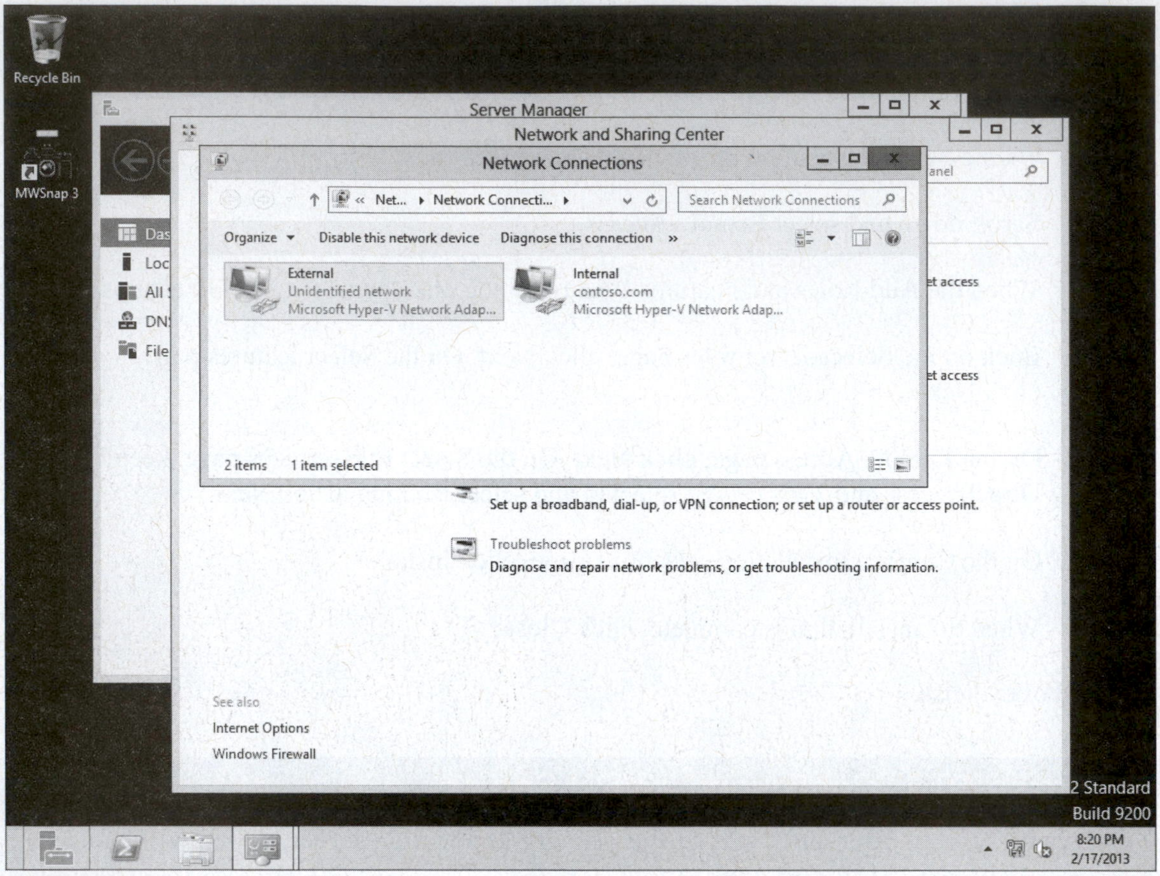

Figure 10-1
Viewing network connections

5. Right-click External and click Properties.

6. When the External Properties dialog box opens, double-click *Internet Protocol Version 4 (TCP/IPv4)*.

7. Click Use the following options and specify the following:

   IP address: **192.168.2.1**

   Subnet mask: **255.255.255.0**

   Click OK. If it says the DNS server list is empty, click OK.

8. Click OK to close the External Properties dialog box.

9. Close Network Connections.

10. On Server01, Server Manager, click Tools > Routing and Remote Access. The Routing and Remote Access console opens as shown in Figure 10-2.

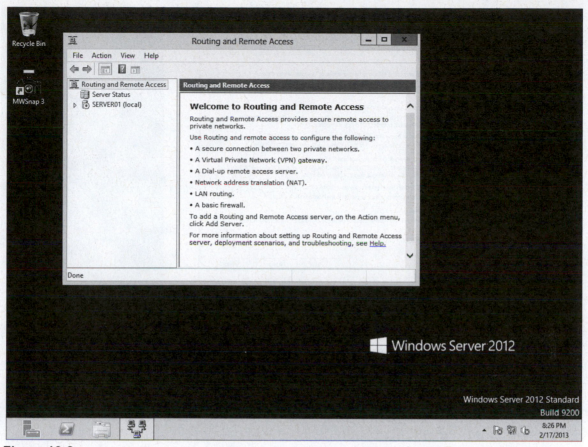

Figure 10-2
Opening the Routing and Remote Access console

11. Right-click Server01 and select *Configure and Enable Routing and Remote
    Access*. The Routing and Remote Access Server Setup Wizard opens.

12. On the Welcome page, click Next.

13. On the Configuration page, select *Virtual private network (VPN) access and NAT*
    as shown in Figure 10-3 and click Next.

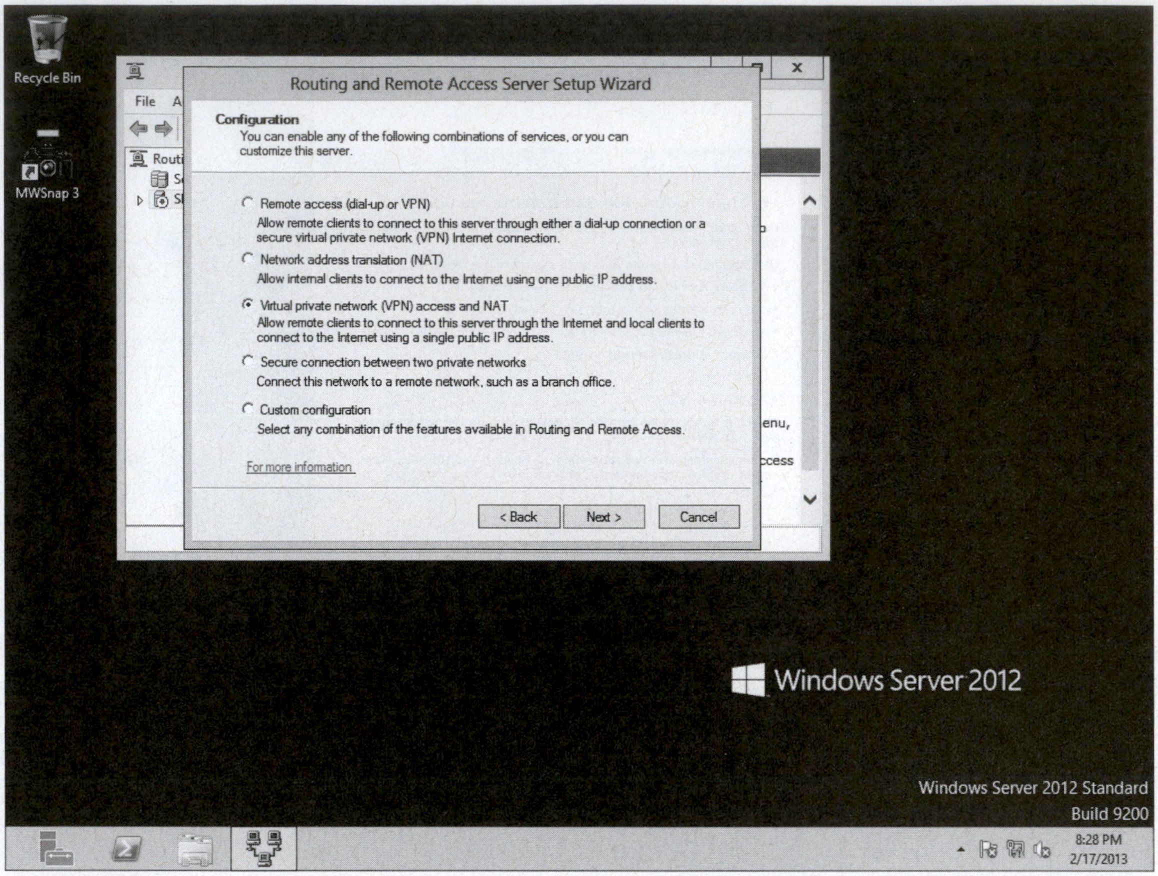

Figure 10-3
Specifying the Routing and Remote Access configuration

14. On the VPN Connection page, select External and click Next.

15. On the IP Address Assignment page, click *From a specified range of addresses* and click Next.

16. On the Address Range Assignment page, click New.

17. When the New IPv4 Address Range dialog box opens, specify the Start IP address as **192.168.1.40** and the End IP address as **192.168.1.45**. Click OK.

18. Back on the Address Range Assignment page, click Next.

19. On the *Managing Multiple Remote Access Servers* page, click Next.

20. On the Completing the Routing and Remote Access Server Setup Wizard page, click Finish.

21. When is says that you have to open a port of Routing and Remote access in the Windows Firewall, click OK.

22. When it asks to support the relaying of DHCP messages from remote access clients message, click OK.

23. Take a screen shot of the Routing and Remote Access window by pressing Alt+Prt Scr and then paste it into your Lab 10 worksheet file in the page provided by pressing Ctrl+V.

24. After RRAS starts, click the Start button, and click Administrative Tools. When theAdministrative Tools opens, double-click *Windows Firewall with Advanced Security*.

25. When Windows Firewall with Advanced Security opens, under Actions, click Properties.

26. When the *Windows Firewall with Advanced Security on Local Computer* dialog box opens, change the Firewall state to Off.

27. Change the Firewall state to Off in the Private profile and Public Profile tabs.

28. Click OK to close the *Windows Firewall with Advanced Security on Local Computer* dialog box.

29. Close *Windows Firewall with Advanced Security* and *Administrative Tools*.

30. Right-click Server01 in Routing and Remote Access, and click Properties.

Question 1	Which tab would you use to specify a preshared key for RRAS?

Question 2	Which VPN method requires a digital ceritificate to provide a SSL connection?

31. Click OK to close the Server01 (local) Properties dialog box.

32. Right-click Ports and click Properties. The Ports Properties dialog box opens.

Question 3	By default, how many IKEv2 connections are available?

33. Click OK to close the Ports Properties dialog box.

34. Log on to RWDC01 as Contoso**administrator**.

35. On Server Manager, from Tools, click *Active Directory Users and Computers*.

36. Expand contoso.com, if needed, and then click Users.

37. Double-click the Administrator account. The Administrator Properties dialog box opens.

38. Click the Dial-in tab.

Question 4	What is the default setting for Network Access Permission?

39. In the Network Access Permission section, click to select Allow access, as shown in Figure 10-4.

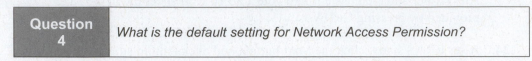

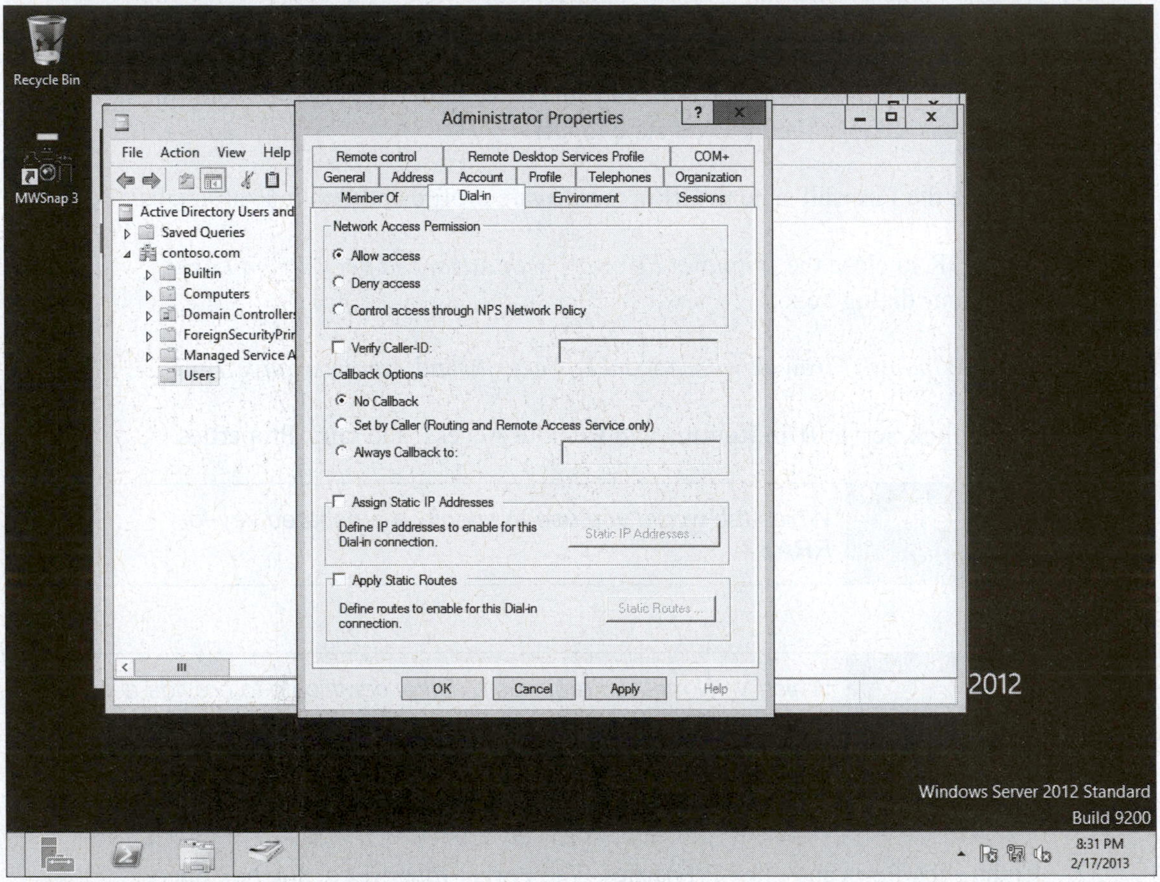

Figure 10-4
Allowing access to Dial-in for Administrator

40. Click OK to close the Administrator Properties dialog box.

41. Close Active Directory Users and Computers.

End of exercise.

Exercise 10.3	Configuring a VPN Client
Overview	Now that you have configured the VPN server, you need to configure a client to connect to the VPN server. During this exercise, you use Server02 to act as a VPN client.
Completion time	30 minutes

1. Log in to Server02 as the **Contoso\Administrator** user account. The Server Manager console opens.

2. On Server02, on the Taskbar, right-click Network and Sharing Center icon and click Open Network and Sharing Center.

3. Click Change adapter settings.

4. Right-click Ethernet and click Disable.

5. Right-click Ethernet2 and click Properties.

6. When the Ethernet Properties dialog box opens, double-click *Internet Protocol Version 4 (TCP/IPv4)*.

7. Click Use the following options and specify the following:

    IP address: **192.168.2.10**

    Subnet mask: **255.255.255.0**

    Click OK.

8. Click OK to close the Ethernet 2 Properties dialog box.

9. Go back to Network and Sharing Center, and choose *Set up a new connection or network*.

10. On the Set Up a Connection or Network page, choose Connect to a workplace. Click Next.

11. On the Connect to a Workplace page, click Use my Internet connection.

12. If it asks if you want to set up Internet connection, click *I'll set up an Internet connection later*.

13. When it asks you to type the Internet address to connect to, type **192.168.2.1** in the Internet address text box. Click Create.

14. When the Networks pane appears as shown in Figure 10-5, click VPN Connection and click Connect.

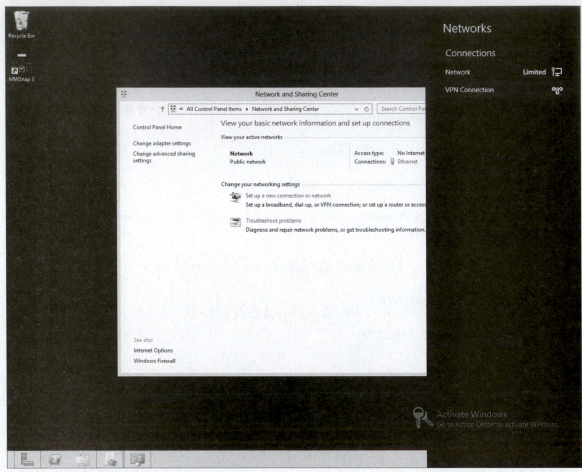

Figure 10-5
Clicking VPN Connection

15. For the user name and password, use **Contoso\Administrator** and **Password01**. Click OK.

16. Take a screen shot of the Networks pane showing a successful connection by pressing Alt+Prt Scr and then paste it into your Lab 10 worksheet file in the page provided by pressing Ctrl+V.

17. Click the VPN Connection and click Disconnect.

18. Click the Desktop.

19. On RWDC01, using Active Directory Users and Computers, double-click the Administrator account.

20. When the Administrator Properties dialog box opens, click the Dial-in tab.

21. In the Network Access Permission section, click Control access through NPS Network Policy.

22. Click OK to close the Administrator Properties dialog box.

23. On Server02, click the Network and Sharing Center icon on the taskbar, click VPN Connection and click Connect.

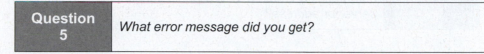

Question 5	What error message did you get?

24. Click Close and click the Desktop.

25. On RWDC01, using Active Directory Users and Computers, double-click the Administrator account.

26. When the Administrator Properties dialog box opens, click the Dial-in tab.

27. In the Network Access Permission section, click Allow access.

28. Click OK to close the Administrator Properties dialog box.

29. On Server01, open the Administrative Tools and double-click Windows Firewall with Advanced Security.

30. When the Windows Firewall with Advanced Security console opens, click Properties under Actions.

31. On the Domain Profile tab, change the Firewall state to On.

32. Using the Private Profile and Public Profile tabs, turn the Firewall state to On.

33. Click OK to close the Windows Firewall with Advanced Security console.

34. On Server02, click the Network and Sharing Center icon on the taskbar.

35. Click VPN Connection and click Connect.

Question 6	What error message did you get?

36. Click Close and click the Desktop.

37. On Server01, using Windows Firewall with Advanced Security, click Properties under Actions.

38. On the Domain Profile tab, change the Firewall state to Off.

39. Using the Private Profile and Public Profile tabs, turn the Firewall state to Off.

40. Click OK to close the Windows Firewall with Advanced Security console.

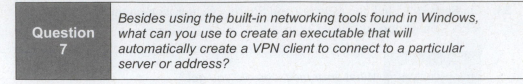

Question 7	Besides using the built-in networking tools found in Windows, what can you use to create an executable that will automatically create a VPN client to connect to a particular server or address?

End of exercise.

Exercise 10.4	Configuring Split Tunneling
Overview	During this exercise, you take the current VPN connection that you created in Exercise 10.3, and enable split tunneling, so that corporate traffic will go through the Internet and Internet traffic will go out the local Internet connection.
Completion time	5 minutes

Mindset Question: **During this exercise, you configure split tunneling. Why is split tunneling not recommended for corporate networks?**

1. On Server02, click the Network and Sharing Center icon on the Task bar. When the Networks pane opens, right-click VPN Connection and click View connection properties. The VPN Connection Properties dialog box opens.

2. Click the Networking tab.

3. Double-click the Internet Protocol Version 4 (TCP/IPv4).

4. On the Internet Protocol Version 4 (TCP/IPv4) Properties dialog box, click the Advanced button.

5. On the Advanced TCP/IP Settings dialog box, on the IP Settings tab, deselect the *Use default gateway on remote network*.

6. Take a screen shot of the Advanced TCP/IP Settings dialog box by pressing Alt+Prt Scr and then paste it into your Lab 10 worksheet file in the page provided by pressing Ctrl+V.

7. Click OK to close the Advanced TCP/IP Settings dialog box.

8. Click OK to close the Internet Protocol Version 4 (TCP/IPv4) Properties dialog box.

9. Click OK to close the VPN Connection Properties dialog box.

End of exercise.

Exercise 10.5 Configuring Routing

Overview	During this exercise, you configure one of the more basic routing protocols to Server01.
Completion time	20 minutes

Mindset Question: **So far, you have built a simple network architecture that consists of two subnets connected together with Server01. If you had additional subnets, what simple routing protocol in Windows Server 2012 can you choose that takes little configuration and what are the limits of this routing protocol?**

1. On Server02, right-click the Network and Sharing Center icon on the taskbar, and click Open network and Sharing Center.

2. When the Network and Sharing Center, click Ethernet 2.

3. When the Ethernet 2 Status dialog box opens, click Properties.

4. When the Ethernet 2 Properties dialog box opens, double-click Internet Protocol Version 4 (TCP/IPv4).

5. In the Internet Protocol Version 4 (TCP/IPv4) Properties dialog box, configure the Default gateway to 192.168.2.1.

6. Click OK to close the Internet Protocol Version 4 (TCP/IPv4) Properties dialog box.

7. Click OK to close the Ethernet 2 Properties dialog box.

8. Click Close to close the Ethernet 2 Status dialog box.

9. Open a command prompt and try to ping 192.168.1.60.

Question 8	Did the ping succeed?

10. On Server01, using Routing and Remote Access, right-click Server01 and click Disable Routing and Remote Access.

11. When you are prompted to continue, click Yes. It will take a couple minutes to stop Routing and Remote Access.

12. Right-click Server01, and click Configure and Enable Routing and Remote Access.

13. When the Routing and Remote Access Server Setup Wizard starts, click Next.

14. On the Configuration page, click Custom configuration and click Next.

15. On the Custom Configuration page, click to select LAN routing and click Next.

16. When the wizard is complete, click Finish.

17. When the Routing and Remote Access dialog box opens, click Start service.

18. Expand the IPv4 node. Then right-click General under IPv4 and click New Routing Protocol.

19. When the New Routing Protocol dialog box opens as shown in Figure 10-6, click *RIP Version2 for Internet Protocol* and and click OK.

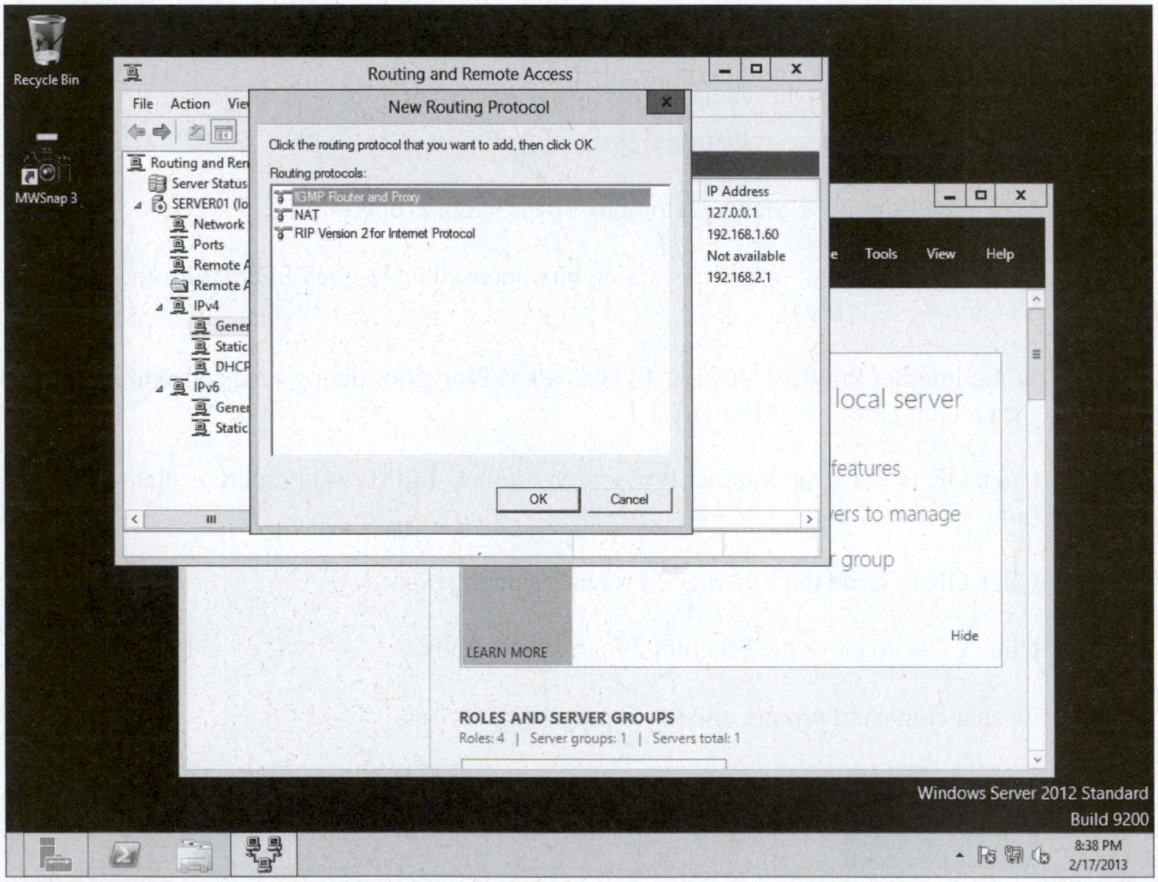

Figure 10-6
Adding a new routing protocol

20. Right-click RIP and click New Interface.

21. Click External and click OK.

22. When the RIP Properties – External Properties dialog box opens, click OK.

23. Right-click RIP and click New Interface.

24. Click Internal and click OK.

25. When the RIP Properties – Internal Properties dialog box opens, click OK.

26. On Server02, using the command prompt, execute the following command:

    Ping 192.168.1.60

Question 9	Did the ping succeed?

End of exercise.

Exercise 10.6   Resetting Servers

Overview	Before you can continue to the next exercise, you need to disable Routing and Remote Access.
Completion time	5 minutes

1. On Server01, with Routing and Remote Access, right-click Server01 and click Disable Routing and Remote Access.

2. When you are prompted to continue, click Yes.

3. After RRAS stops, close Routing and Remote Access.

4. On Server02, open Network and Sharing Center, if needed.

5. Click Change adapter settings.

6. Right-click Ethernet and click Enable.

7. Close *Network Connections and Network and Sharing Center.*

End of exercise.

LAB REVIEW QUESTIONS

Completion time   10 minutes

1. In Exercise 10.2, what software included with Windows Server 2012 allows you to create a VPN server used with PPTP and L2TP?

2. In Exercise 10.2, what program did you use to allow the Administrator to connect using RRAS?

3. In Exercise 10.3, where do you define VPN connections in Windows Server 2012 when a server needs to act as a VPN client?

4. In Exercise 10.4, which option was used to enable or disable split tunneling?

5. In Exercise 10.5, what version of RIP does Windows Server 2012 support?

Lab Challenge	Using the Route Command
Overview	To complete this challenge, you will demonstrate how to use the Route command.
Completion time	10 minutes

By default, routes are automatically created within Windows. However, you can create static routes by using the route.exe command. Therefore, specify the commands that you would use to perform the following tasks?

1. What command would you to display the routing table in Windows?

2. What command would you to create a route to the 172.25.1.x (mask 255.255.255.0) that goes out the 192.168.1.20 router?

3. What option makes a static router permanent so that the route will remain after a computer is rebooted?

4. What command would use to delete the route defined in Question 2?

End of lab.

LAB 11
CONFIGURING DIRECTACCESS

THIS LAB CONTAINS THE FOLLOWING EXERCISES AND ACTIVITIES:

Exercise 11.1	Implementing Client Configuration
Exercise 11.2	Implementing DirectAccess Server
Exercise 11.3	Implementing the Infrastructure Servers
Exercise 11.4	Implementing the Application Servers
Lab Challenge	Configuring Certificates for DirectAccess

BEFORE YOU BEGIN

The lab environment consists of student workstations connected to a local area network, along with a server that functions as the domain controller for a domain called *contoso.com*. The computers required for this lab are listed in Table 11-1.

Table 11-1
Computers Required for Lab 11

Computer	Operating System	Computer Name
Server (VM 1)	Windows Server 2012	RWDC01
Server (VM 2)	Windows Server 2012	Server01

In addition to the computers, you also require the software listed in Table 11-2 to complete Lab 11.

Table 11-2
Software Required for Lab 11

Software	Location
Lab 11 student worksheet	Lab11_worksheet.docx (provided by instructor)

Working with Lab Worksheets

Each lab in this manual requires that you answer questions, take screen shots, and perform other activities that you will document in a worksheet named for the lab, such as Lab11_worksheet.docx. You will find these worksheets on the book companion site. It is recommended that you use a USB flash drive to store your worksheets, so you can submit them to your instructor for review. As you perform the exercises in each lab, open the appropriate worksheet file, fill in the required information, and save the file to your flash drive.

After completing this lab, you will be able to:

- Configure DirectAccess

- Prepare for DirectAccess Deployment

- Configure certificates for DirectAccess

Estimated lab time: 50 minutes

Exercise 11.1	Implementing Client Configuration
Overview	To implement DirectAccess, the installation and configuration is divided into four steps. During this exercise, you perform Step 1 - Client Configuration.
Completion time	10 minutes

Mindset Question: **During this lab, you configure the servers to support DirectAccess. What are the minimum requirements for the DirectAccess server?**

1.   Log in to Server01 as the **Contoso\Administrator** user account. The Server Manager console appears.

2.   On Server Manager, click Tools > Remote Access Management. The Remote Access Management console opens as shown in Figure 11-1.

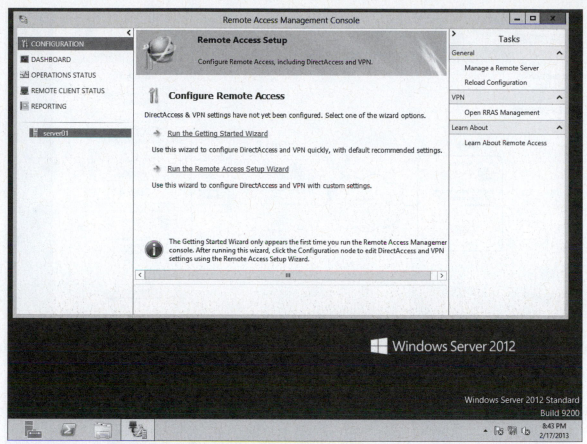

Figure 11-1
Opening the Remote Access Management console

3.   Click the Run the Remote Access Setup Wizard link.

4.   When the Configure Remote Access Wizard starts, click Deploy DirectAccess only. The
     Remote Access Setup console opens as shown in Figure 11-2.

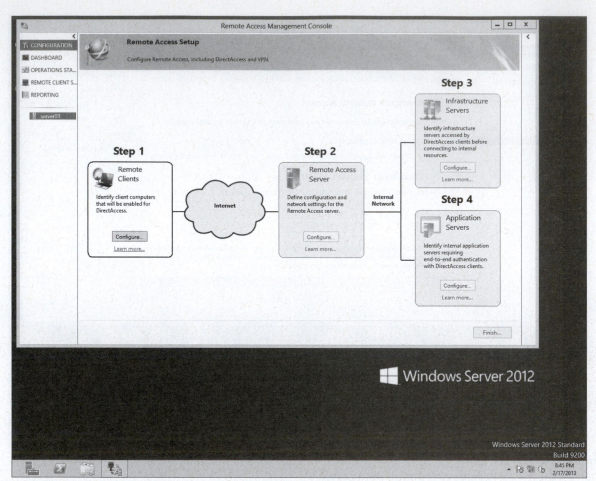

Figure 11-2
Using the Remote Access Setup to configure DirectAccess

5. Under Step 1, Remote Clients, click Configure. The DirectAccess Client Setup Wizard opens.

6. On the Deployment Scenario page, select *Deploy full DirectAccess for client access and remote management*. Click Next.

7. On the Select Groups page, select Add. Type **Domain Computers** in the *Enter the object names to select* text box and and click OK. Click Next.

8. On the Network Connectivity Assistant page as shown in Figure 11-3, double-click a blank resource space. When the Configure Corporate Resources for NCA dialog box opens, change the HTTP to PING and type **RWDC01.CONTOSO.COM** in the text box. Click Add.

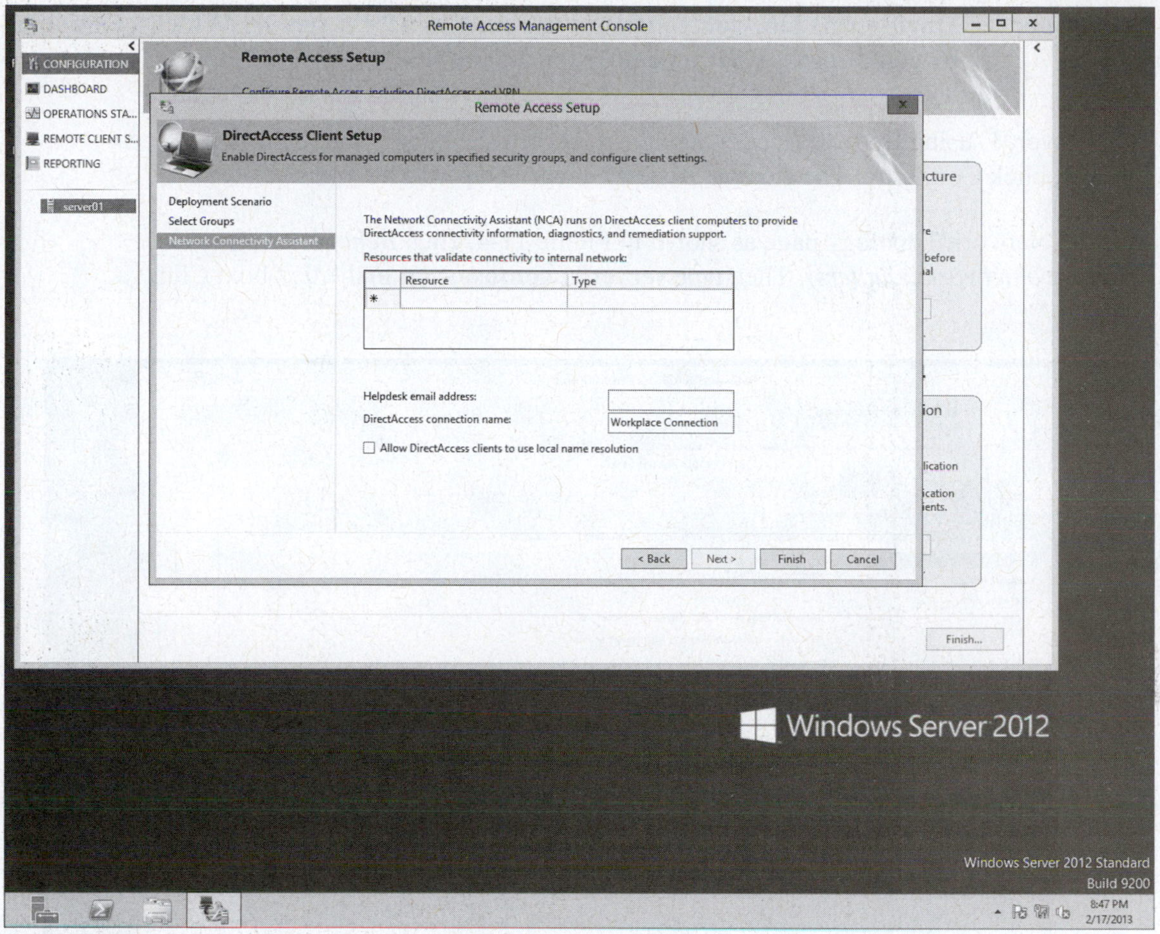

Figure 11-3
Configure the Network Connectivity Assistant

Question 1	*What tool is included with Windows 8 that will help you connect to the DirectAccess server when you have problems and can be used to perform diagnostics for client access to Direct Access?*

9. Back on the Network Connectivity Assistant page, click Finish.

10. Keep Remote Access Management console open for the next exercise.

End of exercise.

Exercise 11.2   Implementing DirectAccess Server

Overview	During this exercise, you configure DirectAccess configuration Step 2 - Configuring the Remote Access Server.
Completion time	10 minutes

Mindset Question: During this lab, you configure the remote access server. Which component or components will you configure during this step?

1. On Server01, using Remote Access Management console, under Step 2, Remote Access Server, click Configure. The Remote Access Server Setup Wizard starts.

2. On the Network Topology page as shown in Figure 11-4, click *Behind an edge device (with two network adapters)*. Then type **server01.contoso.com** in the text box. Click Next.

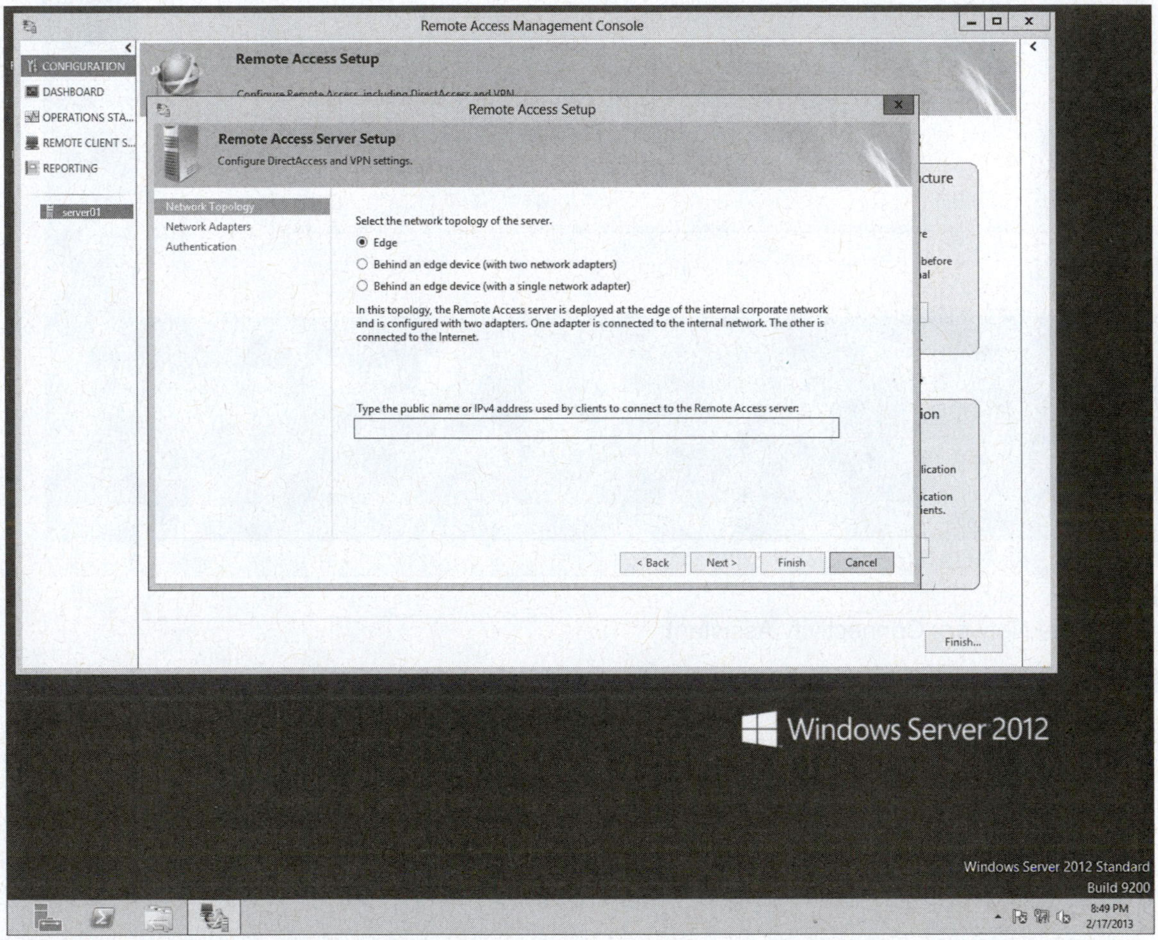

Figure 11-4
Selecting the topology

3. On the Network Adapters page, select External for the Adapter connected to the external network and select Internal for the Adapter connected to the internal network.

4. Click to select the *Use a self-signed certificate created automatically by DirectAccess*. Click Next.

5. On the Authentication page, with Active Directory credentials (username/password) already selected, click Finish.

Question 2	What type of user authentication is selected by default?

6.   Keep Remote Access Management console open for the next exercise.

End of exercise.

Exercise 11.3   Implementing the Infrastructure Servers

Overview	During this exercise, you perform Step 3, where you specify the infrastructure servers that are necessary for DirectAccess to function properly.
Completion time	10 minutes

Mindset Question: **When configuring Direct Access, what do you configure during Step 3?**

1.   On Server01, continuing with the Remote Access Setup Configuration page, under Step 3, Infrastructure Server, click Configure. The Infrastructure Server Setup Wizard starts.

2.   On the Network Location Server page, click *The network location server is deployed on the Remote Access server*. Click to select the *Use a self-signed certificate*.

3.   Take a screen shot of the DNS Manager window by pressing Alt+Prt Scr and then paste it into your Lab 11 worksheet file in the page provided by pressing Ctrl+V.

4.   Click Next.

5.   On the DNS page, click Next.

6.   On the DNS Suffix Search List page, click Next.

7.   On the Management page, double-click the first line of the Management Servers box to open the Add a Management Server dialog box.

Question 3	Which management servers would you include?

8.   In the Computer name text box, type **rwdc01.contoso.com** and click OK.

9.   Click Finish.

10.   Keep Remote Access Management console open for the next exercise.

End of exercise.

Exercise 11.4   Implementing the Application Servers

Overview	Lastly, during Step 4, you need to configure any application servers and apply all the changes that you have configured for Steps 1 through 4.
Completion time	5 minutes

Mindset Question: **When configuring Direct Access, what do you configure during Step 4?**

1.   On Server01, continuing with the Remote Access Setup Configuration page, under Step 4, Application Servers, click Configure. The DirectAccess Application Server Setup Wizard starts.

2.   On the DirectAccess Application Server Setup page, click Finish, accepting the default option selected – Do not extend authentication.

3.   At the bottom of the Remote Access Management console, click Finish to apply all the changes for Steps 1 through 4.

4.   Take a screen shot of the Remote Access Management Console window by pressing Alt+Prt Scr and then paste it into your Lab 11 worksheet file in the page provided by pressing Ctrl+V.

5.   When the Remote Access Review dialog box opens, click Apply.

6.   When the settings have been applied, click Close. Close the Remote Access Management Console.

End of exercise.

LAB REVIEW QUESTIONS

Completion time   5 minutes

1.   In Exercise 11.1, what tool is used to configure DirectAccess?

2.   In Exercise 11.2, in which step did you specify the certificate authority?

3.   In Exercise 11.3, what is the function of the Network Location Server?

Lab Challenge	Configuring Certificates for DirectAccess
Overview	To complete this challenge, you will demonstrate how to configure certificates for DirectoAccess by writing the high-level steps to complete the tasks described in the scenerio.
Completion time	10 minutes

For DirectAccess to function, you must install and configure a Certificate Authority so that it can hand out digital certificates for the clients. You also need to install and configure digital certificates for the IP-HTTPS listener. Explain in general steps what is needed to configure the certificate requirements needed for DirectAccess.

End of lab.

LAB 12
CONFIGURING A NETWORK POLICY SERVER

THIS LAB CONTAINS THE FOLLOWING EXERCISES AND ACTIVITIES:

Exercise 12.1   Installing and Configuring Network Policy Server

Exercise 12.2   Configuring NPS for RADIUS Server for VPN Connections

Exercise 12.3   Managing RADIUS Templates

Exercise 12.4   Configuring RADIUS Accounting

Lab Challenge   Add Workstation Authentication Certificates to All Workstations

BEFORE YOU BEGIN

The lab environment consists of student workstations connected to a local area network, along with a server that functions as the domain controller for a domain called *contoso.com*. The computers required for this lab are listed in Table 12-1.

Table 12-1
Computers Required for Lab 12

Computer	Operating System	Computer Name
Server (VM 1)	Windows Server 2012	RWDC01
Server (VM 2)	Windows Server 2012	Server01

In addition to the computers, you also require the software listed in Table 12-2 to complete Lab 12.

Table 12-2
Software Required for Lab 12

Software	Location
Lab 12 student worksheet	Lab12_worksheet.docx (provided by instructor)

Working with Lab Worksheets

Each lab in this manual requires that you answer questions, shoot screen shots, and perform other activities that you will document in a worksheet named for the lab, such as Lab12_worksheet.docx. You will find these worksheets on the book companion site. It is recommended that you use a USB flash drive to store your worksheets, so you can submit them to your instructor for review. As you perform the exercises in each lab, open the appropriate worksheet file, fill in the required information, and save the file to your flash drive.

After completing this lab, you will be able to:

- Install and configure Network Policy Server

- Configure RADIUS clients

- Manage RADIUS templates

- Configure RADIUS accounting

Estimated lab time: 65 minutes

Exercise 12.1	Installing and Configuring Network Policy Server
Overview	In this exercise, you install and configure Microsoft's RADIUS server known as *Network Policy Server*.
Completion time	15 minutes

Mindset Question: **During this lab, you install and configure the Network Policy Server. What is the Network Policy Server used for?**

Installing Network Policy and Access Services

1. Log in to RWDC01 as the **Contoso\Administrator** user account. The Server Manager console opens.

2. On Server Manager, select Manage and click Add Roles and Features. The Add Roles and Features Wizard opens.

3. On the Before you begin page, click Next.

4. Select *Role-based or feature-based installation*, and then click Next.

5. On the Select destination server page, click Next.

6. On the Select server roles page, select *Network Policy and Access Services*.

7. When it asks you to add features that are required for Network Policy and Access Services, click Add Features.

8. Back on the Select server roles page, click Next.

9. On the Select features page, click Next.

10. On the Network Policy and Access Services page, click Next.

11. On the Select role services page, with the Network Policy Server selected, click Next.

12. On the Confirm installation page, click Install.

13. When the installation is complete, click Close.

Adding a Remote RADIUS Server Group

1. On RWDC01, with Server manager, click Tools > Network Policy Server. The Network Policy Server console opens.

2. Expand the Network Policy Server console to fill the entire screen.

3. In the console tree, double-click RADIUS Clients and Servers, right-click Remote RADIUS Server Groups, and then click New. The New Remote RADIUS Server Group dialog box opens.

4. In Group name, type **RADIUS Servers** in Group name text box. Click Add. The Add RADIUS Servers dialog box opens as shown in Figure 12-1.

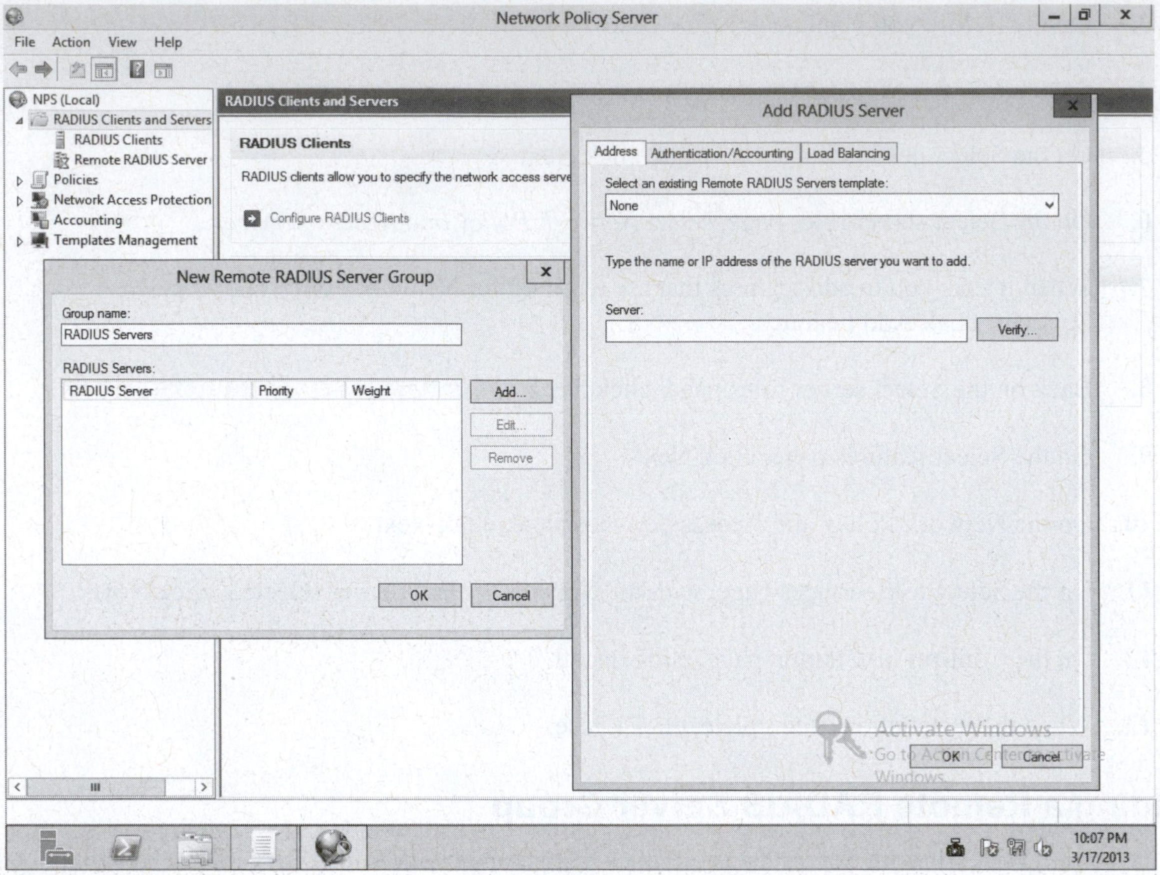

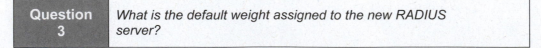

Figure 12-1
Adding a RADIUS server

5. In the Server text box, type the IP address of RWDC01, **192.168.1.50**.

6. Click the Authentication/Accounting tab.

Question 1	*What is the default authentication port used with RADIUS servers?*

Question 2	*What is the default accounting port used with RADIUS servers?*

7. Take a screen shot of the Add RADIUS Server dialog box by pressing Alt+Prt Scr and then paste it into your Lab 12 worksheet file in the page provided by pressing Ctrl+V.

8. Click OK to close the Add RADIUS Server dialog box.

Question 3	*What is the default weight assigned to the new RADIUS server?*

9. Click OK to close the New Remote RADIUS Server group.

10. Leave the Network Policy Server console open for the next exercise.

End of exercise.

Exercise 12.2	Configuring NPS for RADIUS Server for VPN Connections
Overview	During this exercise, you configure NPS to support VPN connections.
Completion time	10 minutes

Mindset Question: **During this lab, you install and configure Microsoft's RADIUS server. What is a RADIUS client and how does it differ from an access client?**

1. On RWDC01, using the Network Policy Server console, click NPS (Local).

2. Use the down arrow under Standard Configuration in the main panel, and select *RADIUS server for Dial-Up or VPN Connections*.

3. Click Configure VPN or Dial-Up. The Configure VPN or Dial-Up Wizard opens.

4. On the Select Dial-up or Virtual Private Network Connections Type page, select *Virtual Private Network (VPN) Connections*. Click Next.

5. On the Specify Dial-Up or VPN Server page as shown in Figure 12-2, click Add.

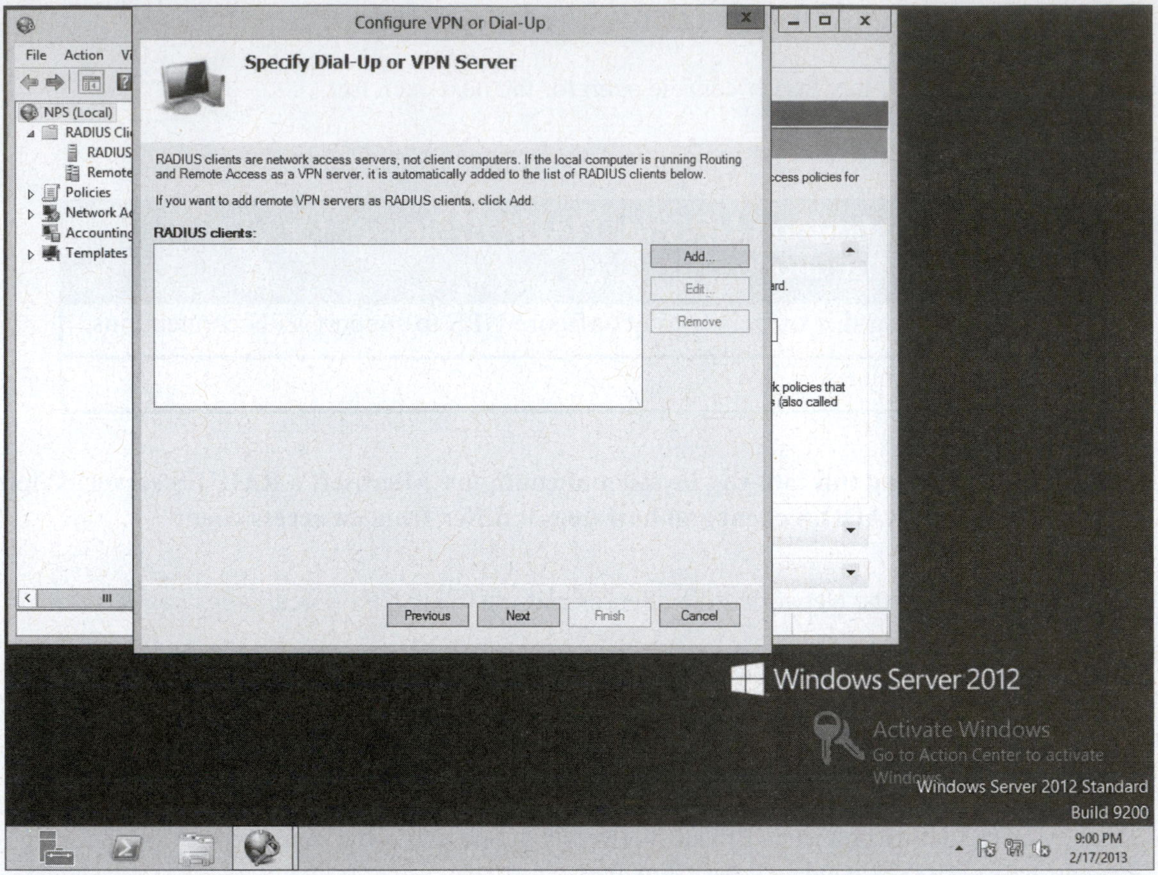

Figure 12-2
Adding RADIUS clients (VPN server)

6. When the New RADIUS Client dialog box opens as shown in Figure 12-3, type **Server01** in the Friendly name text box. In the Address (IP or DNS) text box, type **192.168.1.60**.

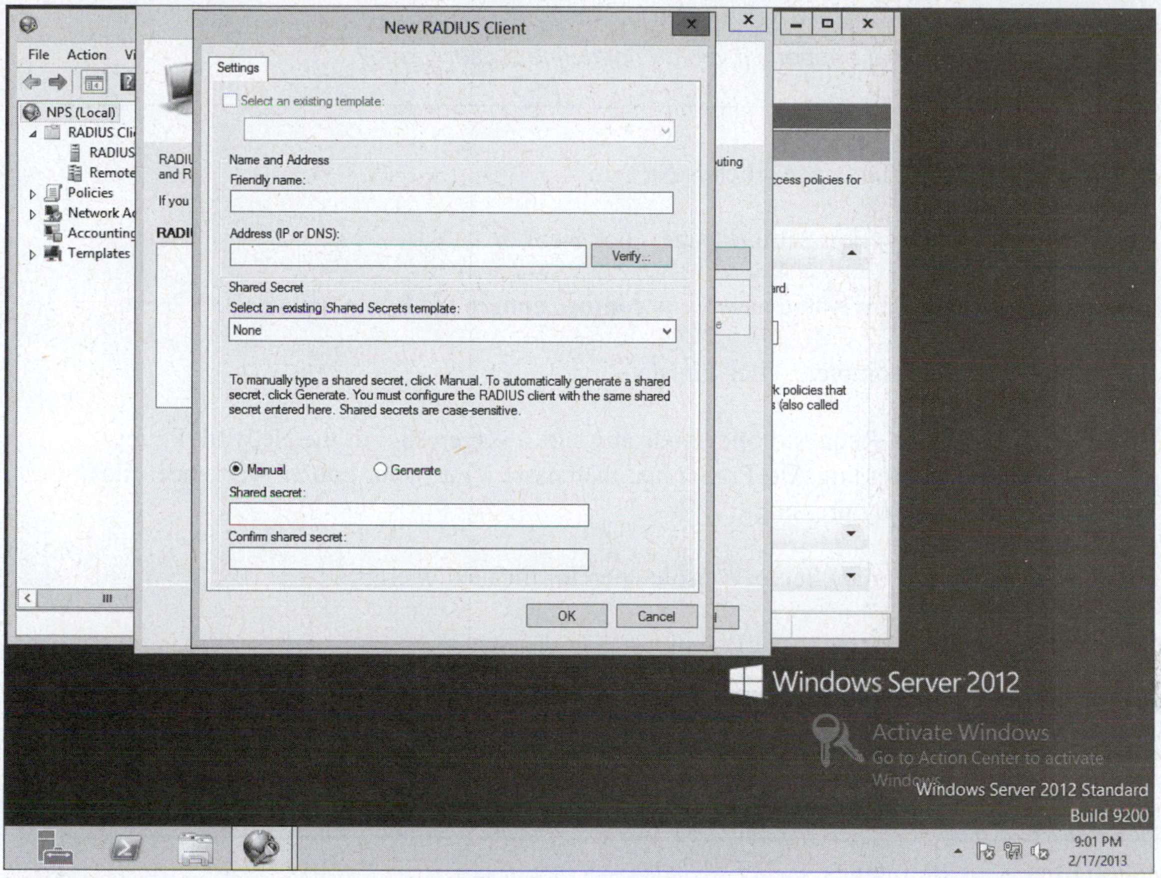

Figure 12-3
Configuring the new RADIUS client

7. At the bottom of the dialog box, type **Password01** in the Shared secret and Confirm shared secret text box. Click OK to close the Remote Access Properties dialog box.

8. Back on the Specify Dial-Up or VPN Server page, click Next.

9. On the Configure Authentication Methods page, answer the following question, and click Next.

Question 4	*By default, what was the authentication method selected?*

10. Take a screen shot of the Configure Authentication Methods by pressing Alt+Prt Scr and then paste it into your Lab 12 worksheet file in the page provided by pressing Ctrl+V.

11. On the Specify User Groups page, answer the following question, and click Next.

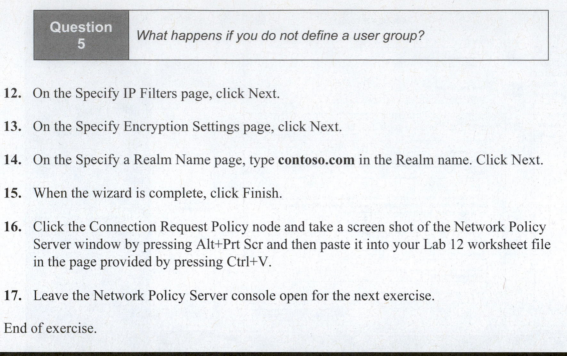

Question 5	*What happens if you do not define a user group?*

12. On the Specify IP Filters page, click Next.

13. On the Specify Encryption Settings page, click Next.

14. On the Specify a Realm Name page, type **contoso.com** in the Realm name. Click Next.

15. When the wizard is complete, click Finish.

16. Click the Connection Request Policy node and take a screen shot of the Network Policy Server window by pressing Alt+Prt Scr and then paste it into your Lab 12 worksheet file in the page provided by pressing Ctrl+V.

17. Leave the Network Policy Server console open for the next exercise.

End of exercise.

Exercise 12.3	Managing RADIUS Templates
Overview	During this exercise, you use RADIUS templates to simplify the deployment of RADIUS in the future.
Completion time	10 minutes

Mindset Question: **During this exercise, you work with RADIUS templates. What are the benefits of RADIUS templates?**

1. On RWDC01, using Network Policy Server console, double-click Templates Management.

2. Right-click Shared Secrets and click New. The New RADIUS Shared Secret Template opens.

3. In the Template name text box, type **Shared Secret Template**.

4. In the Shared secret and Confirm shared secret text boxes, type **Password01** and click OK.

5. Under RADIUS Clients and Servers, click RADIUS Clients.

6. In the RADIUS Clients pane, double-click Server01. The Server01 Properties dialog box opens.

7. In the Shared Secret section, in the drop-down arrow list, select the Shared Secret Template. Click OK.

8.   Right-click Templates Management and click Export Templates to a File.

9.   In the File Name text box, type **Templates** and click Save.

10.   Right-click Templates Management and click Import Templates from a File.

11.   Scroll down and click Templates.xml, then click Open.

12.   Leave the Network Policy Server console open for the next exercise.

End of exercise.

Exercise 12.4	Configuring RADIUS Accounting
Overview	Although RADIUS is used for central authentication, it can also be used for accounting. Therefore, during this exercise, you configure RADIUS accounting.
Completion time	5 minutes

Mindset Question: **What are the two uses of RADIUS accounting?**

1.   On RWDC01, using the Network Policy Server console, on the NPS tree, click Accounting.

2.   In the Accounting section, click Configure Accounting. When the Accounting Configuration Wizard starts, click Next.

3.   On the Select Accounting Options page as shown in Figure 12-4, click *Log to a text file on the local computer* and click Next.

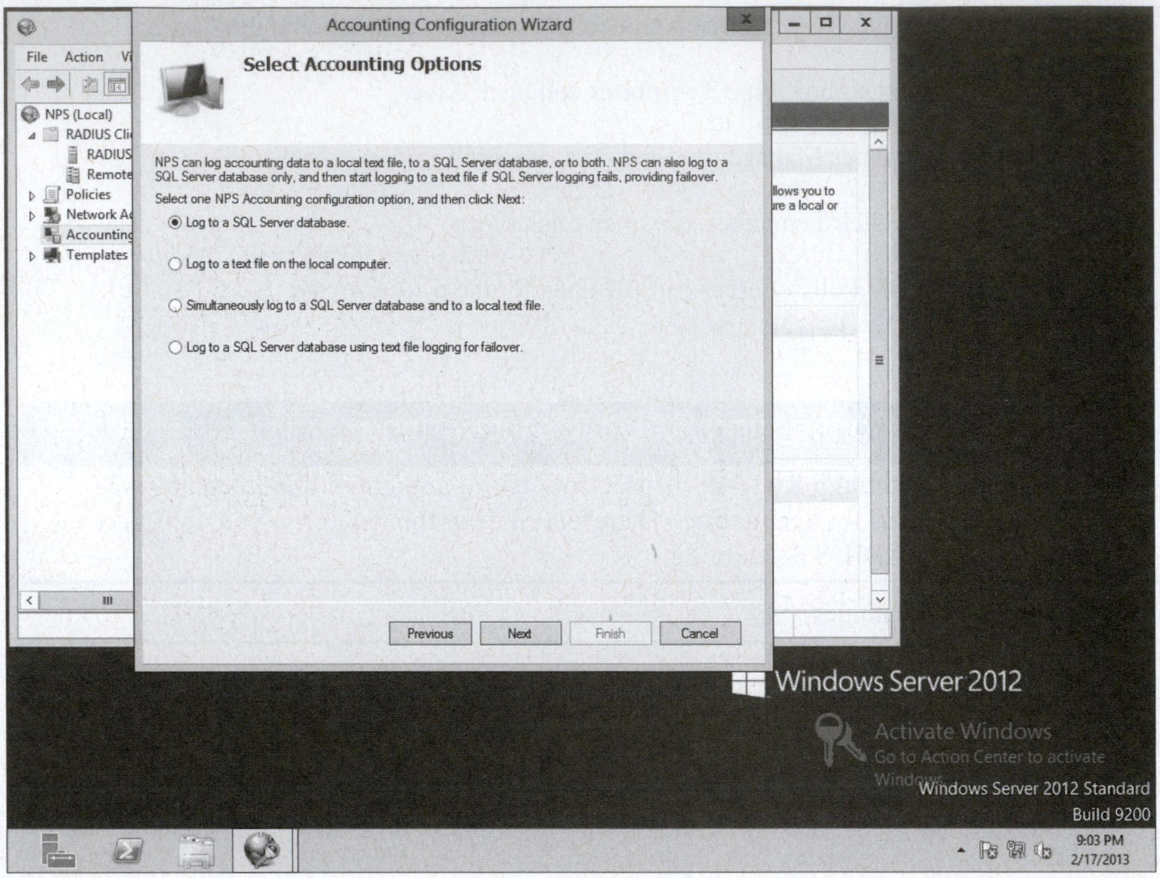

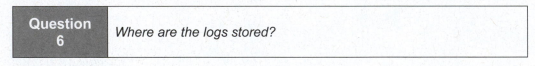

Figure 12-4
Selecting accounting options

4. On the Configure Local File Logging page, click Next.

Question 6	*Where are the logs stored?*

5. On the Summary page, click Next.

6. On the Conclusion page, click Close.

End of exercise.

LAB REVIEW QUESTIONS

Completion time	10 minutes

1. In Exercise 12.1, what program is used as the RADIUS server in Microsoft Windows servers?

2. In Exercise 12.2, what is a VPN server or wireless access point from the point-of-view of the NPS server?

3. In Exercise 12.2, when a user, using his or her laptop, connects to a VPN server, what is the laptop considered when discussing RADIUS?

4. In Exercise 12.3, if you decide to deploy several RADIUS servers, what can you use to help manage the deployment and configuration of servers?

5. In Exercise 12.4, what are the two methods used to record events used in RADIUS accounting?

Lab Challenge	Add Workstation Authentication Certificates to All Workstations
Overview	To complete this challenge, you will demonstrate how to add workstation authentication certificates to all workstations by writing the steps to complete the tasks described in the scenerio.
Completion time	15 minutes

You decide to use RADIUS for your organization. To ensure a secure environment, you decide to use digital certificates. How would you automatically add workstation authentication certificates to all client computers within your organization?

Write out the steps you performed to complete the challenge.

End of lab.

LAB 13
CONFIGURING NPS POLICIES

THIS LAB CONTAINS THE FOLLOWING EXERCISES AND ACTIVITIES:

Exercise 13.1   Creating and Configuring Connection Request Policies

Exercise 13.2   Creating and Configuring Network Policies

Exercise 13.3   Exporting and Importing the NPS Configuration

Lab Challenge   Processing Network Policies

BEFORE YOU BEGIN

The lab environment consists of student workstations connected to a local area network, along with a server that functions as the domain controller for a domain called *contoso.com*. The computers required for this lab are listed in Table 13-1.

Table 13-1
Computers Required for Lab 13

Computer	Operating System	Computer Name
Server (VM 1)	Windows Server 2012	RWDC01

In addition to the computers, you also require the software listed in Table 13-2 to complete Lab 13.

Table 13-2
Software Required for Lab 13

Software	Location
Lab 13 student worksheet	Lab13_worksheet.docx (provided by instructor)

Working with Lab Worksheets

Each lab in this manual requires that you answer questions, take screen shots, and perform other activities that you will document in a worksheet named for the lab, such as Lab13_worksheet.docx. You will find these worksheets on the book companion site. It is recommended that you use a USB flash drive to store your worksheets, so you can submit them to your instructor for review. As you perform the exercises in each lab, open the appropriate worksheet file, fill in the required information, and save the file to your flash drive.

After completing this lab, you will be able to:

- Create and Configure connection request policies

- Create and Configure network policies

- Import and export the NPS configuration

- Understand how network policies are processed

Estimated lab time: 55 minutes

Exercise 13.1	Creating and Configuring Connection Request Policies
Overview	In this exercise, you start using NPS policies, specifically the Connection Request Policies.
Completion time	15 minutes

Mindset Question: **During this lab, you start using NPS Policies. What are connection request policies used for?**

1. Log in to RWDC01 as the **Contoso\administrator** user account. The Server Manager console opens.

2. On Server Manager, click Tools > Network Policy Server. The Network Policy Server console opens.

3. Double-click Policies in the NPS tree.

Question 1	*What does the default connection request policy do?*

4. Right-click Connection Request Policies, and then click New. The New Connection Request Policy Wizard starts.

5. In the Policy name text box, type **Connection Request Policy 1** in the Policy name text box.

6. Under Type of network access server, select *Remote Access Server (VPN-Dial up)*. Click Next.

7. Take a screen shot of the New Connection Request Policy window by pressing Alt+Prt Scr and then paste it into your Lab 13 worksheet file in the page provided by pressing Ctrl+V.

8. On the Specify Conditions page, click Add.

9. When the Select condition dialog box opens, click Tunnel Type and click Add.

10. When the Tunnel Type dialog box opens, click *IP Encapsulating Security Payload in the Tunnel-mode (ESP)*, *Layer Two Tunneling Protocol (L2TP)*, and *Secure Socket Tunneling Protocol (SSTP)*. Click OK.

11. Click Add again, click Day and Time Restrictions, and click Add.

12. When the Day and time restrictions dialog box opens click Monday through Friday, 8 AM to 5 PM, and click Permitted. A blue box should appear as shown in Figure 13-1. Click OK.

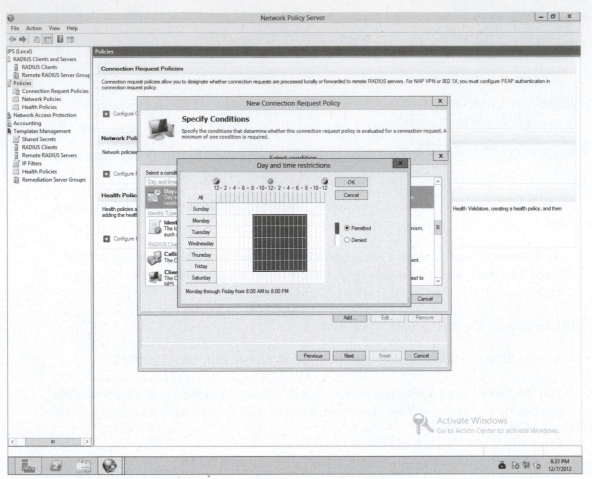

Figure 13-1
Restricting access by day and time

13. Back on the Specify Conditions page, click Next.

14. On the Specify Connection Request Forwarding page, click Next.

15. On the Specify Authentication Methods page, click Next.

16. On the Configure Settings page, click Next.

17. On the Completing Connection Request Policy Wizard page, click Finish. When created, the Connection Policy is listed in the Network Policies pane.

18. Leave the Network Policy Server console open for the next exercise.

End of exercise.

Exercise 13.2	Creating and Configuring Network Policies
Overview	During this exercise, you continue to use NPS policies by creating and configuring Network Policies.
Completion time	10 minutes

Mindset Question: **During this lab, you start using NPS Policies. What are network policies used for?**

1.   On RWDC01, using the Network Policy Server, right-click Network Policies, and then click New. The New Network Policy Wizard opens as shown in Figure 13-2.

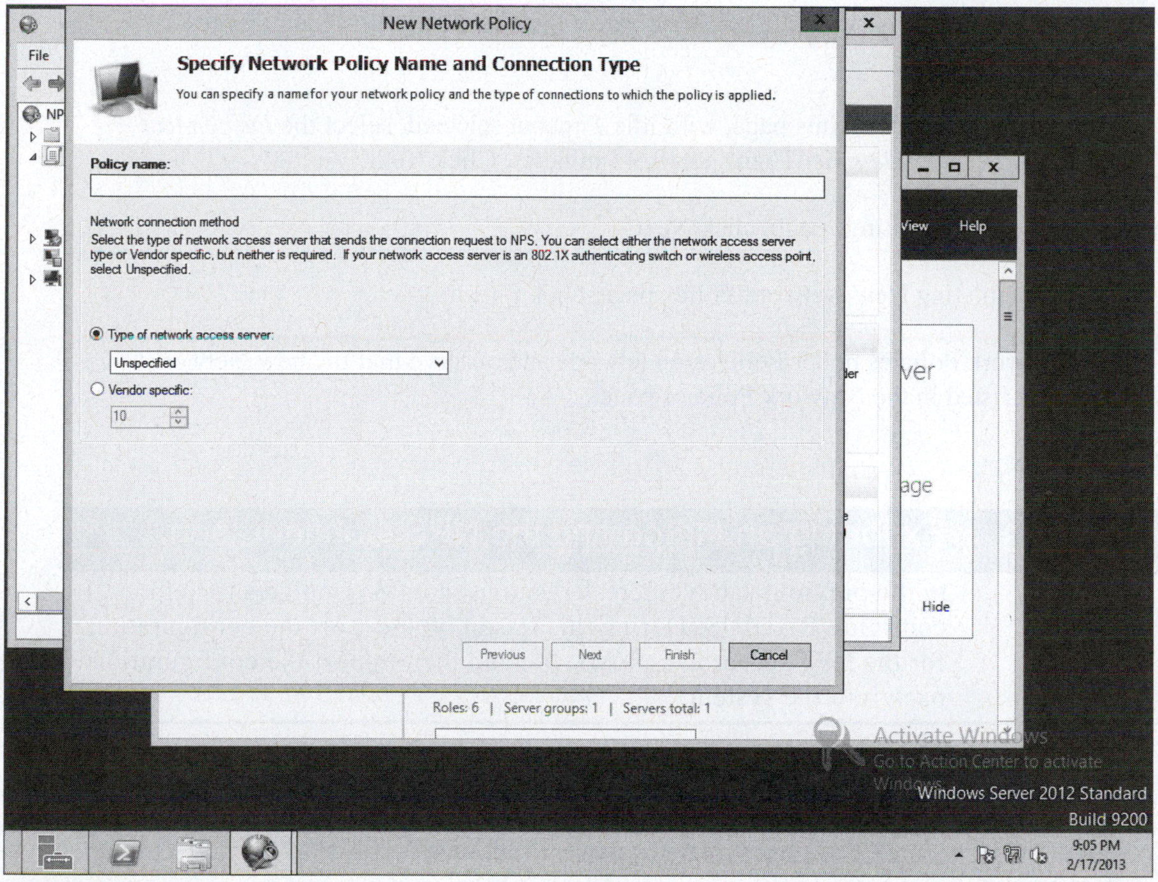

Figure 13-2
Creating a new network policy

2.   In the Policy name text box, type **Network Policy 1** in the Policy name text box.

3.   For the type of network access server, select *Remote Access Server (VPN-Dial up)*. Click Next.

Question 2	*What are the three components that make up a NPS network policy?*

4. On the Specify Conditions page, click Add.

5. When the Select conditions dialog box opens, click Windows Groups and click Add.

6. Click Add Groups. In the Enter the object name to select text box, type **domain guests** and click OK. Click OK to close the Windows Groups dialog box. Click Next.

7. On the Specify Access Permission page, click Next.

Question 3	What is the default access permission?

8. On the Configure Authentication Methods page, take a screen shot by pressing Alt+Prt Scr and then paste it into your Lab 13 worksheet file in the page provided by pressing Ctrl+V. Click Next.

9. On the Configure Constraints page, with Idle Timeout selected, select the *Disconnect after the maximum idle time*. Then specify 15 minutes. Click Next.

10. On the Configure Settings page, click Next.

11. On the Completing New Network Policy page, click Finish.

12. Click Network Policies under Policies on left side and observe that the new Network Policy 1 is listed in the Network Policies pane.

End of exercise.

Exercise 13.3	Exporting and Importing the NPS Configuration
Overview	In the previous lab, you created and used NPS templates to help configure RADIUS. During this lesson, you export the configuration for the NPS server to an XML file and then import the configuration back into the system.
Completion time	10 minutes

1. On RWDC01, open a Command Prompt (Admin) window.

2. Type **netsh**, and then press Enter.

3. At the netsh prompt, type **nps**, and then press Enter.

4. At the netsh nps prompt, type **export filename="C:\Bak.xml" exportPSK=YES**. Press Enter.

Question 4	What does the warning say?

5. At the command prompt, type **exit** and press Enter.

6. To import back in, type **netsh nps import filename="C:\Bak.xml"**, and then press Enter. A message appears indicating whether the import from the XML file was successful.

7. Take a screen shot of the Command Prompt window by pressing Alt+Prt Scr and then paste it into your Lab 13 worksheet file in the page provided by pressing Ctrl+V.

8. When the import is complete, close the Administrator: command prompt and the Network Policy console.

End of exercise.

LAB REVIEW QUESTIONS

Completion time	10 minutes

1. In Exercise 13.1, if you want to configure a RADIUS proxy and forward connection requests to another NPS or RADIUS server, what must you do?

2. In Exercise 13.1, when you create a connection request policy, what parameters do you configure?

3. In Exercise 13.2, if you had multiple network policies, why does order matter?

4. In Exercise 13.2, where would you configure multilink and bandwidth allocation?

Lab Challenge	Processing Network Policies
Overview	To complete this challenge, you will describe hohw network policies are processed by writing the high-level steps of processing network policies.
Completion time	10 minutes

During this lab, you started to use NPS policies, specifically the Connection Request policies and Network Policies. Although the connection request policy specified settings for the RADIUS server, the network policy will allow or disallow the remote access.

What are the steps used when processing network policies?

End of lab.

LAB 14
CONFIGURING NETWORK ACCESS PROTECTION (NAP)

THIS LAB CONTAINS THE FOLLOWING EXERCISES AND ACTIVITIES:

Exercise 14.1   Installing Health Registration Authority Role on an NPS Server

Exercise 14.2   Configuring NAP Enforcement for DHCP

Exercise 14.3   Configuring SHV and Health Policies

Lab Challenge   Configuring Clients for NAP

BEFORE YOU BEGIN

The lab environment consists of student workstations connected to a local area network, along with a server that functions as the domain controller for a domain called *contoso.com*. The computers required for this lab are listed in Table 14-1.

Table 14-1
Computers Required for Lab 14

Computer	Operating System	Computer Name
Server (VM 1)	Windows Server 2012	RWDC01
Server (VM 2)	Windows Server 2012	Server01

In addition to the computers, you also require the software listed in Table 14-2 to complete Lab 14.

Table 14-2
Software Required for Lab 14

Software	Location
Lab 14 student worksheet	Lab14_worksheet.docx (provided by instructor)

Working with Lab Worksheets

Each lab in this manual requires that you answer questions, take screen shots, and perform other activities that you will document in a worksheet named for the lab, such as Lab14_worksheet.docx. You will find these worksheets on the book companion site. It is recommended that you use a USB flash drive to store your worksheets, so you can submit them to your instructor for review. As you perform the exercises in each lab, open the appropriate worksheet file, fill in the required information, and save the file to your flash drive.

After completing this lab, you will be able to:

- Install Health Registration Authority role on an NPS server

- Install and configure NAP Enforcement using DHCP

- Configure System Health Validators (SHVs)

- Configure health policies

- Configure NAP client settings

Estimated lab time: 60 minutes

Exercise 14.1	Installing Health Registration Authority Role on an NPS Server
Overview	Network Access Protection (NAP), which is used to control who can access a network based on the security health of a client, is one of the more complicated installations during this course. Before you can configure NAP, you must add the Health Registration Authority role to the current NPS installation on RWDC01 so that it can monitor the connections on the NPS server.
Completion time	10 minutes

Mindset Questions:	So far, you have configured NPS. However, NPS also supports Network Access Protection. Explain what NAP is and how it is used to protect your network?

1. Log in to RWDC01 as the **Contoso\administrator** user account. The Server Manager console opens.

2. On Server Manager, click Manage and click Add Roles and Features. The Add Roles and Feature Wizard opens.

Question 1	To use NAP with DHCP, which server do you need to install NPS on?

3. On the Before you begin page, click Next.

4. Select *Role-based or feature-based installation*, and then click Next.

5. On the Select destination server page, click Next.

6. On the Select server roles page, expand *Network Policy and Access Services (Installed)*, click to select Health Registration Authority and click Next.

7. When you are asked to add features that are required for Health Registration Authority, click Add Features.

8. On the Select server roles page, click Next.

9. On the Select features page, click Next.

10. On the Network Policy and Access Services page, click Next.

11. Click *Use the local CA to issue health certificates for this HRA server*. Click Next.

12. On the Authentication Requirements page, select the *Yes, required requestors to be authenticated as members of a domain. (recommended)*. Click Next.

13. On the Server Authentication Certificate page, make sure Choose an existing certificate for SSL encryption (recommended) is already selected. Click to highlight RWDC01.contoso.com, then click Next.

14. On the Confirm installation selection page, click Install.

15. When the installation is complete, click Close.

End of exercise.

Exercise 14.2	Configuring NAP Enforcement for DHCP
Overview	During this exercise, you configure NAP enforcement for DHCP, specify the remediation servers, and enable NAP for a DHCP scope.
Completion time	20 minutes

Mindset Question: **When you configure NAP enforcement for DHCP, what are the basic steps that must be performed?**

1. On RWDC01, right-click the Start button, and select Command Prompt (Admin).

2. At the command prompt, execute the **`napclcfg.msc`** command. The NAP Client Configuration console opens, as shown in Figure 14-1.

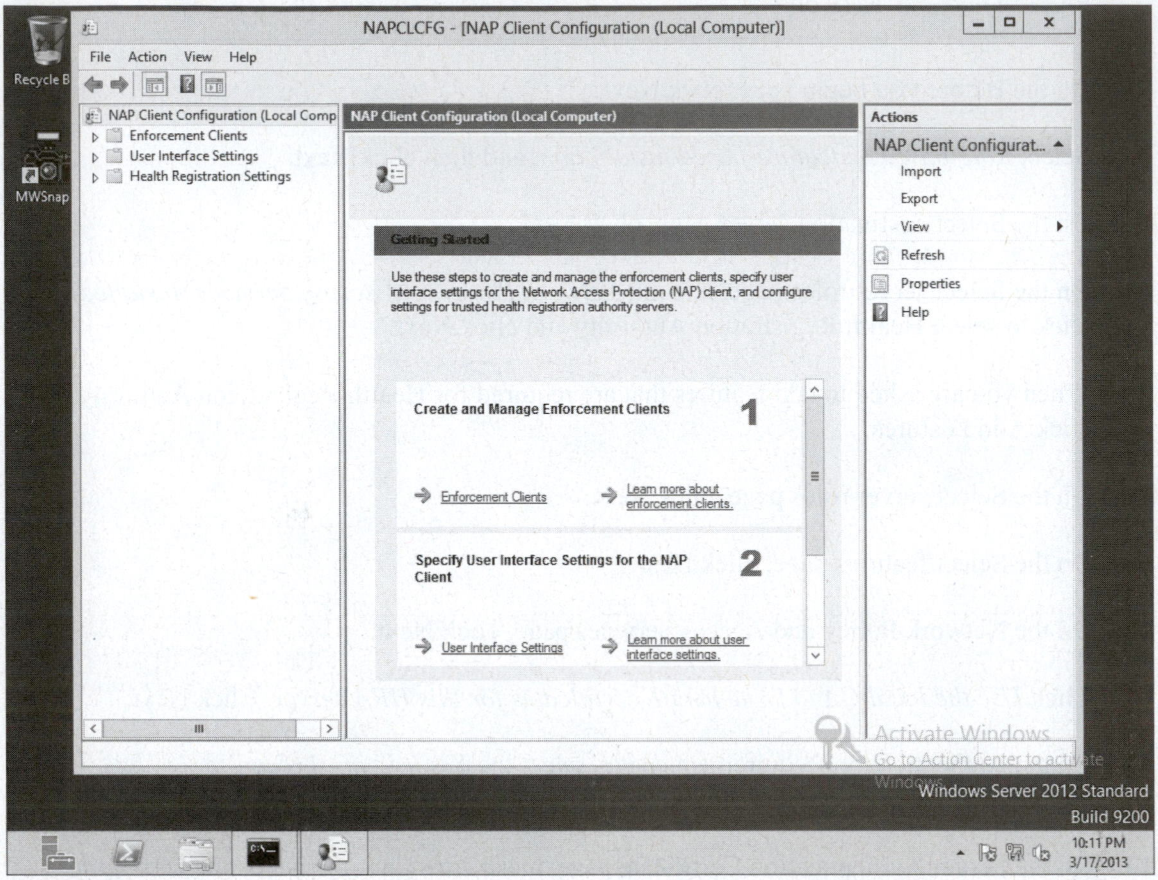

Figure 14-1
Opening the NAP Client Configuration

3. In the left pane, click Enforcement Clients.

4. In the center pane, double-click DHCP Quarantine Enforcement Client to open the DHCP Quarantine Enforcement Client Properties dialog box.

5. Select the Enable this enforcement client option. Click OK to close the DHCP Quarantine Enforcement Client Properties dialog box.

6. Take a screen shot of the NAP Client Configuration window by pressing Alt+Prt Scr and then paste it into your Lab 14 worksheet file in the page provided by pressing Ctrl+V.

7. Close the NAP Client Configuration Client console.

8. At the command prompt, execute the **`services.msc`** command.

9. Scroll down and find the Network Access Protection Agent. Then double-click the Network Access Protection Agent service to open the Network Access Protection Agent Properties dialog box.

10. Change the Startup type to Automatic.

11. Take a screen shot of the Network Access Protection Agent Properties dialog box by pressing Alt+Prt Scr and then paste it into your Lab 14 worksheet file in the page provided by pressing Ctrl+V.

12. Click the Start button.

13. After the service is started, click OK to close the Network Access Protection Agent Properties dialog box.

14. Close the Services console and close the command prompt.

15. Using Server Manager, open the Tools menu and click Network Policy Server. The Network Policy Server console opens.

16. In the main pane, click Configure NAP to start the Configure NAP Wizard as shown in Figure 14-2.

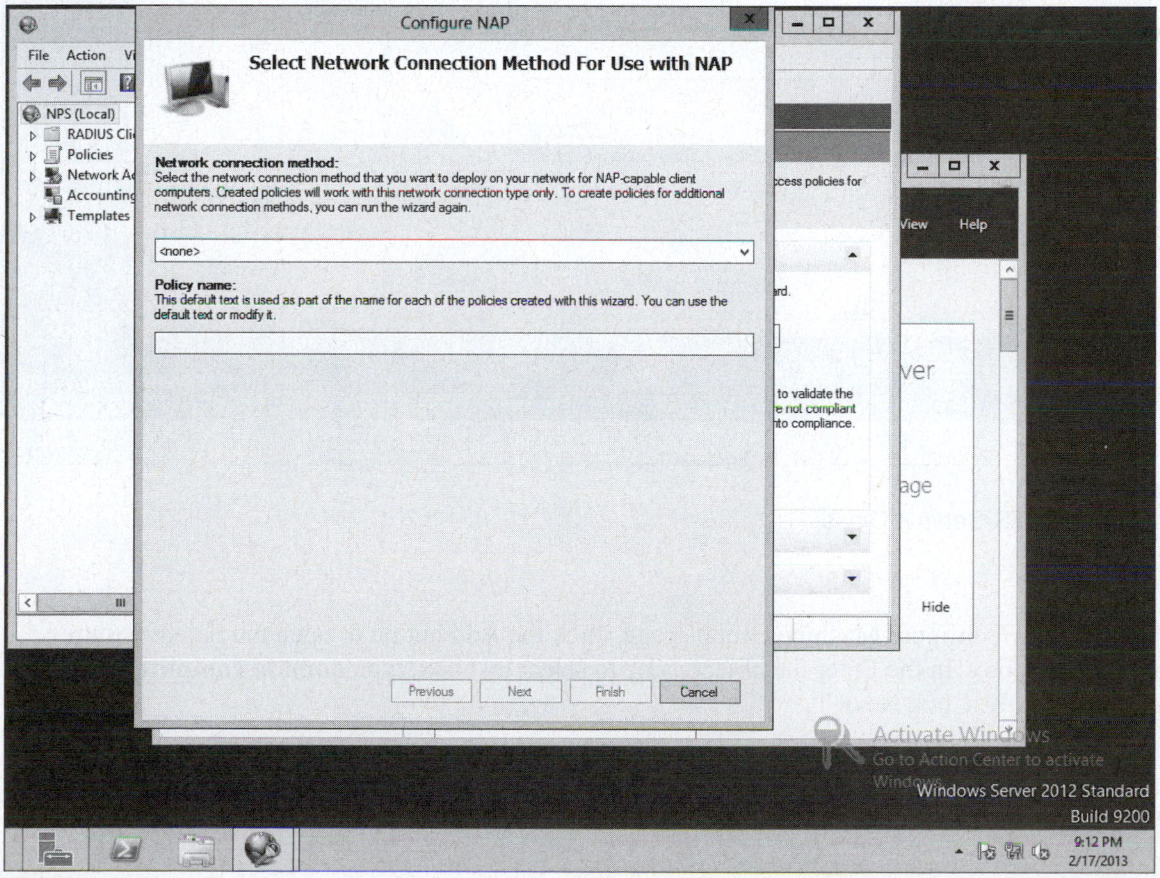

Figure 14-2
Configuring NAP

17. When the Select Network Connection Method For Use with NAP Wizard opens, select the Dynamic Host Configuration Protocol (DHCP) for the network connection method from the drop-down list. Click Next.

18. On the Specify NAP Enforcement Servers Running DHCP Server page, because this server is already running DHCP, click Next.

19. On the Specify DHCP Scopes page, click the Add button to open the MS-Server Class page as shown in Figure 14-3. Type **NAP DHCP** in the text box and click OK. On the Specify DHCP Scopes page, click Next.

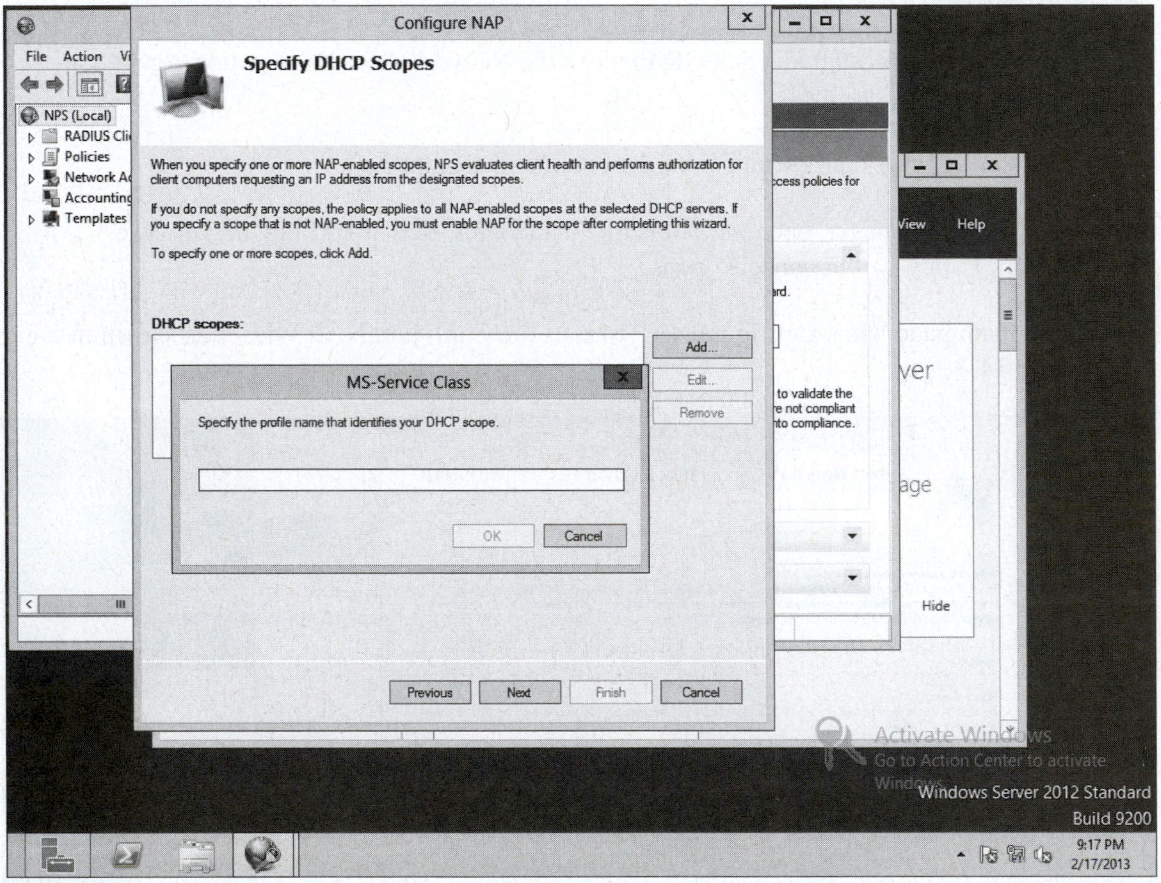

Figure 14-3
Configure the MS-Service Class

20. On the Configure Machine Groups page, click the Add button to open the Select Group dialog box. In the Enter the object name to select text box, type **domain computers** and click OK. Click Next.

21. On the Specify a NAP Remediation Server Group and URL page as shown in Figure 14-4, click New Group. In the Group Name text box, type **Remediation Servers**.

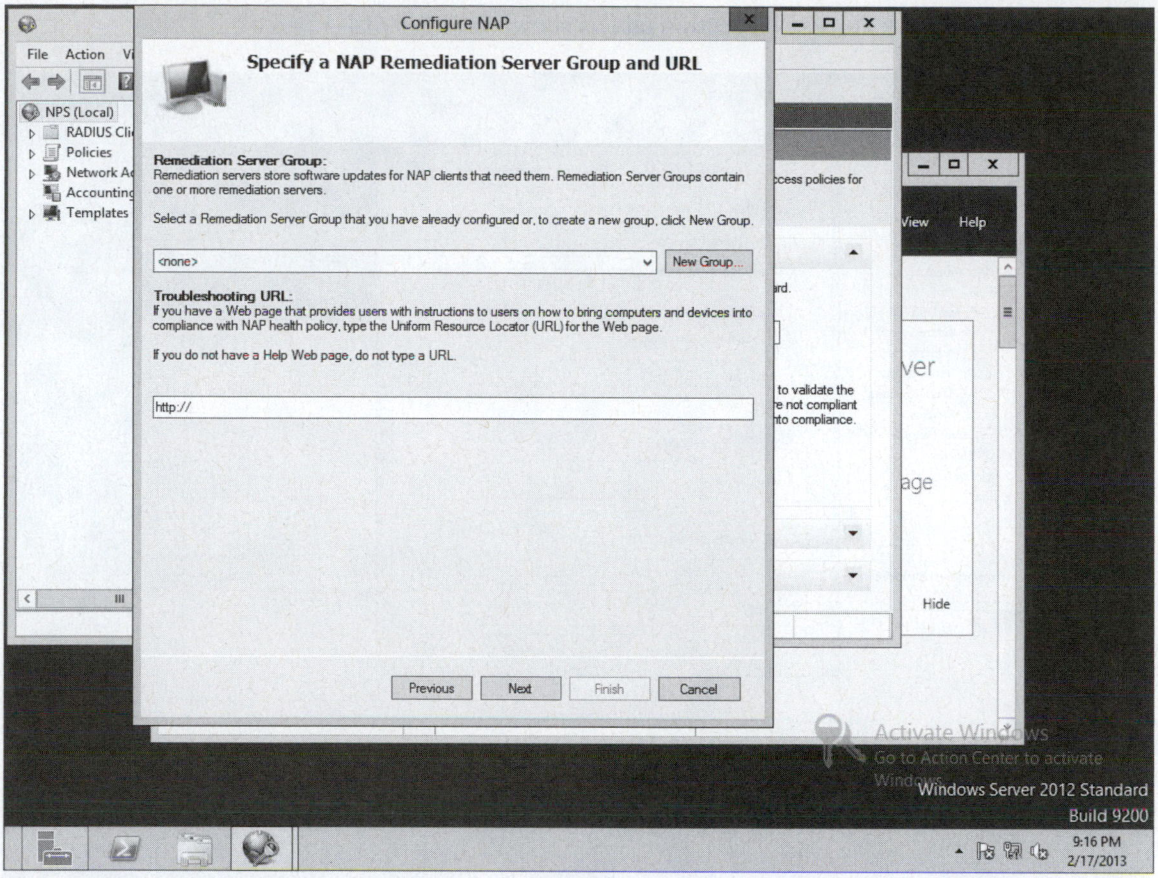

Figure 14-4
Specifying the NAP remediation server group and URL

Question 2	What remediation servers should you include?

22. Click the Add button. In the Friendly name text box, type **Server01**. For the IP address or DNS name, type **Server01.contoso.com** and click Resolve. Click OK to close the Add New Server and click OK to close the New Remediation Server Group dialog box. Click Next.

23. On the Define NAP Health Policy page, click Next.

24. On the Completing NAP Enforcement Policy and RADIUS Client Configuration page, click Finish.

25. Using Server Manager, open the Tools menu and click DHCP. The DHCP console opens.

26. Expand the server node and expand the IPv4 node.

27. Click Scope [192.168.1.0]. Then right-click Scope [192.168.1.0] and click Properties. A Scope Properties dialog box opens.

28. Click the Network Access Protection tab, as shown in Figure 14-5.

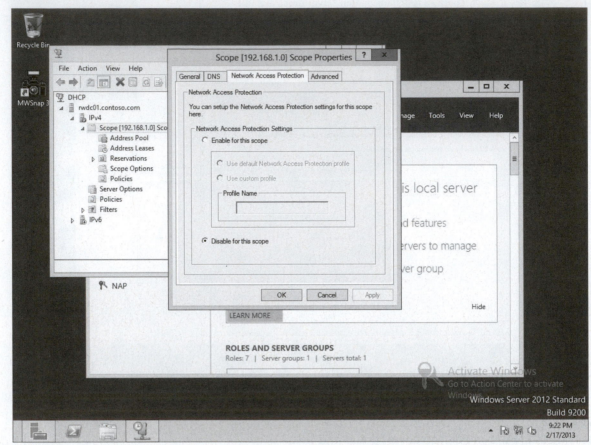

Figure 14-5
Enabling Network Access Protection

29. Click Enable for this scope.

30. Click OK to close Scope Properties dialog box.

31. Close DHCP console.

End of exercise.

Exercise 14.3	Configuring SHV and Health Policies
Overview	During this exercise, to enforce NAP, you configure System Health Validator and Health Policies.
Completion time	10 minutes

1. On RWDC01, using Server Manager, open Tools, and open Network Policy Server.

2. Expand Network Access Protection, expand System Health Validators, expand Windows Security Health Validator, and click Windows Security Health Validator.

3. Click Settings, then double-click Default Configuration. The Windows Security Health Validator dialog box opens as shown in Figure 14-6.

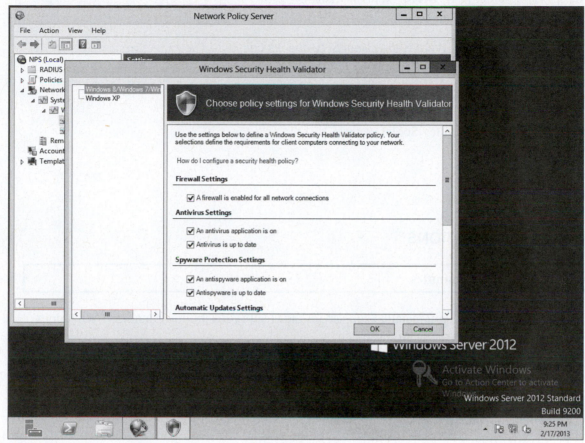

Figure 14-6
Configuring the Windows Security Health Validator

Question 3	Which options are already selected for the Windows Security Health Validator?

4. Click OK to close the Windows Security Health Validator.

5. In the NPS console, under Policies, click Health Policies.

6. Double-click NAP DHCP Compliant.

Question 4	Which Windows Security Health Validator is configured?

Question 5	What is the Client SHV checks configured as?

7.   Click OK to close the NAP DHCP Compliant Properties.

8.   Double-click NAP DHCP Noncompliant.

Question 6	*What is the Client SHV checks configured as?*

9.   Click OK to close the NAP DHCP Noncompliant Properties.

10.   Close Network Policy Server console.

End of exercise.

LAB REVIEW QUESTIONS

Completion time   10 minutes

1.   In Exercise 14.1, you installed support for the Health Registration Authority. What does the Health Registration Authority do?

2.   In Exercise 14.2, what command opened the NAP Client Configuration console?

3.   In Exercise 14.2, what allows a computer to get Windows update so that it can be compliant when using NAP?

4.   In Exercise 14.3, when using NAP, what defines the requirements for client computers that connect to the network?

Lab Challenge	Configuring Clients for NAP
Overview	To complete this challenge, you will explain how to configure clients for NAP by writing the highlevel steps to complete the tasks described in the scenerio.
Completion time	10 minutes

So far, you have configured NAP on the servers. You now need to configure NAP for the clients. Explain how to enable Security Center and to automatically start Network Access Protection Agent services.

Write out the steps you performed to complete the challenge.

End of lab.

LAB 15
CONFIGURING SERVER AUTHENTICATION

THIS LAB CONTAINS THE FOLLOWING EXERCISES AND ACTIVITIES:

Exercise 15.1   Creating a Service Account

Exercise 15.2   Creating a Managed Service Account

Exercise 15.3   Configuring Kerberos and Kerberos Delegation

Lab Challenge   Configuring Kerberos with the Setspn Command

BEFORE YOU BEGIN

The lab environment consists of student workstations connected to a local area network, along with a server that functions as the domain controller for a domain called *contoso.com*. The computers required for this lab are listed in Table 15-1.

Table 15-1
Computers Required for Lab 15

Computer	Operating System	Computer Name
Server (VM 1)	Windows Server 2012	RWDC01
Server (VM 2)	Windows Server 2012	Server01

In addition to the computers, you also require the software listed in Table 15-2 to complete Lab 15.

Table 15-2
Software Required for Lab 15

Software	Location
Lab 15 student worksheet	Lab15_worksheet.docx (provided by instructor)

Working with Lab Worksheets

Each lab in this manual requires that you answer questions, take screen shots, and perform other activities that you will document in a worksheet named for the lab, such as Lab15_worksheet.docx. You will find these worksheets on the book companion site. It is recommended that you use a USB flash drive to store your worksheets, so you can submit them to your instructor for review. As you perform the exercises in each lab, open the appropriate worksheet file, fill in the required information, and save the file to your flash drive.

After completing this lab, you will be able to:

- Create a service account

- Create a Group Service Account

- Configure Kerberos and Kerberos Delegation

Estimated lab time: 60 minutes

Exercise 15.1	Creating a Service Account
Overview	In this exercise, you create a traditional service account.
Completion time	10 minutes

1. Log on to RWDC01 as the **Contoso\administrator** user account with Password, **Password01**. The Server Manager console opens.

2. On Server Manager, click Tools > Active Directory Users and Computers.

3. In the console tree, expand contoso.com, if needed.

4. Right-click contoso.com, click New, and click Organizational Unit. The New Object – Organizational Unit dialog box opens.

5. In the Name text box, type **Service Accounts** and click OK.

6. Right-click the Service Accounts organizational unit, click New, and then click User. The New Object – User Wizard starts.

7. In the First name text box, type **App1**. In the Last name text box, type **Service**. In the User logon name text box, type **App1Service**. Click Next. The password options appear.

8. In the Password and Confirm password dialog boxes, type **Password01**. Select the Password never expires option. When a dialog box opens saying that the password should never expire and that the user will not be required to change the password at next logon, click OK.

9. Click Next.

10. Click Finish to complete creating a service account.

End of exercise.

Exercise 15.2	Creating a Managed Service Account
Overview	During this exercise, you create and deploy a Managed Service Account (MSA).
Completion time	25 minutes

Mindset Question: **What is the advantage of using a Managed Service Account over the traditional service account that was created in Exercise 15.1?**

1. On RWDC01, using Server Manager, open the Tools menu and click Active Directory Users and Computers, if needed.

2. In Active Directory Users and Computers, right-click the Computers OU, click New, and click Group. For the Group name, type **ServerGroup** and click OK.

3. In the Computers OU, Right-click ServerGroup and click Properties.

4. When the Properties dialog box opens, click the Members tab.

5. Click Add. In the text box, type **Server01.**

6. Click Object Types, select Computers, and click OK.

7. Click OK to close the ServerGroup Properties.

8. On RWDC01, using Server Manager, open the Tools menu and select Active Directory Module for Windows PowerShell. The Active Directory Module for Windows Powershell opens.

9. To create a key distribution services root key for the domain, run the following command in PowerShell:

```
Add-KDSRootKey -EffectiveTime ((Get-Date).AddHours
(-10))
```

10. To create an Active Directory AD service account, execute the following command:

```
New-ADServiceAccount -Name App2Service -DNSHostname
rwdc01.contoso.com
-PrincipalsAllowedToRetrieveManagedPassword ServerGroup
```

11. Take a screen shot of the Active Directory Users and Computers showing the Managed Service Account OU by pressing Alt+Prt Scr and then paste it into your Lab 15 worksheet file in the page provided by pressing Ctrl+V.

Question 1	*In which OU was the account created?*

12. To associate an MSA to a computer account, execute the following command in PowerShell:

```
Add-ADComputerServiceAccount -identity server01
-ServiceAccount App2Service
```

13. Log in to Server01 as the **Contoso\administrator** user account. The Server Manager console opens.

14. Open the Manage menu and click Add Roles and Features.

15. When the Add Roles and Features Wizard opens, click Next.

16. On the Select installation type page, click Next.

17. On the Select destination server page, click Next.

18. Click Active Directory Domain Services. When it asks to add features, click Add Features. Then click Next.

19. On the Select features page, click Next.

20. On the Active Directory Domain Services page, click Next.

21. On the Confirm installation selections page, click Install.

22. When the installation is complete, click Close.

23. On Server01, with Server Manager, open the Tools menu and click *Active Directory Module for Windows PowerShell*.

24. When PowerShell starts, execute the following command to add the computer account to Server01:

```
Add-ADComputerserviceaccount -Identity Server01
-ServiceAccount App2Service
```

25. On Server01, with Server Manager, open the Tools menu and click Services. The Services console opens.

26. Double-click the SNMP Trap service. The SNMP Trap Properties dialog box opens.

27. Click the Log On tab.

28. Select This account option and type **contoso\app2service$**.

Question 2	*Why is the $ used?*

29. Clear the password in the Password and Confirm password text boxes.

30. Click OK.

31. When it says that the account has been granted the Log On As Service, click OK.

32. If it states that the new logon name will not take effect until you stop and restart the service, click OK.

End of exercise.

Exercise 15.3	Configuring Kerberos and Kerberos Delegation
Overview	In this exercise, you create a Service Principal Name (SPN) for an account and configure Kerberos Delegation.
Completion time	10 minutes

Mindset Question: **When you want to use Kerberos, what names are used to represent users and what format does it follow?**

1. On RWDC01, with Server Manager, click Tools > ADSI Edit. The ADSI Edit console opens.

2. Right-click ADSI Edit in the console tree, and then click Connect To. When the Connection Settings dialog displays, click OK.

3. Double-click Default Naming Context in the console tree, expand the DC=contoso,DC=com, and then click OU=Service Account.

4. In the Details pane, right-click the App1 Service and then click Properties. The CN=App1 Service Properties dialog box opens as shown in Figure 15-1.

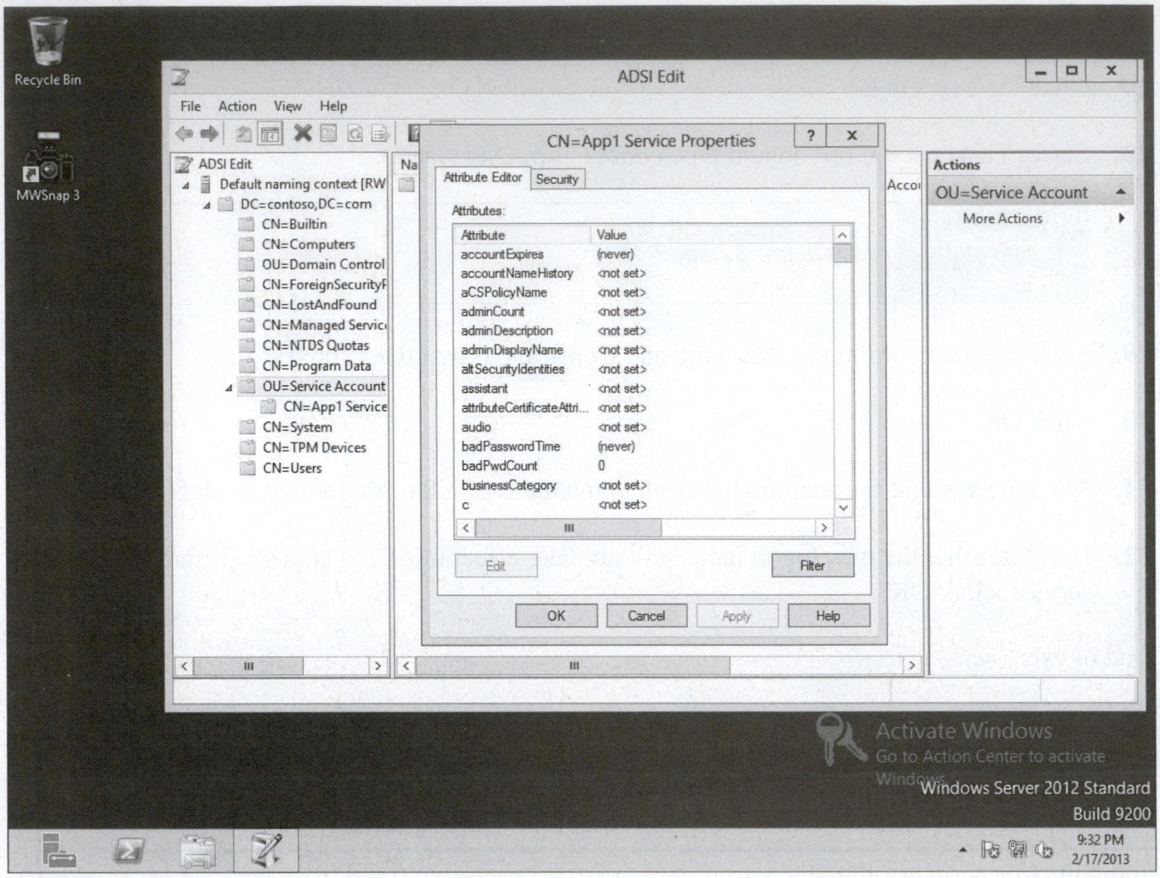

Figure 15-1
Editing the properties of a user

5. In the Attributes list, double-click servicePrincipalName to display the Multi-valued
   String Editor dialog box as shown in Figure 15-2.

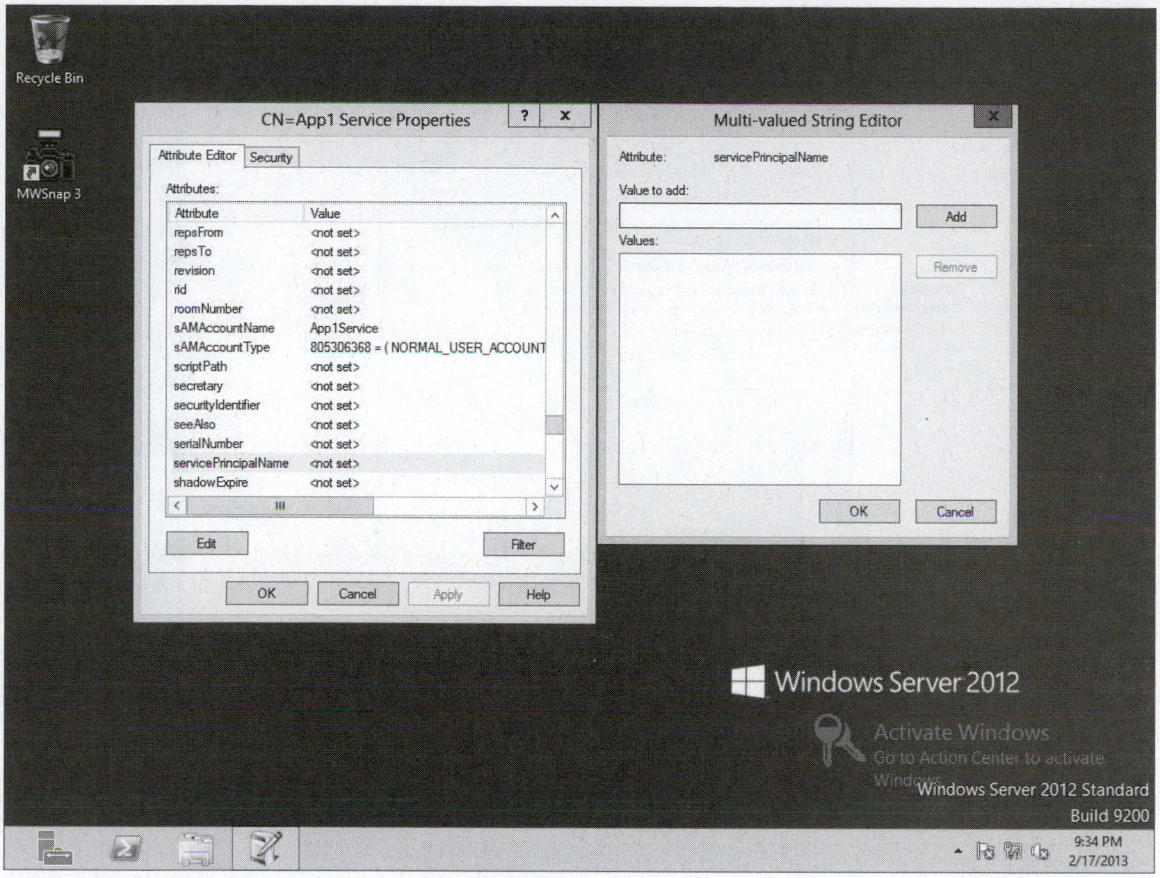

Figure 15-2
Modifying the servicePrincipalName

6. In the Value to add field, type **http/portal.contoso.com:443** and then click Add.

7. Click OK twice.

8. Using Server Manager, open the Tools menu, and click *Active Directory Users and Computers*.

9. Navigate to and click the Service Accounts organizational unit.

10. Right-click App1 Service and click Properties. The Properties dialog box opens.

11. Click the Delegation tab.

12. To allow this account to be delegated for a service, click *Trust this user for delegation to any service (Kerberos only)*, as shown in Figure 15-3.

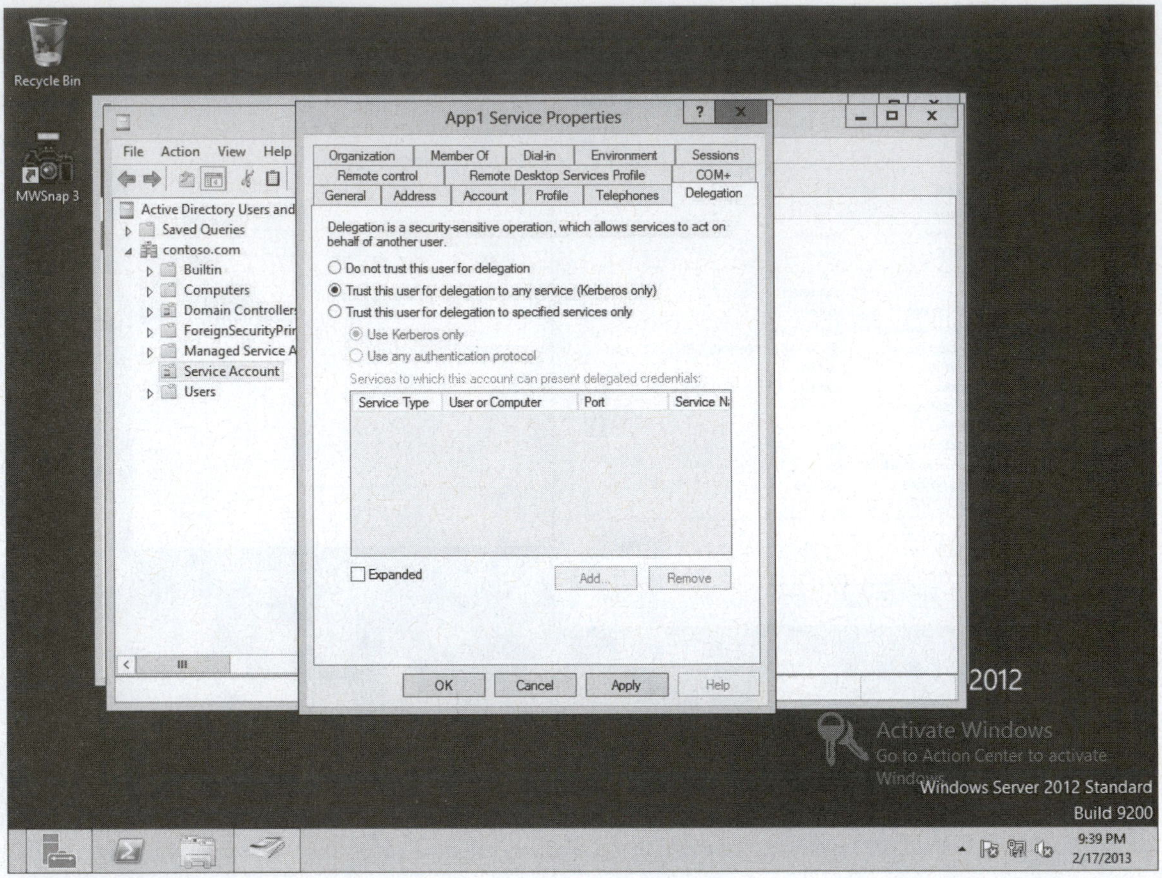

Figure 15-3
Configuring Kerberos delegation

13. Click OK to close the Properties dialog box.

End of exercise.

LAB REVIEW QUESTIONS

Completion time	10 minutes

1. In Exercise 15.2, what are the minimum requirements for Managed Service Accounts?

2. In Exercise 15.2, when using the PrincipalsAllowedToRetrieveManagedPassword option, what kind of objects can you specify?

3. In Exercise 15.2, what do you use to create a Managed Service Account?

4. In Exercise 15.3, what was used to define an SPN for an account?

Lab Challenge	Configuring Kerberos with the SetSPN Command
Overview	To complete this challenge, you will demonstrate how to configure Kerberos with the SetSPN command writing the step to complete the tasks described in the scenerio.
Completion time	5 minutes

You need to configure an SPN for an account. You decide that you want to create the SPN using the command prompt. What command would you use to configure the SPN in the same way that you did in Exercise 15-3.

Take a screen shot of the netsh command prompt window by pressing Alt+Prt Scr and then paste it into your Lab 15 worksheet file in the page provided by pressing Ctrl+V.

End of lab.

LAB 16
CONFIGURING DOMAIN CONTROLLERS

THIS LAB CONTAINS THE FOLLOWING EXERCISES AND ACTIVITIES:

Exercise 16.1   Promoting Server01 to a Domain Controller

Exercise 16.2   Configuring Universal Group Membership Caching

Exercise 16.3   Moving Operations Masters

Exercise 16.4   Seizing Operations Masters

Exercise 16.5   Creating an RODC

Lab Challenge   Cloning a Domain Controller

BEFORE YOU BEGIN

The lab environment consists of student workstations connected to a local area network, along with a server that functions as the domain controller for a domain called *contoso.com*. The computers required for this lab are listed in Table 16-1.

Table 16-1
Computers Required for Lab 16

Computer	Operating System	Computer Name
Server (VM 1)	Windows Server 2012	RWDC01
Server (VM 2)	Windows Server 2012	Server01
Server (VM 3)	Windows Server 2012	Server02

In addition to the computers, you also require the software listed in Table 16-2 to complete Lab 16.

Table 16-2
Software Required for Lab 16

Software	Location
Lab 16 student worksheet	Lab16_worksheet.docx (provided by instructor)

Working with Lab Worksheets

Each lab in this manual requires that you answer questions, shoot screen shots, and perform other activities that you will document in a worksheet named for the lab, such as Lab16_worksheet.docx. You will find these worksheets on the book companion site. It is recommended that you use a USB flash drive to store your worksheets, so you can submit them to your instructor for review. As you perform the exercises in each lab, open the appropriate worksheet file, fill in the required information, and save the file to your flash drive.

After completing this lab, you will be able to:

- Configure universal group membership caching (UGMC)

- Transfer and seize operations masters

- Install and configure a Read-Only Domain Controller

- Clone a Domain Controller

Estimated lab time: 95 minutes

Exercise 16.1	Promoting Server01 to a Domain Controller
Overview	During this exercise, you promote Server01 to a domain controller.
Completion time	10 minutes

1. Log in to Server01 as the Contoso\administrator user account. The Server Manager console opens.

2. Click the *Yellow triangle with the black exclamation point (!)* and click *Promote this server to a domain controller.*

3. When the Deployment Configuration page opens, click Next.

4. On the Domain Controller Options page, type **Password01** in the Password and Confirm password text boxes and click Next.

5. On the DNS Options page, click Next.

6. On the Additional Options page, click Next.

7. On the Paths page, click Next.

8. On the Review Options page, click Next.

9. After the prerequisites are checked, click Install.

10. When the promotion is done, the system restarts automatically.

End of exercise.

Exercise 16.2	Configuring Universal Group Membership Caching
Overview	During this exercise, you promote Server01 to a domain controller.
Completion time	10 minutes

Mindset Question: **For users to be able to log in, they, of course, need a domain controller. What component is needed for users to log in and why?**

1. Log in to RWDC01 as the **Contoso\administrator** user account. The Server Manager console opens.

2. On Server Manager, click Tools > Active Directory Sites and Services. The Active Directory Sites and Services console opens.

Question 1	What program is used to enable or disable global catalogs?

3. Expand Sites, and click Default-First-Site-Name.

4. Right-click NTDS Site Settings and click Properties. The NTDS Site Settings Properties dialog box opens as shown in Figure 16-1.

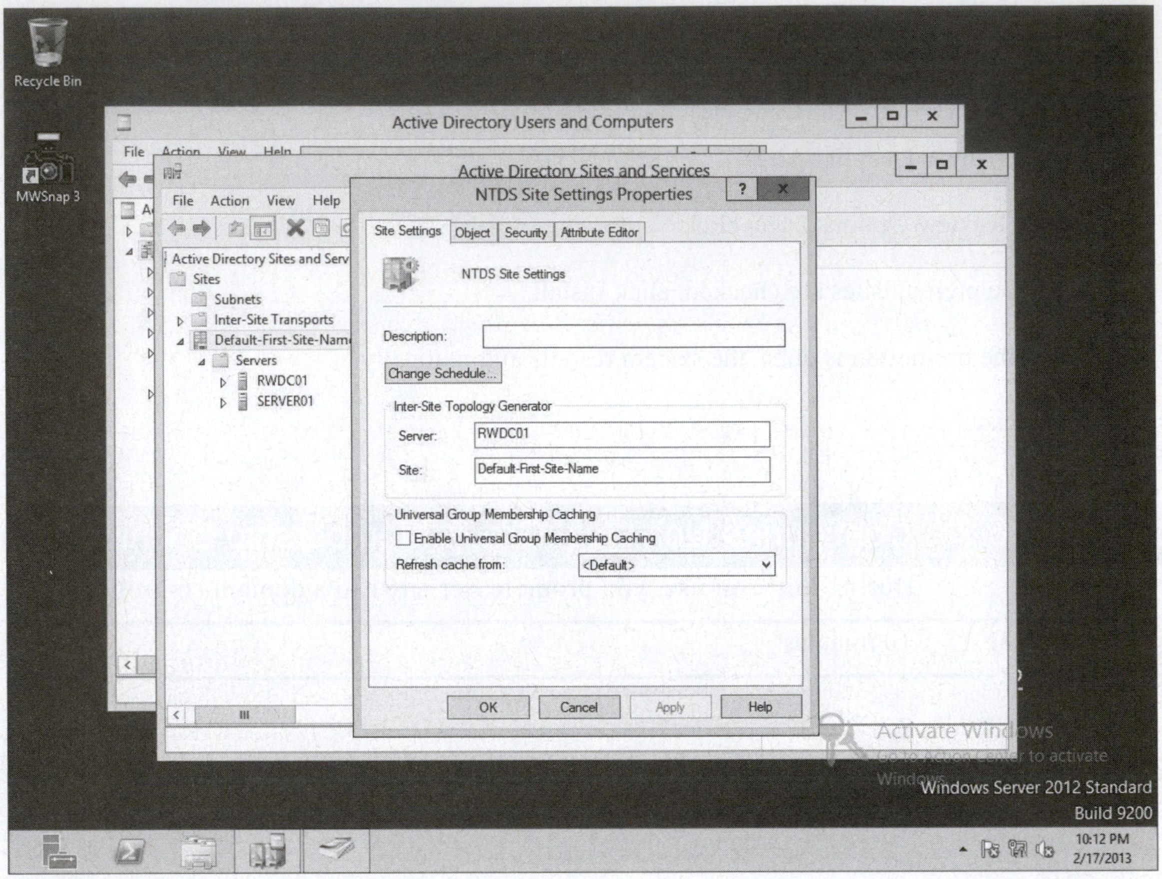

Figure 16-1
Modifying site settings

5. Select the *Enable Universal Group Membership Caching* option.

6. Click OK to close the NTDS Settings Properties dialog box.

7. Close Active Directory Sites and Services.

End of exercise.

Exercise 16.3	Moving Operations Master
Overview	During this exercise, you transfer the Operations Masters to another domain controller.
Completion time	20 minutes

Mindset Question: You have multiple sites. During a weekend, you will perform maintenance on the corporate network, which would make those domain controllers (which are also the Operations Masters) unavailable for an extended period of time. What effect will this have on the users on the network and what should you do to minimize down time for the other sites?

1. Log in to Server01 as the **Contoso\administrator** user account. The Server Manager console opens.

2. On Server Manager, click Tools > Active Directory Users and Computers. The Active Directory Users and Computers console opens.

3. Right-click contoso.com and click Change Domain Controller. Click Server01.contoso.com and click OK.

4. Right-click contoso.com and click Operations Masters. The Operations Masters dialog box opens as shown in Figure 16-2.

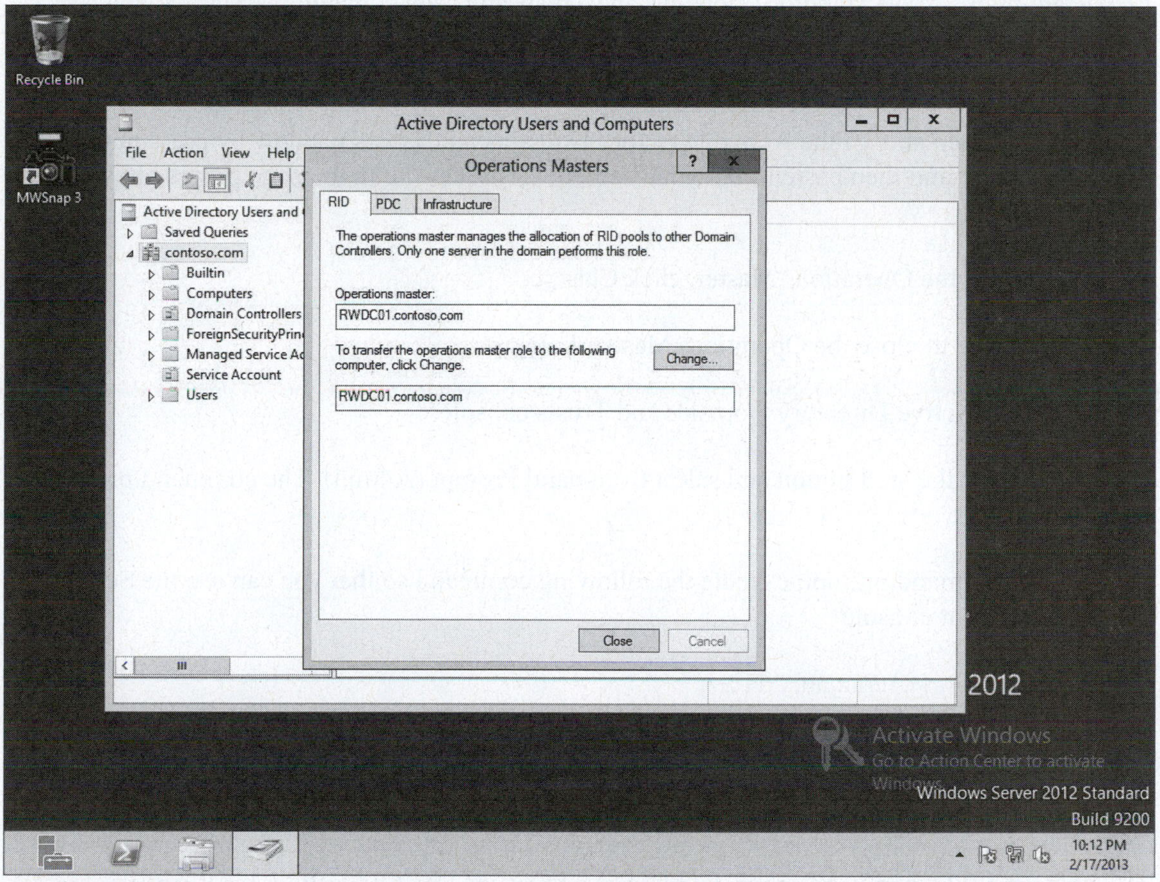

Figure 16-2
Viewing the current domain-level operations masters

5. To transfer the RID from RWDC01 to Server01, click Change on the RID tab. When it asks if you are sure, click Yes. When the Operations Master role is transferred, click OK.

6. Click the PDC tab. Transfer the PDC Emulator to Server01.

Question 2	*Which Operations Master acts as the master time server and is considered authorative for account passwords?*

7.   Click the Infrastructure tab. Transfer the Infrastructure to Server01.

8.   Close the Operations Masters dialog box.

9.   Close the Active Directory Users and Computers console.

10.   On Server01, using Server Manager, click Tools > Active Directory Domains and Trusts. The Active Domains and Trusts console opens.

11.   Right-click Active Directory Domains and Trusts and click Change Active Directory Domain Controller. Click Server01.contoso.com. Click OK.

12.   Right-click Active Directory Domains and Trusts and select Operations Master. The Operations Master dialog box showing current Domain Naming Operations Master opens.

13.   Take a screen shot of the Active Directory Domains and Trusts window by pressing Alt+Prt Scr and then paste it into your Lab 16 worksheet file in the page provided by pressing Ctrl+V.

14.   To transfer the Operations Master, click Change.

15.   Click Close to close the Operations Master dialog box.

16.   Close the Active Directory Domains and Trusts console.

17.   Right-click the start button and select Command Prompt (Admin). The command prompt opens.

18.   At the command prompt, execute the following command so that you can use the Schema Management console.

```
Regsvr32 schmmgmt.dll
```

19.   When the schmmgmt.dll is registered, click OK.

20.   At the command prompt, execute the mmc command. The MMC console opens.

21.   Open the File menu and select Add/Remove Snap-in. The Add or Remove Snap-ins dialog box opens.

22.   Select Active Directory Schema and click Add. Then click OK to close the Add/Remove Snap-ins dialog box.

23.   Right-click Active Directory Schema and click Change Active Directory Domain Controller. Click Server01.contoso.com and click OK. When it gives you a warning, click OK.

24.   Right-click Active Directory Schema and select Operations Master. The Change Schema Master dialog box opens.

25. To transfer the Schema Master to Server01, click Change. When it asks if you are sure, click Yes. When the Operations Master is transferred, click OK.

26. Click Close to close the Change Schema Master dialog box.

27. Close the MMC console. If you are asked to save the console settings, click No. Close the command prompt window.

End of exercise.

Exercise 16.4	Seizing Operations Masters
Overview	In this exercise, instead of transfering the Operations Master, you seize the Operations Masters and move them to another domain controller.
Completion time	10 minutes

Mindset Question: **The ntdsutil is a powerful tool when managing Active Directory. When should you transfer roles and when should you seize roles?**

1. On RWDC01, right-click the Start button and select Command Prompt (Admin). The command prompt opens.

2. From the command prompt, execute the `ntdsutil` command.

3. At the ntdsutil prompt, execute the `roles` command.

4. At the fsmo maintenance prompt, execute the `connections` command.

5. At the server connections prompt, execute the following command:

   `connect to server rwdc01`

6. At the server connections prompt, execute the `quit` command.

7. To see the available options for fsmo maintenance, press the ? key and press the Enter key.

8. To seize the roles, at the fsmo maintenance prompt, type the following commands:

   seize schema master

   seize naming master

   seize RID master

   seize PDC

```
seize infrastructure master
```

If an "Are you sure?" dialog box appears, click Yes to continue.

> **NOTE**
>
> *When you use the Ntdsutil.exe to seize an operations master role, Ntdsutil.exe will first try to transfer from the current role owner. If the current role owner is not available, the tool seizes the role. Remember, in production, you should only seize a role when the current holder will not be coming back any time soon.*

9. At the fsmo maintenance prompt, execute the `quit` command.

10. At the ntdsutil prompt, execute the `quit` command.

11. Close the command prompt.

End of exercise.

Exercise 16.5	Creating an RODC
Overview	In this exercise, you create and deploy a read-only domain controller (RODC).
Completion time	20 minutes

Mindset Question: **So far, we have not had a need for a Read-Only Domain Controller (RODC). When is an RODC necessary?**

1. Log in to Server02 as the **Contoso\administrator** user account. The Server Manager console opens.

2. On Server Manager, open the Manage menu and click Add Roles and Features.

3. When the Add Roles and Features Wizard opens, click Next.

4. On the Select installation type page, click Next.

5. On the Select destination server page, click Next.

6. Click Active Directory Domain Services. When it asks to add features, click Add Features. Then click Next.

7. On the Select features page, click Next.

8. On the Active Directory Domain Services page, click Next.

9. On the Confirm installation selections page, click Install.

10. When the installation is complete, click Close.

11. On the left pane, click AD DS. On the right-pane click More in the yellow bar.

12. When the All Servers Task Details window open, click *Promote this server to a domain controller*. The Active Directory Domain Services Configuration Wizard starts.

13. On the Deployment Configuration page, confirm that *Add a domain controller to an existing domain* is already selected, click Next.

14. On the Domain Controllers Options page, select Read only domain controller (RODC), as shown in Figure 16-3. Select the correct site name (Default-First-Site-Name, in this case). In the Password and Confirm Password text boxes, type **Password01**. Click Next.

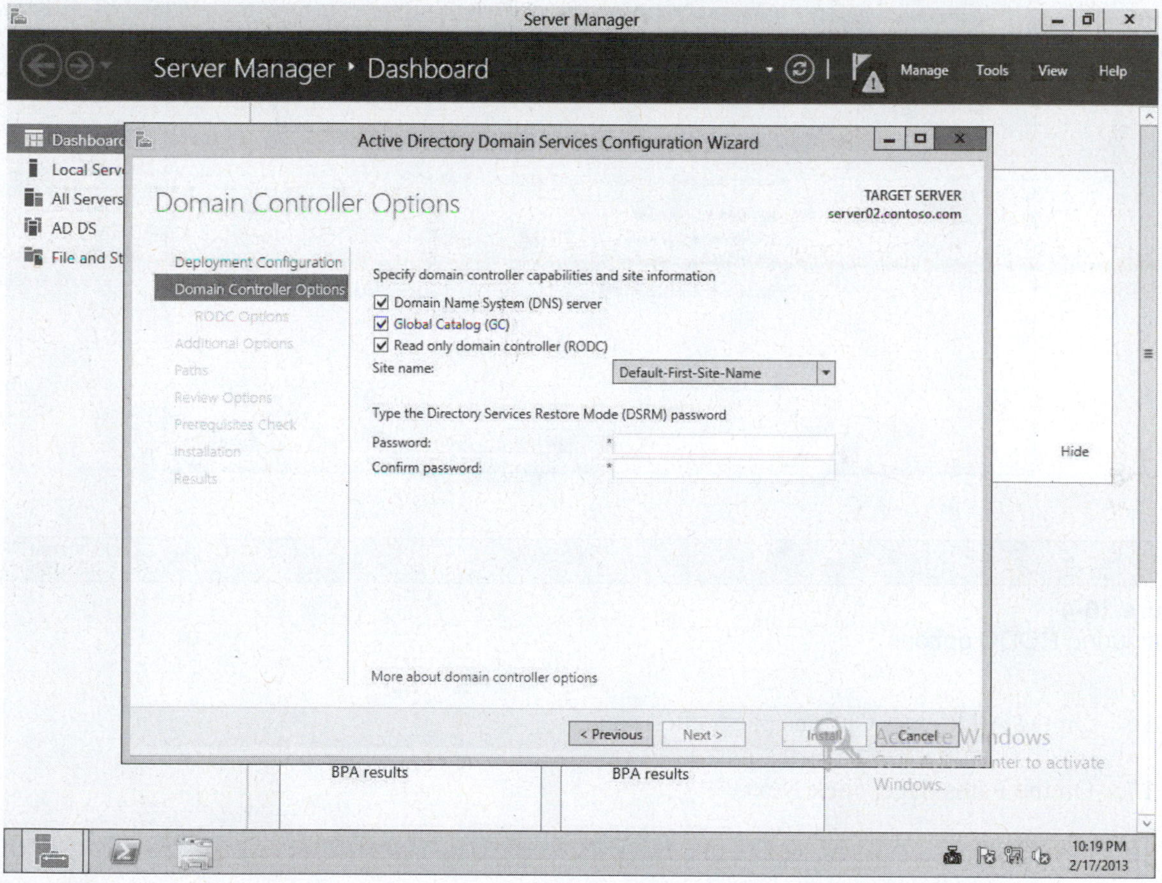

Figure 16-3
Promoting a server to a read-only domain controller

Question 3	*What accounts can replicate passwords to the RODC?*

Question 4	*What accounts are denied from replicating passwords?*

15. On the RODC Options page as shown in Figure 16-4, under Delegated administrator account click Select. In the text box, type **App1Service** and click OK. Click Next.

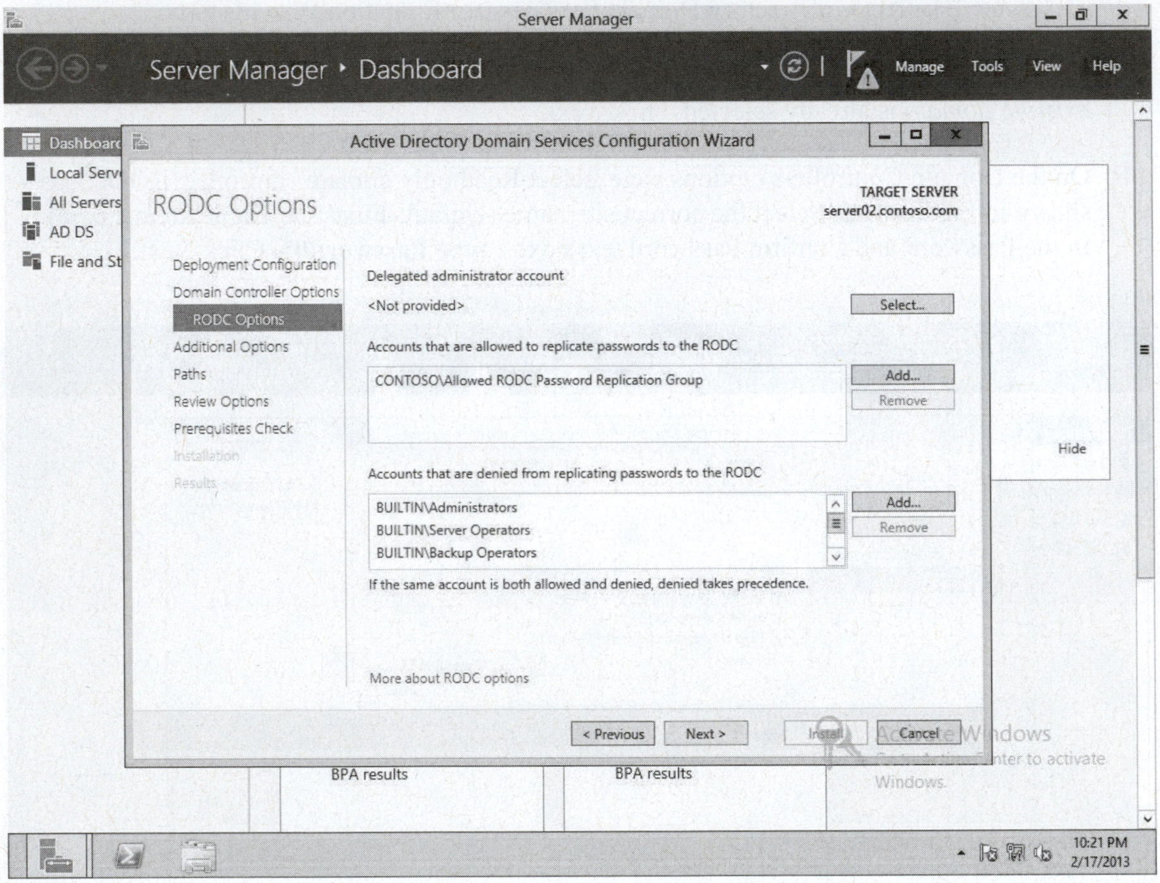

Figure 16-4
Configuring RODC options

16. On the Additional Options page, click Next.

17. On the Paths page, click Next.

18. On the Review Options page, click Next.

19. On the Prerequisites Check page, click Install.

20. When the installation is complete, Windows automatically restarts the domain controller.

21. On RWDC01, using Server Manager, Tools, open Active Diretory Users and Computers.

22. Navigate to the Domain Controllers OU. Wait for Server02 to reboot. Then right-click Server02 and click Properties. The Properties dialog box opens.

23. Click the Password Replication Policy tab to view the current password replication policies.

24. Take a screen shot of the Password Replication Policy tab by pressing Alt+Prt Scr and then paste it into your Lab 16 worksheet file in the page provided by pressing Ctrl+V.

25. Click OK to close the Server02 Properties dialog box.

End of exercise.

LAB REVIEW QUESTIONS

Completion time   10 minutes

1. In Exercise 16.2, what tool was used to enable Universal Group Membership Caching

2. In Exercise 16.3, how many PDC emulators are there within a typical organization?

3. In Exercise 16.3, when you try to transfer an operations master to another domain controller using an MMC and the source and target domain controllers are the same, what do you have to do?

4. In Exercise 16.3, to be able to access the Active Directory Schema console, what must you do first?

5. In Exercise 16.3, what did you use to transfer the PDC Emulator role?

6. In Exercise 16.4, what did you use to seize the operation masters?

7. In Exercise 16.5, where woiuld you go if you need to modify which accounts are replicated to the RODC?

Lab Challenge	Cloning a Domain Controller
Overview	To complete this challenge, you must demonstrate how to clone a domain controller by writing the steps to complete the tasks described in the scenerio. Due to time, this is a written-only exercise.
Completion time	20 minutes

Write out the steps you performed to complete the challenge.

End of lab.

LAB 17
MAINTAINING ACTIVE DIRECTORY

THIS LAB CONTAINS THE FOLLOWING EXERCISES AND ACTIVITIES:

Exercise 17.1   Backing Up System State

Exercise 17.2   Restoring the System State

Exercise 17.3   Using an Active Directory Snapshot

Exercise 17.4   Restoring a Deleted Object Using the Active Directory Recycle Bin

Exercise 17.5   Managing the Active Directory Database

Lab Challenge   Removing Server02 from Active Directory

BEFORE YOU BEGIN

The lab environment consists of student workstations connected to a local area network, along with a server that functions as the domain controller for a domain called *contoso.com*. The computers required for this lab are listed in Table 17-1.

Table 17-1
Computers Required for Lab 17

Computer	Operating System	Computer Name
Server (VM 1)	Windows Server 2012	RWDC01
Server (VM 2)	Windows Server 2012	Server01
Server (VM 3)	Windows Server 2012	Server02

In addition to the computers, you also require the software listed in Table 17-2 to complete Lab 17.

Table 17-2
Software Required for Lab 17

Software	Location
Lab 17 student worksheet	Lab17_worksheet.docx (provided by instructor)

Working with Lab Worksheets

Each lab in this manual requires that you answer questions, take screen shots, and perform other activities that you will document in a worksheet named for the lab, such as Lab17_worksheet.docx. You will find these worksheets on the book companion site. It is recommended that you use a USB flash drive to store your worksheets, so you can submit them to your instructor for review. As you perform the exercises in each lab, open the appropriate worksheet file, fill in the required information, and save the file to your flash drive.

After completing this lab, you will be able to:

- Back up the System State including Active Directory

- Perform an Active Directory restore

- Configure Active Directory snapshots

- Restore a Deleted Object using the Active Directory Recycle Bin

- Perform Active Directory maintenance

Estimated lab time: 130 minutes

Exercise 17.1	Backing Up System State
Overview	As a system administrator, it is important to have good backups. Therefore, during this exercise, you use Windows Server Backup to back up the system state of Server01, which includes the Active Directory.
Completion time	30 minutes

Mindset Question: **What is the system state and how does it relate to Active Directory?**

Installing Windows Server Backup

Question 1	*What is the best method for disaster recovery?*

1. Log in to Server01 as the **Contoso\administrator** user account. The Server Manager console opens.

2. On Server Manager, click Manage and click Add Roles and Features.

3. When the Add Roles and Features Wizard starts, click Next.

4. On the Select installation type page, click Next.

5. On the Select destination server page, click Next.

6. On the Select server roles page, click Next.

7. On the Select features page, click to select the Windows Server Backup and click Next.

8. On the Confirm installation selections page, click Install.

9. When the installation is complete, click Close.

Performing a Back Up of the System State

1. Log in to RWDC01 as the **Contoso\Administrator** user account. The Server Manager console opens.

2. On RWDC01, open Windows Explorer and create a **C:\BAK** folder.

3. Right-click the BAK folder and click Properties.

4. When the Properties dialog box opens, click the Sharing tab.

5. Click Advanced Sharing.

6. When the Advanced Sharing dialog box opens, click Share this folder. Click Permissions. Click to select the Allow Change permission for Everyone. Click OK to close the Permissions for BAK dialog box. Click OK to close the Advanced Sharing dialog box.

7.   Click Close to close the Properties dialog box.

8. On Server01, using Server Manager, click Tools > Windows Server Backup. The Windows Server Backup console opens.

9. Click Local Backup in the left pane.

10. Under Actions, click Backup Once.

11. When the Backup Once Wizard starts, click Different Options and click Next.

12. On the Select Backup Configuration page, click Custom and click Next.

13. On the Select Items for Backup page, click Add Items. The Select Items dialog box opens as shown in Figure 17-1.

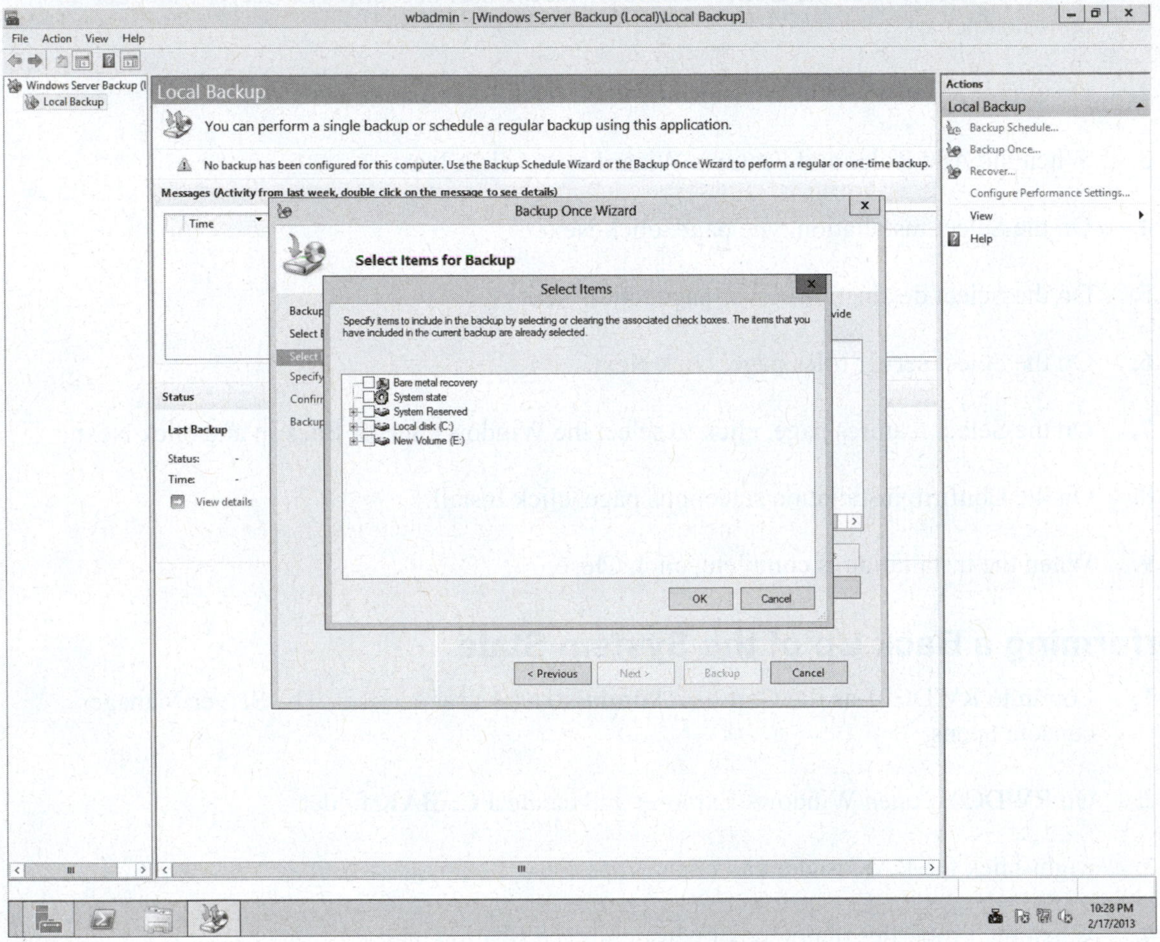

Figure 17-1
Selecting items for backup

14. Select System state and click OK.

15. On the Select Items for Backup page, click Next.

16. On the Specify Destination Type page, select Remote shared folder. Click Next.

17. On the Specify Remote Folder page, type **\\RWDC01\BAK** and click Next.

18. On the Confirmation page, click Backup. The backups will take a few minutes.

19. When the backup is completed, take a screen shot of the Backup Once Wizard window by pressing Alt+Prt Scr and then paste it into your Lab 17 worksheet file in the page provided by pressing Ctrl+V.

20. Click Close.

End of exercise.

Exercise 17.2	Restoring the System State
Overview	In the previous exercise, you performed a backup. During this exercise, you perform a restore of the system state. However, before you perform the final reboot, you make an OU as authoritative so that the OU will not be overwritten by other domain controllers.
Completion time	30 minutes

Mindset Question: **When you need to restore Active Directory, what are the two types of restores and how do they differ?**

1. On a physical server, you would normally press F8 during reboot. However, because you are running on a virtual environment on Server01, right-click Start, select Run, and then enter msconfig.exe, opening System Configuration. Click the Boot tab, click to select Safe boot, and select Active Directory repair. Click OK. Then restart the computer.

2. Log in as the local administrator (DSRM), using the password of **Password01**.

3. On Server01, using Server Manager, click Tools > Windows Server Backup. The Windows Server Backup console opens.

4. Click Local Backup. Under Actions, click Recover.

5. When the Recovery Wizard starts, select *A backup stored on another location* and click Next.

6. On the Specify Location Type page, click Remote shared folder and click Next.

7. On the Specify Remote Folder page, type **\\RWDC01\BAK** and click Next.

8. On the Select Backup Date page, select today's date of the backup that you want to restore from and click Next.

9. On the Select Recovery Type page, click System state. Click Next.

10. On the Select Location for System State Recovery page, select *Perform an authoritative restore of Active Directory files* and click Next.

11. When the warning appears that this recovery option will cause all replicated content on the local server to re-synchronize after recovery, click OK.

12. When it asks for you to continue, click OK.

13. On the Confirmation page, click Recover.

14. When it asks if you want to continue again, click Yes.

15. When the restore is completed, do not click Restart. Instead, close the Windows Backup program.

16. Right-click the Start Menu button and select Command Prompt (Admin). The command prompt window opens.

17. Execute the `ntdsutil` command.

18. From the ntdsutil prompt, execute the flowing command:

    ```
    activate instance NTDS
    ```

19. At the ntdsutil prompt, execute the following command:

    ```
    authoritative restore
    ```

20. To mark the Service Accounts OU to be restored with an authoritative restore, execute the following command:

    ```
    restore subtree "OU=Service Accounts,DC=contoso,DC=com"
    ```

21. When the Authoritative Restore Confirmation dialog box opens, click Yes to perform the authoritative restore. When the record or records have been updated, the names of the back-link files are displayed.

22. Take a screen shot of the ntdsutil Command Prompt window by pressing Alt+Prt Scr and then paste it into your Lab 17 worksheet file in the page provided by pressing Ctrl+V.

23. Execute the `quit` command twice to get back to the command prompt.

24. Open System Configuration (msconfig.exe). Click the Boot tab, deselect the Safe boot option, and click OK. When it asks you to restart, click Restart.

End of exercise.

Exercise 17.3	Using an Active Directory Snapshot
Overview	In this exercise, you create a snapshot of Active Directory. You then mount and access the snapshot.
Completion time	20 minutes

Mindset Question: **Active Directory has the ability to create snapshots. How can snapshots be used and what are their limits?**

1. Log in to Server01 as the **Contoso\Administrator** user account. The Server Manager console opens.

2. Right-click the Start button and select Command Prompt (Admin). The command prompt window opens.

3. At the command prompt, execute the `ntdsutil` command.

4. At the ntdsutil prompt, execute the `snapshot` command.

5. At the snapshot prompt, execute the `activate instance ntds` command.

6. Execute the `create` command.

Question 2	What is the Guid (without the braces ({})) of the snapshot created?

7. To return a list of all snapshots, at the snapshot prompt, execute the `list all` command.

8. Execute the `mount {GUID}` command, where GUID is the one that you recorded.

9. Take a screen shot of the ntdsutil Command Prompt window by pressing Alt+Prt Scr and then paste it into your Lab 17 worksheet file in the page provided by pressing Ctrl+V.

10. Execute the quit command twice to exit ntdsutil.

11. To mount the snapshot, execute the following command:

```
dsamain -dbpath
c:\$snap_datetime_volumec$\windows\ntds\ntds.dit
-ldapport 5000
```

You need to specify the date-time when you performed the mount command. The port number, 5000, can be any open and unique TCP port number (see Figure 17-2).

Figure 17-2
Mounting a snapshot

12. A message indicates that Active Directory Domain Services startup is complete. Do not close the command prompt window and leave the command you just ran, dsamain.exe, running while you continue to the next step.

13. Using Server Manager, click Tools > Active Directory Users and Computers. The Active Directory Users and Computers console opens.

14. Right-click the contoso.com, and then click Change Domain Controller. The Change Directory Server dialog box appears.

15. Click <Type a Directory Server name[:port] here>, type **Server01.contoso.com:5000**, and press Enter.

16. Click OK. You are now viewing the users and computers that are stored in the snapshot.

17. Switch to the command prompt in which the snapshot is mounted.

18. Press Ctrl+C to stop DSAMain.exe.

19. Execute the `ntdsutil` command.

20. Execute the `activate instance ntds` command.

21. Execute the `snapshot` command.

22. Type **unmount <GUID>**, where GUID is the GUID of the snapshot, and then press Enter.

23. Execute the `list all` command.

24. Because the snapshot is the first entry in the list, execute the following command:

```
delete 1
```

25. Execute the `quit` command twice.

26. Take a screen shot of the ntdsutil Command Prompt window by pressing Alt+Prt Scr and then paste it into your Lab 17 worksheet file in the page provided by pressing Ctrl+V.

27. Close the command prompt window and the Active Directory Users and Computers console.

End of exercise.

Exercise 17.4	Restoring a Deleted Object Using the Recycle Bin
Overview	During this exercise, you activate the Active Directory Recycle Bin. You then delete an object and restore the object from the Recycle Bin.
Completion time	10 minutes

Mindset Question: **Explain how the Active Directory Recycle Bin works.**

1. On Server01, using Server Manager, click Tools > Active Directory Administrative Center. The Active Directory Administrative Center opens.

2. Click contoso (local), as shown in Figure 17-3.

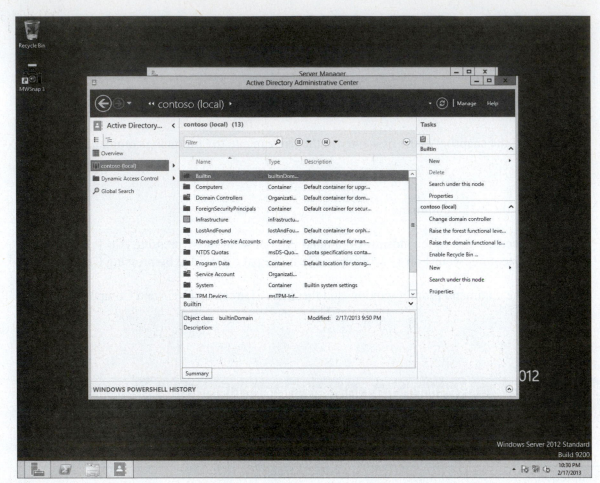

Figure 17-3
Managing the contoso domain with Active Directory Administrator Center

3. In the right pane, click Enable Recycle Bin. When it says that once the Recycle Bin has been enabled, it cannot be disabled and asks if you want to continue, click OK.

4. When is says to refresh the AD Administrative Center now, click OK.

5. Press the F5 key on the keyboard to refresh the Active Directory Administrative Center.

6. Using Server Manager, open Active Directory Users and Computers.

7. Expand contoso.com and click Service Accounts.

8. Delete the App1Service account. Click Yes to continue.

9. Close Active Directory Users and Computers.

10. Go back to the Active Directory Administrative Center.

11. Click the small arrow next to the domain and select Deleted Objects. If the App1Service account does not show in the Deleted Objects folder, press the F5 key to refresh.

12. Take a screen shot of the Active Directory Administrative Center window by pressing Alt+Prt Scr and then paste it into your Lab 17 worksheet file in the page provided by pressing Ctrl+V.

13. Right-click App1Service and click Restore.

14. Close Active Directory Administrative Center.

Question 3	What other method could used to activate the Active Directory Recycle Bin?

15. Confirm that the App1Service account has been restored to Service Accounts OU.

End of exercise.

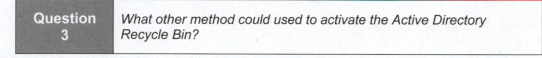

Exercise 17.5	Managing the Active Directory Database
Overview	From time to time, you should perform maintenance on the Active Directory Database. Therefore, during this exercise, you compact the database and perform an integrity check on the database.
Completion time	20 minutes

Mindset Question: **Why does maintenance have to be done on Active Directory?**

1. On Server01, using Server Manager, click Tools > Services. The Services console opens.

2. Right-click the Active Directory Domain Services service and click Stop. When it asks if you want to stop other services, click Yes.

3. Right-click the Start button and select Command Prompt (Admin). The command prompt window opens.

4. Execute the `ntdsutil` command.

5. At the ntdsutil prompt, execute the `activate instance NTDS` command.

6. Execute the `files` command.

7. At the file maintenance prompt, execute the `compact to C:\` command. The database is compacted.

8. Take a screen shot of the ntdsutil Command Prompt window by pressing Alt+Prt Scr and then paste it into your Lab 17 worksheet file in the page provided by pressing Ctrl+V.

9. To check the integrity of the offline database, execute the `integrity` command.

10. At the file maintenance prompt, execute the `quit` command.

11. To perform a semantic database consistency check, execute the `semantic database analysis` command.

12. At the semantic checker prompt, execute the `go` command.

13. Execute the `quit` command twice.

14. Copy the ntdis.dit file from the C:\ folder to the C:\Windows\NTDS folder.

15. Close the command prompt.

16. Go back to the Service console. Right-click the Active Directory Domain Services service and click Start.

17. Close the Services console.

End of exercise.

LAB REVIEW QUESTIONS

Completion time	10 minutes

1. In Exercise 17.1, what did you use to back up the System State?

2. In Exercise 17.2, what type of restore will have changes overwritten by the current Active Directory?

3. In Exercise 17.2, when you restore from backup and you want to make sure that the restored objects in Active Directory do not get removed automatically by Active Directory because they were deleted in the past, what type of of restore must be done?

4. In Exercise 17.2, what tool allowed you to choose selected objects as authoritative restore?

5. In Exercise 17.3, what command did you use to create the Active Directory snapshot?

6. In Exercise 17.4, what did you use to enable the Active Directory Recycle Bin?

7. In Exercise 17.5, what program allowed you to compress the Active Directory database?

Lab Challenge	Remove Server02 from Active Directory
Overview	To complete this challenge, you will remove a domain controller from Active Directory.
Completion time	10 minutes

In Hyper V, you decide to shut down Server02 because it has been giving you problems that you cannot recover from. Assuming the Server02 is not available, how would you remove Server02 from Active Directory?

Write out the steps you performed to complete the challenge.

End of lab.

LAB 18
CONFIGURING ACCOUNT POLICIES

THIS LAB CONTAINS THE FOLLOWING EXERCISES AND ACTIVITIES:

Exercise 18.1   Configuring a Domain Password Policy

Exercise 18.2   Configuring Account Lockout Settings

Exercise 18.3   Configuring a Password Settings Object

Lab Challenge   Managing Password Settings Objects Permissions

BEFORE YOU BEGIN

The lab environment consists of student workstations connected to a local area network, along with a server that functions as the domain controller for a domain called *contoso.com*. The computers required for this lab are listed in Table 18-1.

Table 18-1
Computers Required for Lab 18

Computer	Operating System	Computer Name
Server (VM 1)	Windows Server 2012	RWDC01

In addition to the computers, you also require the software listed in Table 18-2 to complete Lab 18.

Table 18-2
Software Required for Lab 18

Software	Location
Lab 18 student worksheet	Lab18_worksheet.docx (provided by instructor)

Working with Lab Worksheets

Each lab in this manual requires that you answer questions, take screen shots, and perform other activities that you will document in a worksheet named for the lab, such as Lab18_worksheet.docx. You will find these worksheets on the book companion site. It is recommended that you use a USB flash drive to store your worksheets, so you can submit them to your instructor for review. As you perform the exercises in each lab, open the appropriate worksheet file, fill in the required information, and save the file to your flash drive.

After completing this lab, you will be able to:

- Configure a domain user password policy

- Configure account lockout settings

- Configure and apply Password Settings Objects (PSOs)

Estimated lab time: 55 minutes

Exercise 18.1	Configuring a Domain Password Policy
Overview	In this exercise, you define a domain-level password policy including maximum password length and password history.
Completion time	10 minutes

Mindset Question: **How many account policies/password policies can you configure within an organization?**

1. Log in to RWDC01 as the **Contoso\Administrator** user account. The Server Manager console opens.

2. On Server Manager, click Tools > Group Policy Management. The Group Policy Management console opens.

3. Find and right-click Default Domain Policy and click Edit. The Group Policy Management Editor opens.

4. In the left window pane, expand the Computer Configuration node, expand the Policies node, and expand the Windows Settings folder. Then, expand the Security Settings node. In the Security Settings node, expand Account Policies and select Password Policy, as shown in Figure 18-1.

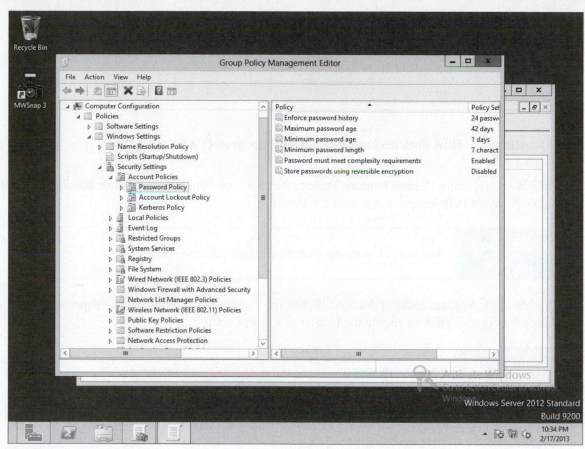

Figure 18-1
Managing Password Policy

Question 1	What is the maximum password age?

Question 2	What is the minimum password length?

Question 3	How does enforce password history and minimum password age work together to keep a network environment secure?

5. Double-click the Minimum password length. When the Minimum password length Properties dialog box opens, change the 7 value to 8 characters. Click OK to close the Minimum password length Properties dialog box.

6. Keep the Default Domain Policy Group Policy Management Editor window open for the next exercise.

End of exercise.

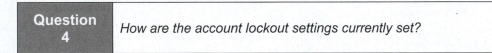

Exercise 18.2	Configuring Account Lockout Settings
Overview	In this exercise, you continue to configure the Default Domain Policy by configuring the account lockout settings.
Completion time	5 minutes

Mindset Question: **How does account lockout settings protect a network?**

1. On RWDC01, using Default Domain Policy Group Policy Management Editor console, under Account Policies, click Account Lockout Policy.

> | Question 4 | *How are the account lockout settings currently set?* |
> |---|---|

2. Double-click Account lockout duration. When the Account lockout duration Properties dialog box opens, click to enable the Define this policy setting.

> | Question 5 | *What is the default value for the Account lockout duration?* |
> |---|---|

3. Click OK to close the Account lockout duration Properties dialog box. When the Suggested Value Changes dialog box opens, look at the suggested settings and click OK.

> | Question 6 | *How many invalid logon attempts can be made that will cause an account to be locked?* |
> |---|---|

4. Close the Group Policy Management Editor window for the Default Domain Policy.

5. Close the Group Policy Management console.

End of exercise.

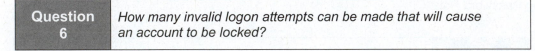

Exercise 18.3	Configuring a Password Settings Object
Overview	In this exercise, you create and apply a Password Settings Object to the Sales group.
Completion time	25 minutes

Mindset Questions: **How are Password Settings Objects (PSOs) used in a domain?**

1. On RWDC01, using Server Manager, click Tools > Active Directory Users and Computers. The Active Directory Users and Computers console opens.

2. Right-click contoso.com, click New, and click Organizational Unit.

3. When the New Object – Organizational Unit dialog box opens, type **Sales** in the Name text box. Click OK to close the New Object – Organizational Unit dialog box.

4. Right-click the Sales organizational unit, click New, and click User. The New Object – User dialog box opens.

5. Type in the following information:

First name: **John**

Last name: **Smith**

User logon name: **JSmith**

Click Next.

6. For the Password and Confirm password text boxes, type **Password01**.

7. Click to deselect the User must change password at next logon. Click Next.

8. Click Finish.

9. Create a user with the following information:

First name: **Stacy**

Last name: **Jones**

User logon name: **SJones**

Password: **Password01**

10. Right-click the Sales OU, click New, and click Group. The New Object – Group dialog box opens.

11. In the Group name text box, type **Sales**. Click OK.

12. Double-click the Sales group. The Sales Properties dialog opens.

13. Click the Members tab.

14. Click Add. The Select Users, Contacts, Computers, Service Accounts, or Groups dialog box opens.

15. In the text box, type **John Smith; Stacy Jones** and click OK.

16. Take a screen shot of the Sales Properties dialog box window by pressing Alt+Prt Scr and then paste it into your Lab 18 worksheet file in the page provided by pressing Ctrl+V.

17. Click OK to close the Sales Properties dialog box.

18. On RWDC01, using Server Manager, click Tools > Active Directory Administrative Center. The Active Directory Administrative Center opens.

19. In the Active Directory Administrative Center navigation pane, click the arrow next to the contoso.com (local) and select the System folder. Then scroll down and double-click Password Settings Container. The Password Settings Container is shown in Figure 18-2.

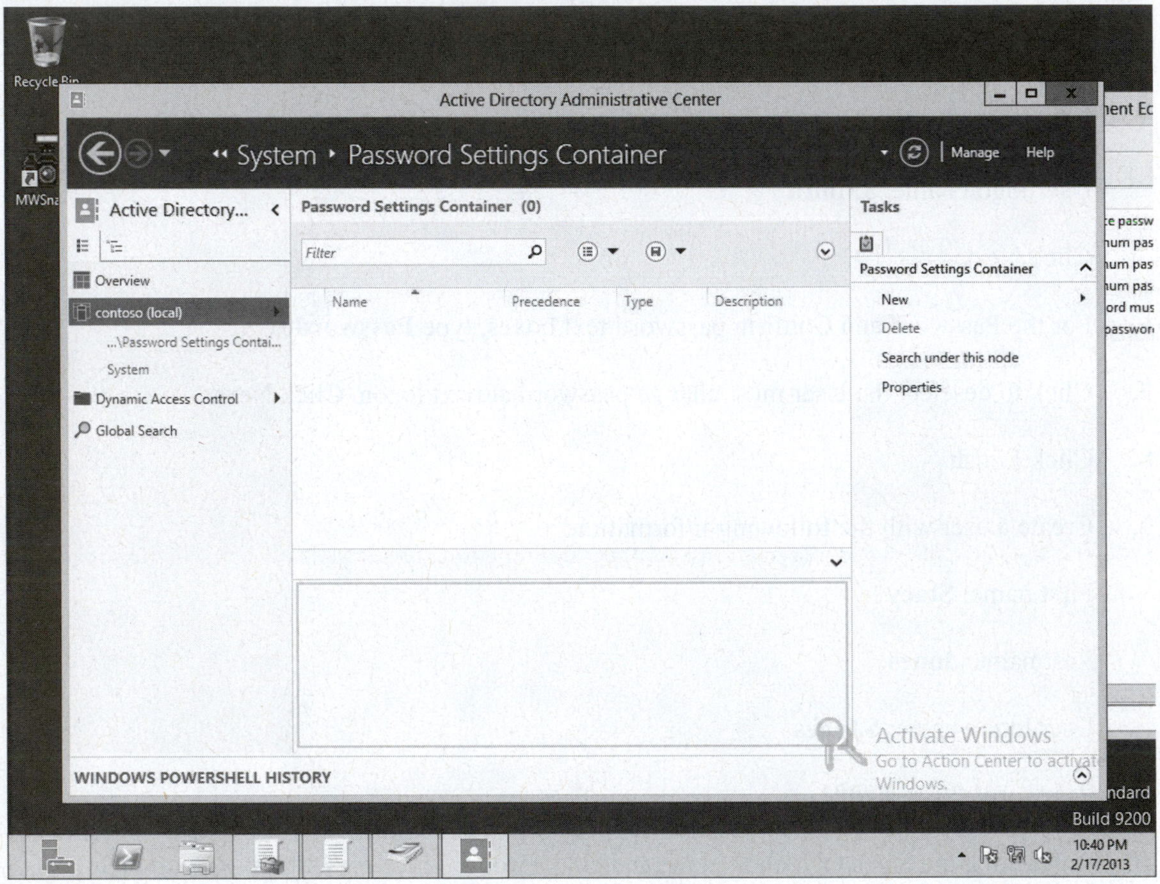

Figure 18-2
Managing Password Settings Container

20. In the Tasks pane, click New, and then click Password Settings. The Create Password Settings window opens as shown in Figure 18-3.

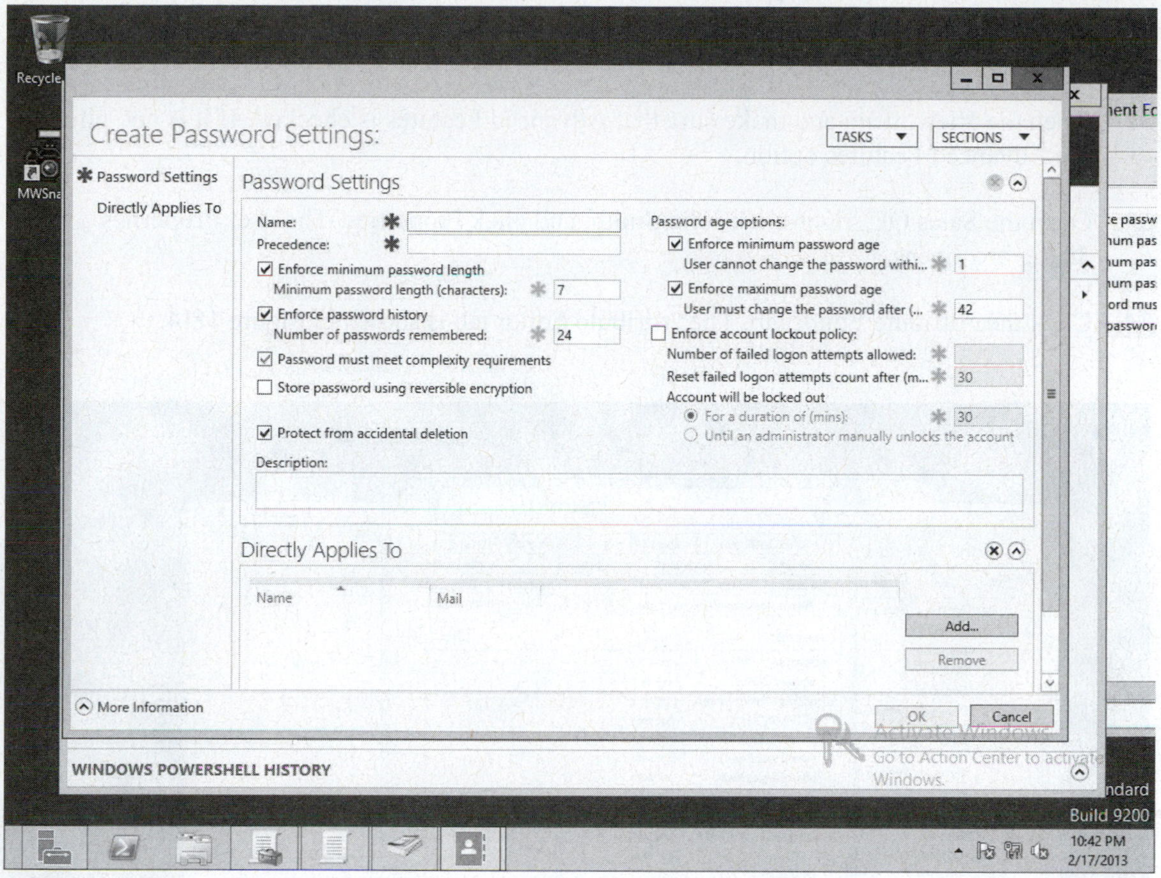

Figure 18-3
Creating Password Settings

21. In the Name text box, type **PSO1**.

22. In the Precedence text box, type **1**.

23. Change the minimum password length to **12**.

24. Click to enable Enforce account lockout policy.

25. Set the Number of failed logon attempts to **3**.

26. Change both the Reset failed logon attempts count after and Account will be locked out for a duration of **15** minutes.

27. In the Directly Applies To section, click the Add button.

28. When the Select Users or Groups dialog box opens, type **Sales** in the text box and click OK.

29. Click OK to submit the creation of the PSO.

30. Close the Active Directory Administrative Center.

31. Using Server Manager, open Tools > Active Directory Users and Computers. The Active Directory Users and Computers console opens.

32. Open the View menu and make sure that Advanced Features is checked. If it is not, click the Advanced Features option.

33. Open the Sales OU, right-click John Smith, and click Properties. The user Properties dialog box opens.

34. Click the Attribute Editor tab. The Attribute Editor tab is shown in Figure 18-4.

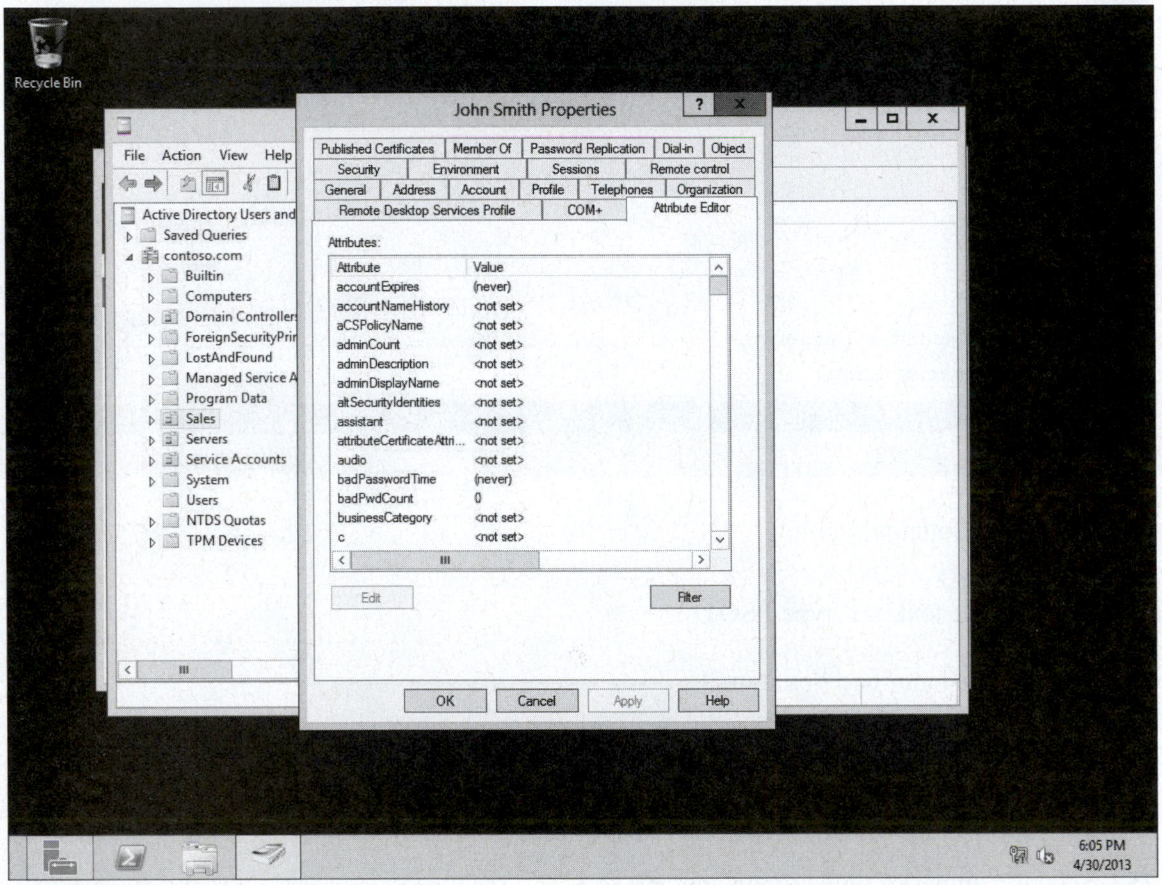

Figure 18-4
Editing a user's attributes

35. Click Filter, and click Constructed.

36. Scroll down and find the msDS-ResultantPSO attribute to see the current PSO being applied.

Question 7	*Which PSO is applied?*

37. Take a screen shot of the Attribute Editor tab by pressing Alt+Prt Scr and then paste it into your Lab 18 worksheet file in the page provided by pressing Ctrl+V.

38. Clicked OK to close the Properties dialog box.

39. Close the Active Directory Users and Computers console.

End of exercise.

LAB REVIEW QUESTIONS

Completion time	5 minutes

1. In Exercise 18.1, what did you use to define Password policies?

2. In Exercise 18.1, for a domain, where do you define password policies?

3. In Exercise 18.3, what are Password Settings Objects assigned to?

4. In Exercise 18.3, what settings are configured with Password Settings Objects?

Lab Challenge	Managing Password Settings Objects Permissions
Overview	To complete this challenge, you must demonstrate how manage Password Settings Object Permissions by writing the steps to complete the tasks described in the scenerio.
Completion time	10 minutes

As an administrator for the Contoso Corporation, how would you delegate permissions so that John Smith could manage the Password Settings Objects for the Contoso.com domain?

Write out the steps you performed to complete the challenge.

End of lab.

LAB 19
CONFIGURING GROUP POLICY PROCESSING

THIS LAB CONTAINS THE FOLLOWING EXERCISES AND ACTIVITIES:

Exercise 19.1   Configuring Processing and Precedence of GPOs

Exercise 19.2   Configuring Blocking Inheritance and Enforced Policies

Exercise 19.3   Configuring Security Filtering and WMI Filtering

Exercise 19.4   Configuring Loopback Processing

Lab Challenge   Using Group Policy Results Wizard

BEFORE YOU BEGIN

The lab environment consists of student workstations connected to a local area network, along with a server that functions as the domain controller for a domain called *contoso.com*. The computers required for this lab are listed in Table 19-1.

Table 19-1
Computers Required for Lab 19

Computer	Operating System	Computer Name
Server (VM 1)	Windows Server 2012	RWDC01

In addition to the computers, you also require the software listed in Table19-2 to complete Lab 19.

Table 19-2
Software Required for Lab 19

Software	Location
Lab 19 student worksheet	Lab19_worksheet.docx (provided by instructor)

Working with Lab Worksheets

Each lab in this manual requires that you answer questions, shoot screen shots, and perform other activities that you will document in a worksheet named for the lab, such as Lab19_worksheet.docx. You will find these worksheets on the book companion site. It is recommended that you use a USB flash drive to store your worksheets, so you can submit them to your instructor for review. As you perform the exercises in each lab, open the appropriate worksheet file, fill in the required information, and save the file to your flash drive.

After completing this lab, you will be able to:

- Configure the processing order and precedence of GPOs

- Configure blocking of inheritance and enforced policies

- Configure security and WMI filtering

- Configure loopback processing

Estimated lab time: 60 minutes

Exercise 19.1	Configuring Processing and Precedence of GPOs
Overview	During this exercise, you create multiple GPOs and look at overall precedence of the GPOs.
Completion time	20 minutes

Mindset Question: **During this lab, you learn how group policies are applied, and how to modify the order in which they are applied. How are group policies processed, and what is the precedence of each GPO?**

1. Log in to RWDC01 as the **Contoso\administrator** user account. The Server Manager console opens.

2. Using Server Manager, click Tools > Active Directory Users and Computers. The Active Directory Users and Computers console opens.

3. Under the Sales OU, create an East OU and a West OU.

4. Using Server Manager, click Tools > Group Policy Management. The Group Policy Management console opens.

5. Navigate to and click the Sales OU.

6. Right-click the Sales OU and click *Create a GPO in this domain, and Link it here*. When the New GPO dialog box opens, type **GPO1**. Click OK.

7. Create a GPO called **GPO2** for West OU.

8. Create a GPO called **GPO3** for the East OU.

9. Create a GPO called **GPO4** for the contoso.com domain.

10. Create a GPO called **GPO5** for the Sales OU.

11. Create a GPO called **GPO6** for the East OU.

12. Create a GPO called **GPO7** for the East OU.

13. Click East OU, as shown in Figure 19-1. In the East pane, click Group Policy Inheritance.

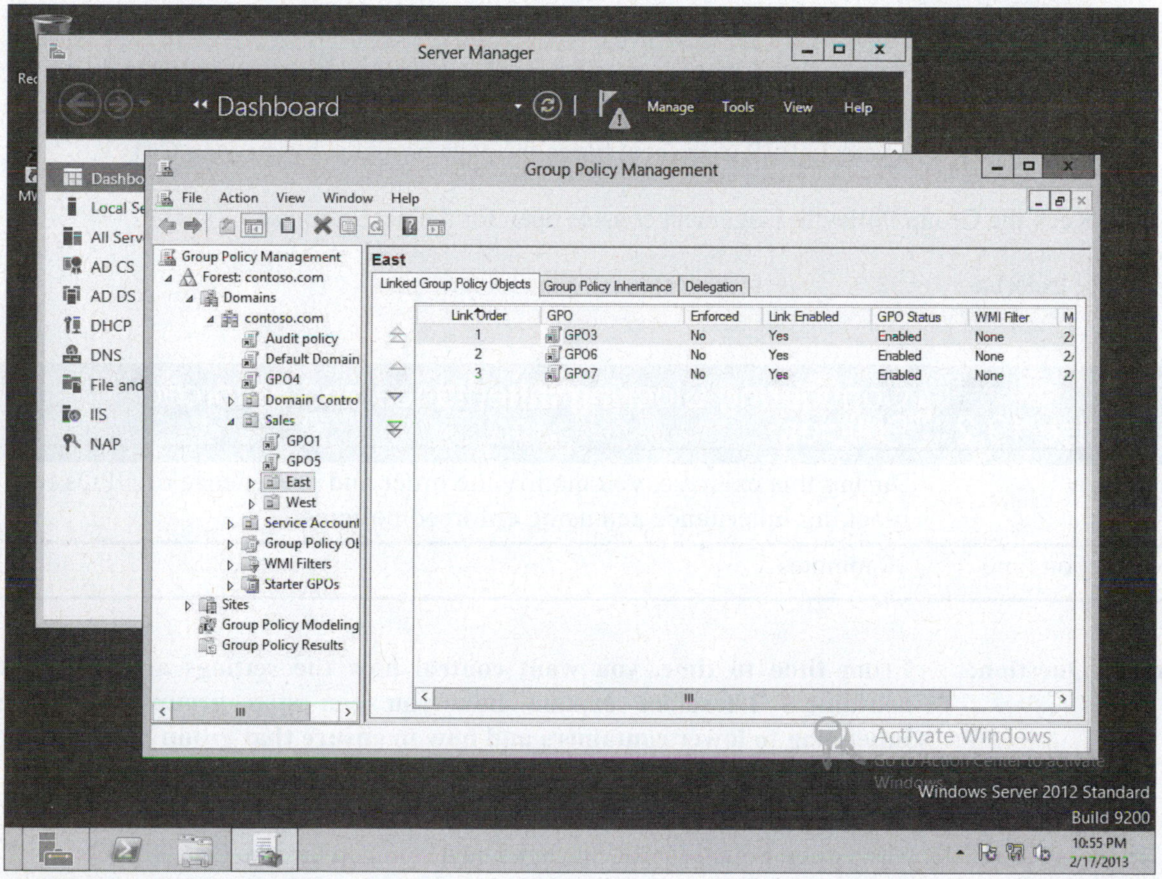

Figure 19-1
Viewing GPOs linked to a OU

Question 1	*What is the order of GPOs that are being applied?*

14. For the East OU, click Linked Group Policy Objects.

Question 2	*What are the three GPOs linked to the East OU? List them in order.*

15. Click GPO7. Then click the double up arrow.

Question 3	*What are the three GPOs linked to the East OU? List them in order.*

16. Click the Group Policy Inheritance tab.

Question 4	*What is the order of GPOs that are being applied?*

17. Take a screen shot of the Group Policy Management window by pressing Alt+Prt Scr and then paste it into your Lab 19 worksheet file in the page provided by pressing Ctrl+V.

18. Keep the Group Policy Management console open for the next exercise.

End of exercise.

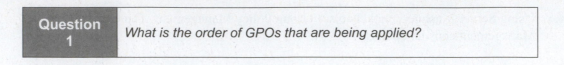

Exercise 19.2	Configuring Blocking Inheritance and Enforced Policies
Overview	During this exercise, you modify the order and precedence of GPOs by blocking inheritance and using enforced policies.
Completion time	10 minutes

Mindset Question: **From time to time, you want control how the settings are applied to a container. Therefore explain how you can stop group policies from inheriting to lower containers and how to ensure that group policies that are processed later will overwrite the specified settings in the earlier GPO?**

1. On RWDC01, with Group Policy Management, navigate to and click the East OU.

2. Right-click the East OU and select Block Inheritance. An exclamation point inside a blue circle appears for the container as shown in Figure 19-2.

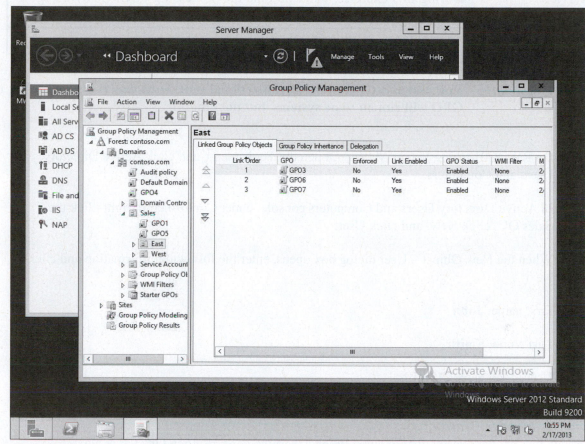

Figure 19-2
Viewing the East OU with block inheritance

3. Click the Group Policy Inheritance tab.

Question 5	What is the order of GPOs that are being applied to the East OU?

4. Right-click GPO4, and click Enforced.

Question 6	What is the order of GPOs that are being applied to the East OU? Note: You might need to press F5 key to refresh the screen.

5. Take a screen shot of the Group Policy Management window by pressing Alt+Prt Scr and then paste it into your Lab 19 worksheet file in the page provided by pressing Ctrl+V.

6. Leave the Group Policy Management console open for the next exercise.

End of exercise.

Exercise 19.3	Configuring Security Filtering and WMI Filtering
Overview	During this exercise, you fine-tune the processing of GPOs by using security filtering and WMI filtering.
Completion time	10 minutes

Mindset Question: **You assign a GPO to an Organizational unit. How can you specify that the GPO will run on some systems, but not others?**

1. On RWDC01, using Server Manager, open the Tools menu, and click Active Directory Users and Computers.

2. In Active Directory Users and Computers console, under Contoso.com, right-click the Sales OU, click New, and click User.

3. When the New Object – User dialog box opens, enter the following information and click Next:

    First name: **John**

    Last name: **Smith**

    User logon name: **JSmith**

4. In the Password and Confirm password text boxes, type **Password01**.

5. Click the Password never expires. When a warning appears, click OK. Click Next.

6. When the wizard is complete, click Finish.

7. Using Group Policy Management, click GPO5 that is assigned to the Sales OU. If needed, click OK on the message box that appears.

8. Click the Delegation tab and click Advanced. The GPO Security Settings dialog box opens as shown in Figure 19-3.

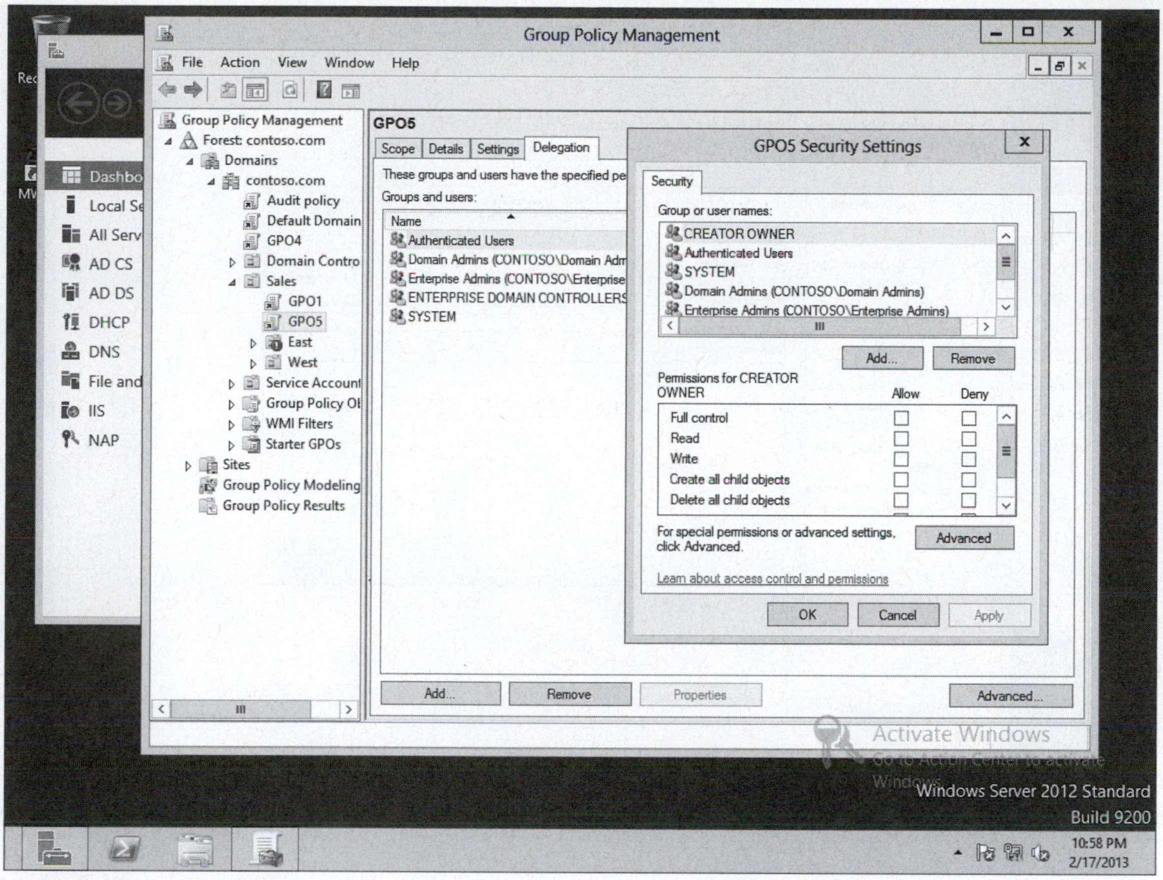

Figure 19-3
Viewing a GPO security settings

Question 7	*What permissions are needed for a GPO to apply to a user?*

9. Click the Add button. The Select users, Computers, Service Accounts, or Groups dialog box opens.

10. In the text box, type **John Smith** and press the Enter key.

11. With John Smith highlighted, assign the Deny Apply group policy and click OK. When it states that Deny entries take precedence and asks whether you want to continue, click Yes.

12. In the left pane, navigate to and click the WMI filters.

13. Right-click the WMI Filters node and click New. The New WMI Filter dialog box opens as shown in Figure 19-4.

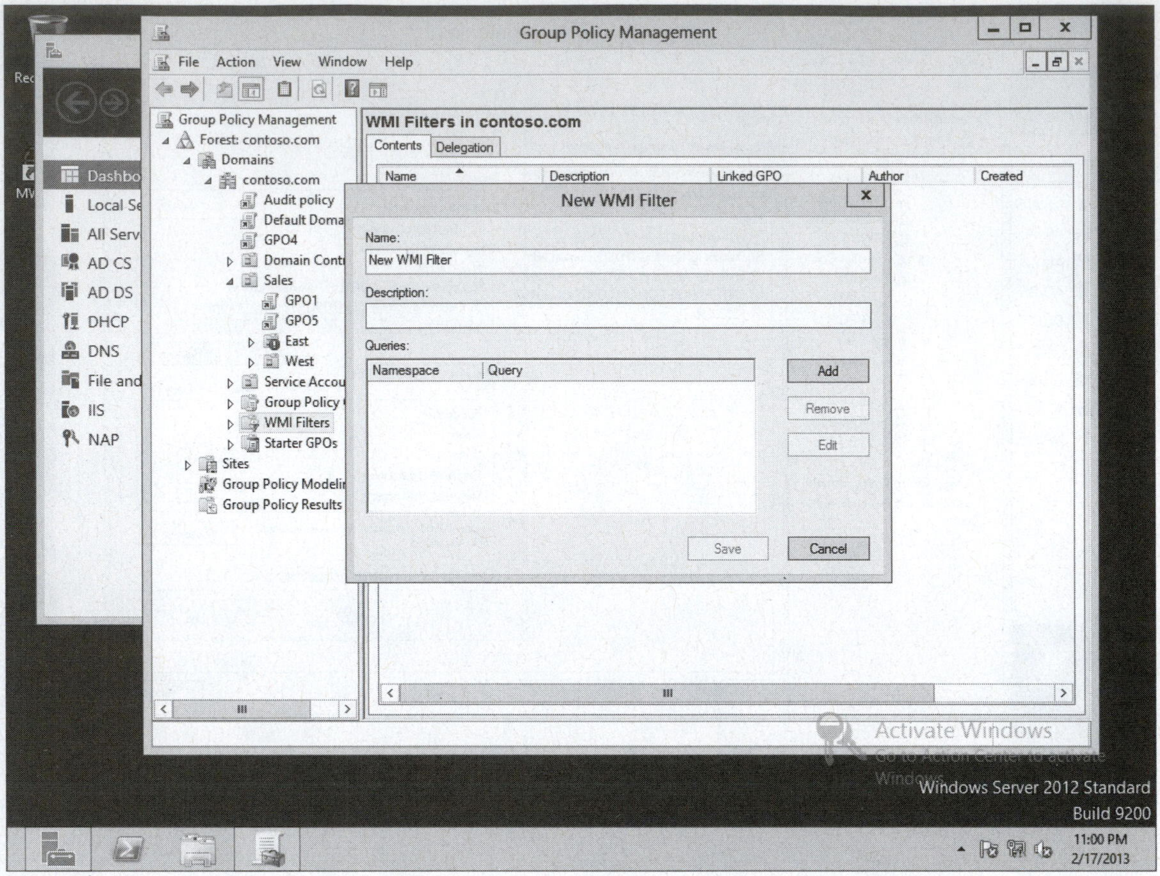

Figure 19-4
Creating a new WMI filter

14. In the Name and Description fields, type **WMIFilter1** in the Name text box.

15. In the Queries section, click Add. The WMI Query dialog box opens.

16. In the Query text box, type the following and click OK:

    ```
    Select * from Win32_Processor where AddressWidth ='32'
    ```

17. Click Save to create the WMI filter.

18. Click GPO5. If a message box appears, click OK. Click the Scope tab.

19. Under WMI Filtering, select WMIFilter1. Click Yes to confirm your changes.

20. Leave the Group Policy Management console open for the next exercise.

End of exercise.

Exercise 19.4	Configuring Loopback Processing
Overview	During this exercise, you have the computer settings overwrite the user settings when applying GPO settings.
Completion time	5 minutes

Mindset Question: **You are responsible for establishing a multiple kiosk computer that will be used within the front lobby of your company. You want to ensure that the configuration of the computer is the same regardless of who logs on. How can you do it?**

1. On RWDC01, with Group Policy Management, click GPO1. If a message box appears, click OK.

2. Right-click GPO1 and click Edit. The Group Policy Management Editor opens.

3. Navigate to and double-click Computer Configuration\Policies\Administrative Templates\System\Group Policy\Configure user Group Policy Loopback processing mode.

4. When the Configure user Group Policy loopback processing mode dialog opens, click Enabled.

Question 8	*What is the difference between Replace and Merge?*

5. Change the mode to Merge and click OK.

6. Close Group Policy Management Editor.

End of exercise.

LAB REVIEW QUESTIONS

Completion time 5 minutes

1. In Exercise 19.1, which policy has the highest precedence?

2. In Exercise 19.2, how do you make sure that a GPO that is assigned at the domain level is not overwritten by GPOs at a lower level?

3. In Exercise 19.3, where do you define the security filtering of GPOs?

4. In Exercise 19.4, how do you ensure computer settings are applied after user settings?

Lab Challenge	Using Group Policy Results Wizard
Overview	To complete this challenge, you will demonstrate how to use the Group Policy Results Wizard to view current GPO settings being applied to a user.
Completion time	10 minutes

Over the last few months, you and your team have created and applied over 30 GPOs. However, you are getting a little bit confused on which GPOs are being applied. What can you do to determine which GPOs are being applied?

Write out the steps you performed to complete the challenge.

End of lab.

LAB 20
CONFIGURING GROUP POLICY SETTINGS

THIS LAB CONTAINS THE FOLLOWING EXERCISES AND ACTIVITIES:

Exercise 20.1	Performing Software Installation with Group Policies
Exercise 20.2	Using Folder Redirection
Exercise 20.3	Using Scripts with Group Policies
Exercise 20.4	Using Administrative Templates
Exercise 20.5	Using Security Templates
Lab Challenge	Using ADM Files

BEFORE YOU BEGIN

The lab environment consists of student workstations connected to a local area network, along with a server that functions as the domain controller for a domain called *contoso.com*. The computers required for this lab are listed in Table 20-1.

Table 20-1
Computers Required for Lab 20

Computer	Operating System	Computer Name
Server (VM 1)	Windows Server 2012	RWDC01
Server (VM 2)	Windows Server 2012	Server01

In addition to the computers, you also require the software listed in Table 20-2 to complete Lab 20.

Table 20-2
Software Required for Lab 20

Software	Location
System Center Monitoring Pack for File and Storage Management.msi	\\RWDC01\Software
ADMX Migrator	\\RWDC01\Software
Lab 20 student worksheet	Lab20_worksheet.docx (provided by instructor)

Working with Lab Worksheets

Each lab in this manual requires that you answer questions, take screen shots, and perform other activities that you will document in a worksheet named for the lab, such as Lab20_worksheet.docx. You will find these worksheets on the book companion site. It is recommended that you use a USB flash drive to store your worksheets, so you can submit them to your instructor for review. As you perform the exercises in each lab, open the appropriate worksheet file, fill in the required information, and save the file to your flash drive.

After completing this lab, you will be able to:

- Perform software installation with group policies

- Use folder redirection

- Run scripts with group policies

- Configure administrative and security templates

Estimated lab time: 75 minutes

Exercise 20.1	Performing Software Installation with Group Policies
Overview	During this exercise, you perform a software installation of an MSI file using group policies.
Completion time	10 minutes

Mindset Question: **When you install software with GPOs, you have the choice to install software to a computer or to a user. You also have the choice to assign the software or publish software. What are the various combinations and what does each combination do?**

1.   Log in to RWDC01 as the **Contoso\Administrator** user account. The Server Manager console opens.

2.   Using Server Manager, under Tools, open Group Policy Management.

3. On Group Policy Management console, under the East GPO, right-click GPO7 and click Edit. If a pop-up window opens, click OK. The Group Policy Management Editor opens.

4. Navigate to Software Settings under the Computer Configuration\Policies\Software Settings.

5. Right-click the Software installation node, select New, and then click Package. The Open dialog box opens.

6. Navigate to the \\RWDC01\Software. Click *System Center Monitoring Pack for File and Storage Management* and click Open.

Question 1	What happens when software is assigned to a computer using a GPO?

Question 2	Why is Published grayed out?

7. When the Deploy Software dialog box opens (as shown in Figure 20-1), click Assigned and click OK. The System Center Monitoring Pack for File and Storage Management appears in the right pane.

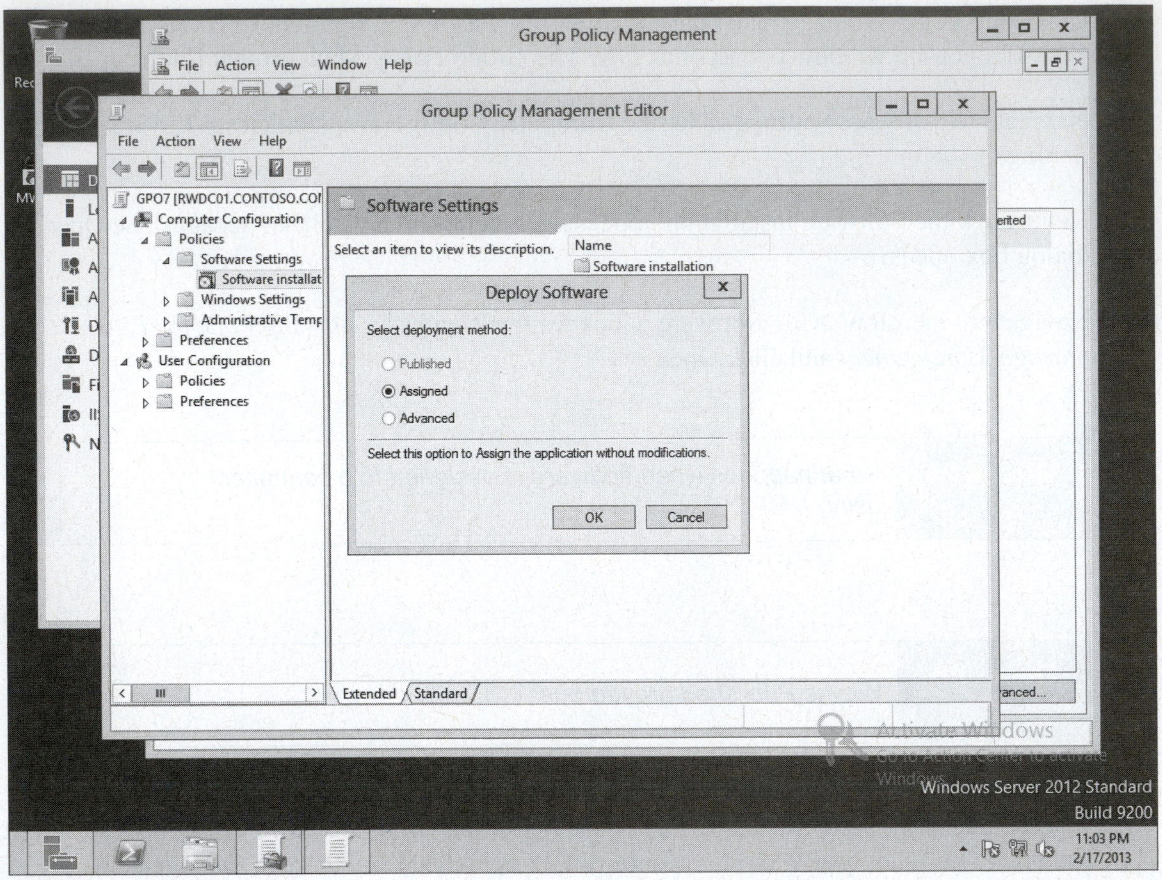

Figure 20-1
Selecting a deployment method

8.   Keep the Group Policy Management Editor window open for the next exercise.

End of exercise.

Exercise 20.2	Using Folder Redirection
Overview	During this exercise, you create a UserData folder on a server and redirect the user's Documents folder to the UserData folder.
Completion time	10 minutes

Mindset Question: **You are thinking of using folder redirection for all documents stored in the Documents folder. What is the advantage of having all the Documents for the users in one location?**

1.   Log in to Server01 as the **Contoso\Administrator** user account. The Server Manager console opens.

2.   On Server01, create the C:\UserData folder.

3.   Right-click the C:\UserData folder and click Properties. The Properties dialog box opens.

4.   Click the Sharing tab and click Advanced Sharing. The Advanced Sharing dialog box opens.

5.   Click Share this folder. Click Permissions. Click Allow Change permission for Everyone

6.   Take a screen shot of the Permissions for UserData dialog box by pressing Alt+Prt Scr and then paste it into your Lab 20 worksheet file in the page provided by pressing Ctrl+V.

7.   Click OK to close the Permissions for UserData dialog box and click OK to close the Advanced Sharing dialog box.

8.   Click Close to close the UserData Properties dialog box.

9.   On RWDC01, using Group Policy Management Editor for GPO7, navigate to the \User Configuration\Policies\Windows Settings\Folder Redirection node.

10.   Right-click the Documents folder in the left window pane and select Properties. The Documents Properties dialog box opens as shown in Figure 20-2.

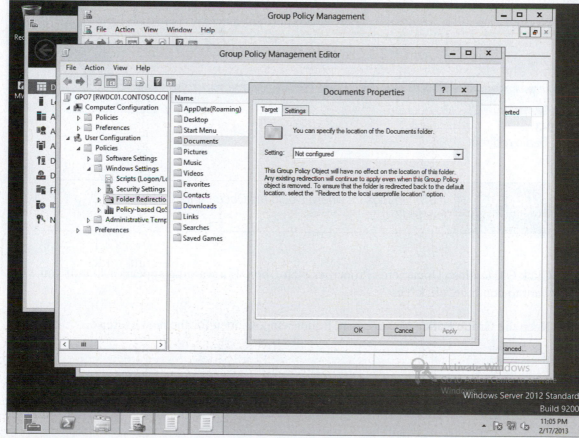

Figure 20-2
Redirecting the Documents folder

11. Under Setting, click *Basic – Redirect everyone's folder to the same location* as shown in Figure 20-3. Under Root Path, type **\\server01\UserData**.

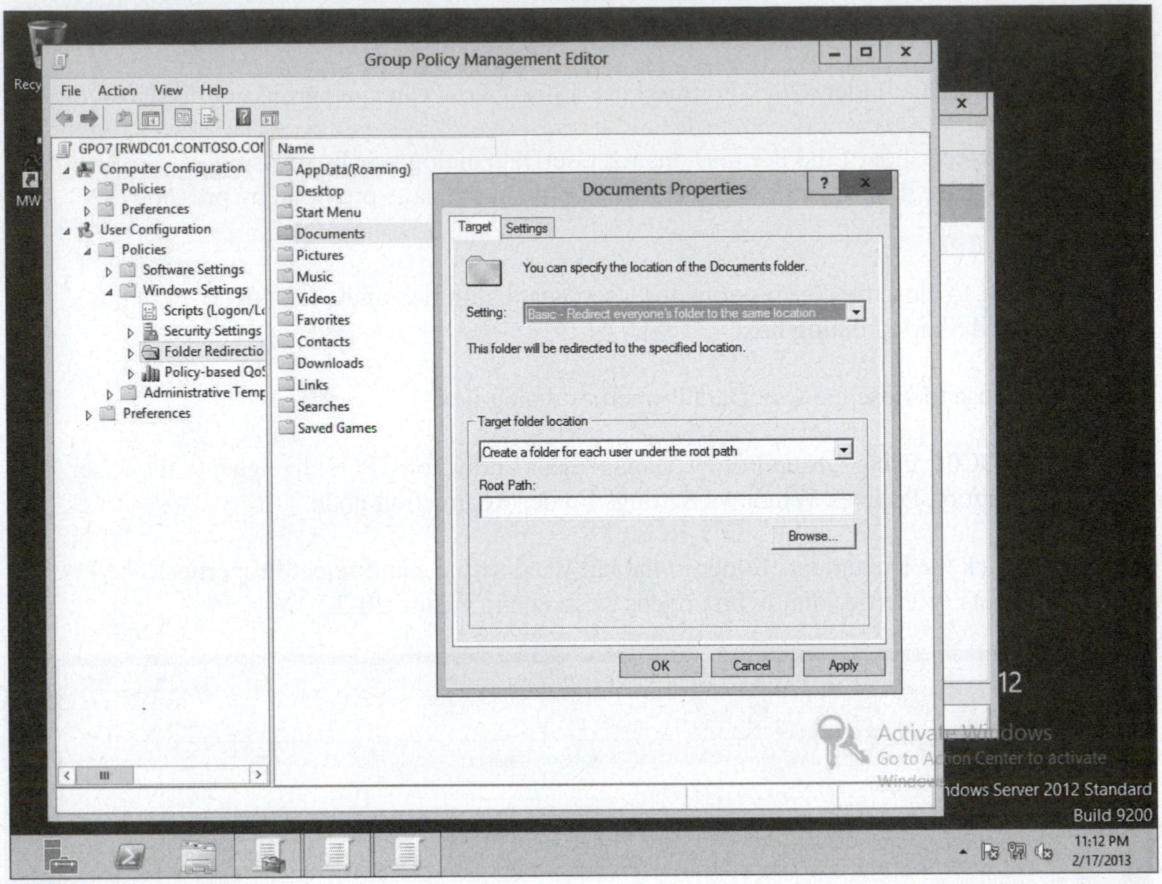

Figure 20-3
Selecting basic redirect

Question 3	*If JSmith logs in, where would his Documents folder be located?*

12. Click OK to close Documents Properties dialog box. If a warning appears asking if you want to continue, click Yes.

13. Keep the Group Policy Management Editor window open for the next exercise.

End of exercise.

Exercise 20.3	Using Scripts with Group Policies
Overview	During this exercise, you create a simple login script that will map the M drive to a shared folder and display "Hello" on the screen.
Completion time	10 minutes

Mindset Question: **List and explain the differences between the various scripts that you can execute with group policies.**

1. On Server01, open the C:\Data folder.

2. Open the View menu and click File name extensions check box.

3. Take a screen shot of the Data windows showing the File name extension option window by pressing Alt+Prt Scr and then paste it into your Lab 20 worksheet file in the page provided by pressing Ctrl+V.

4. Right-click the empty white part of the C:\Data folder, click New, and click Text Document. For the name, highlight the entire filename, type **Hello.bat** and press the Enter key. If it asks are you sure you want to rename the file, click Yes.

5. Right-click Hello.bat and click Edit. Notepad opens.

6. Type in the following text:

   ```
   @echo off
   rem The NET Use command will map the \\Server01\Data rem
   share to the M drive.
   net use m: \\Server01\Data
   echo HELLO
   pause
   ```

7. In Notepad, open the File menu and click Exit. When it asks to save the changes, click Save.

8. On RWDC01, using Group Policy Management Editor for GPO7, navigate to and click *User Configuration\Policies\Windows Settings\Scripts (Logon/Logoff)*.

9. Double-click Logon to open the Logon Properties dialog box, as shown in Figure 20-4.

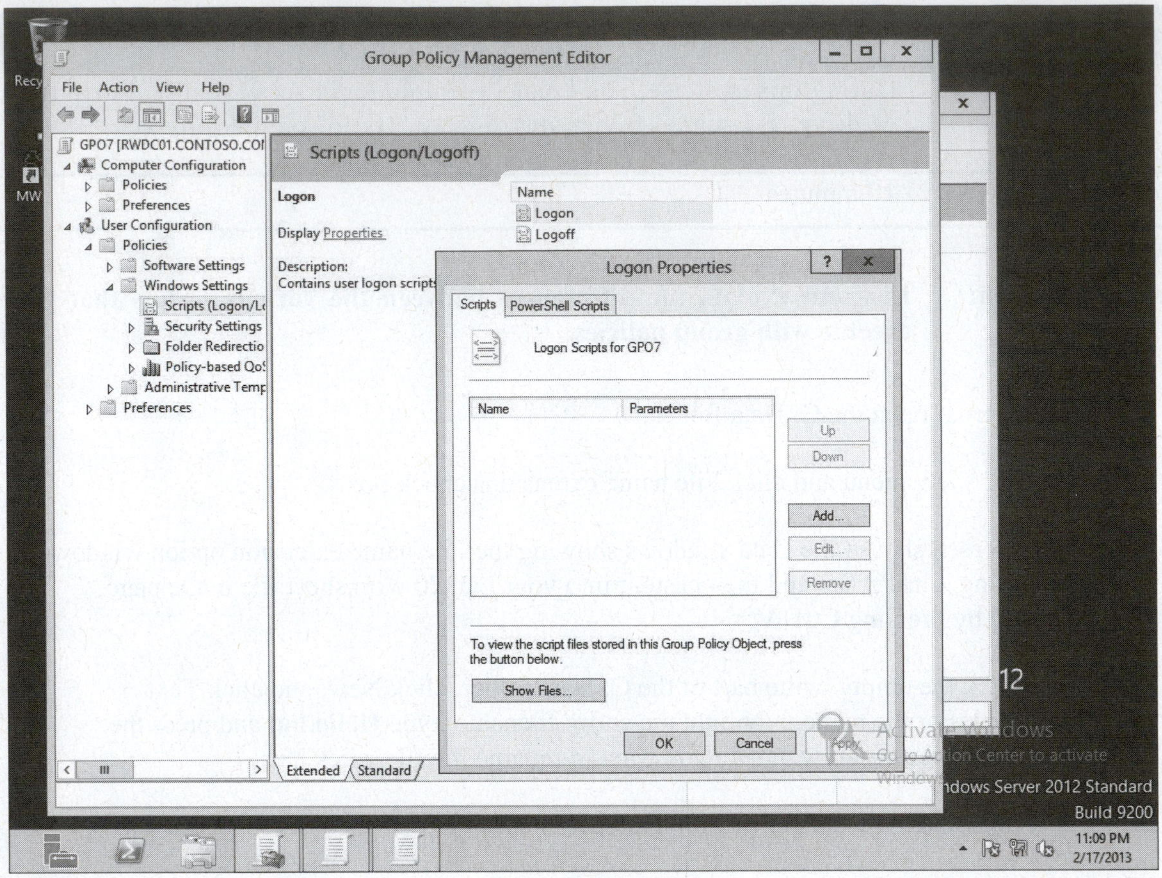

Figure 20-4
Configuring Logon scripts

10. Click Add to open the Add a Script dialog box.

11. In the Script Name text box, type **\\Server01\Data\Hello.bat** and click OK. Click OK to close the Logon Properties dialog box.

12. Keep the Group Policy Management Editor window open for the next exercise.

End of exercise.

Exercise 20.4	Using Administrative Templates
Overview	During this exercise, you configure the desktop wallpaper and screen saver settings. The screen saver settings are used to help protect a system by activating a screen saver when a user walks away from his or her computer for more than 15 minutes. If the screen saver is activated, the user will have to input his or her password to resume.
Completion time	10 minutes

Mindset Question: **What is used to define administrative templates when used with group policies?**

1.   On RWDC01, using Group Policy Management Editor for GPO7, navigate to and click User Configuration\Policies\Administrative Templates\Desktop\Desktop.

2.   Double-click Desktop Wallpaper. The Desktop Wallpaper dialog box opens.

3.   Click Enabled. Then in the Wallpaper Name, type the following:

`C:\Windows\Web\Screen\img101.jpg`

4.   Take a screen shot of the Desktop Wallpaper dialog box by pressing Alt+Prt Scr and then paste it into your Lab 20 worksheet file in the page provided by pressing Ctrl+V.

5.   Click OK to close the Desktop Wallpaper dialog box. The Desktop Wallpaper shows as Enabled.

6.   Navigate to and click User Configuration\Policies\Administrative Templates\Control Panel\Personalization.

7.   Double-click Enable screen saver. The Enable screen saver dialog box opens.

8.   Click Enabled and click OK to close the Enable screen saver dialog box.

9.   Double-click Force specific screen saver. The Force specific screen saver dialog box opens.

10.   Click Enabled. In the Screen Saver executable name, type **scrnsave.scr**. Click OK to close the Force specific screen saver.

11.   In the Personalization node, double-click Screen saver timeout.

12.   Click Enabled. Answer the following question. Then click OK to close the Screen saver timeout dialog box.

Question 4	*What is the default number of seconds?*

13.   Lastly, double-click Password protect the screen saver. The Password protect the screen saver dialog box opens.

14.   Click Enabled. Click OK to close the Password protect the screen saver dialog box.

15.   Close the Group Policy Management Editor window.

End of exercise.

Exercise 20.5	Using Security Templates
Overview	During this exercise, you open a security template for domain controllers and use it to compare settings with RWDC01.
Completion time	10 minutes

Mindset Question: **Why are security templates used and how are they used with group policies?**

1. On RWDC01, right-click the Start menu and select Command Prompt (Admin).

2. At the command prompt, execute the `mmc` command. An empty console opens.

3. Open the File menu, and click Add/Remove Snap-in.

4. When the Add or Remove Snap-ins dialog box opens, scroll down and click Security Templates. Click Add. Click OK. The Security Templates snap-in is available.

5. Select the Security Templates snap-in in the left pane. Open the Action menu and click New Template Search Path. When the Browse For Folder dialog box opens, navigate and click the following folder:

   `C:\Windows\security\templates`

6. Take a screen shot of the Console1 Security Templates windows and Browse For Folder dialog box by pressing Alt+Prt Scr and then paste it into your Lab 20 worksheet file in the page provided by pressing Ctrl+V.

7. Click OK to close the Browse for Folder dialog box. In the MMC console, double-click C:\Windows\security templates, and then double-click the DC security template.

8. Browse the various settings. Be sure to view the System Services.

9. Close the MMC console. When prompted to save the console, click No.

10. Back at the command prompt, execute the `mmc` command again. An empty console opens.

11. Open the File menu, and click Add/Remove Snap-in.

12. When the Add or Remove Snap-ins dialog box opens, scroll down and click Security Configuration and Analysis. Click Add. Click OK. The Security Configuration and Analysis console is available.

13. Right-click Security Configuration and Analysis in the left pane and click Open Database. In the File name text box, type **Test** and click Open.

14. When it asks to import template, in the file name text box, enter the following:
    `C:\Windows\security\templates\DC security.inf`

15. Right-click Security Configuration and Analysis and click Analyze Computer Now. When the Perform Analysis dialog box opens, click OK.

16. When the analysis is done, check the settings looking for settings that are not compliant. Be sure to look at System Services.

17. Close the Security Configuration and Analysis console.

End of exercise.

LAB REVIEW QUESTIONS

Completion time   10 minutes

1. In Exercise 20.1, what type of programs can you install with a GPO?

2. In Exercise 20.1, when you deploy software with group policies, which option allows you to automatically install software when the user clicks the application icon or when a user tries to open a file that is associated with the specified application?

3. In Exercise 20.2, if you decide to redirect the Document folder, what other folder should you consider to redirect for users that might also have user documents?

4. In Exercise 20.3, list some of the types of scripts that you can execute with GPOs?

5. In Exercise 20.4, what is used to customize a user's Windows look and feel?

6. In Exercise 20.5, what is used to check security settings of a computer running Windows Server 2012?

Lab Challenge	Using ADM Files
Overview	To complete this challenge, you must demonstrate how to install and use the ADMX Migrator by writing the steps to complete the tasks described in the scenerio.
Completion time	15 minutes

Write out the steps you performed to complete the challenge.

End of lab.

LAB 21
MANAGING GROUP POLICY OBJECTS

THIS LAB CONTAINS THE FOLLOWING EXERCISES AND ACTIVITIES:

Exercise 21.1   Backing Up and Restoring GPOs

Exercise 21.2   Importing and Copying GPOs

Exercise 21.3   Resetting Default GPOs

Exercise 21.4   Delegating Group Policy Management

Lab Challenge   Using a Migration Table

BEFORE YOU BEGIN

The lab environment consists of student workstations connected to a local area network, along with a server that functions as the domain controller for a domain called *contoso.com*. The computers required for this lab are listed in Table 21-1.

Table 21-1
Computers Required for Lab 21

Computer	Operating System	Computer Name
Server (VM 1)	Windows Server 2012	RWDC01

In addition to the computers, you also require the software listed in Table 21-2 to complete Lab 21.

Table 21-2
Software Required for Lab 21

Software	Location
Lab 21 student worksheet	Lab21_worksheet.docx (provided by instructor)

Working with Lab Worksheets

Each lab in this manual requires that you answer questions, take screen shots, and perform other activities that you will document in a worksheet named for the lab, such as Lab21_worksheet.docx. You will find these worksheets on the book companion site. It is recommended that you use a USB flash drive to store your worksheets, so you can submit them to your instructor for review. As you perform the exercises in each lab, open the appropriate worksheet file, fill in the required information, and save the file to your flash drive.

After completing this lab, you will be able to:

- Back up and restore GPOs

- Import and copy GPOs

- Reset the Default GPOs

- Delegate management of group policies

- Use a migration table

Estimated lab time: 60 minutes

Exercise 21.1	Backing Up and Restoring a GPO
Overview	In this exercise, you back up several GPOs and then restore a single backed-up GPO.
Completion time	10 minutes

Mindset Question: **By now, you probably figured out that GPOs are powerful and can be a valuable tool for any organization. What can you do to make sure that you can roll back to an earlier GPO without restoring the entire server?**

1. Log in to RWDC01 as the **Contoso\Administrator** user account. The Server Manager console opens.

2. On Server Manager, click Tools > Group Policy Management. The Group Policy Management console opens.

3. Navigate to and click the Group Policy Objects container.

Question 1	*Before you make any major changes to a group policy, particularly the Default Domain Policy and Default Domain Controller Policy, what should you consider?*

4. To back up all GPOs, right-click the Group Policy Objects container and then click Back Up All. The Back Up Group Policy Object dialog box opens.

5. In the Location Text Box, type **\\RWDC01\BAK**. In the Description text box, type **GPO Backup <Today's Date>**. Click Back Up.

6. When the backup is complete, take a screen shot of the Backup dialog box by pressing Alt+Prt Scr and then paste it into your Lab 21 worksheet file in the page provided by pressing Ctrl+V.

7. When the backup is complete, click OK.

8. Expand Group Policy Objects.

9. Right-click Audit Policy and click Back Up. In the Description, type **Audit Policy Backup <Today's Date>**. Click Back Up. When the backup is complete, click OK.

10. To restore a GPO, right-click the Audit Policy GPO and click Restore from Backup.

11. When the Restore Group Policy Object Wizard opens, click Next.

12. On the Backup location page, click Next.

13. Choose the first Audit Policy backup and click Next.

14. When the wizard is complete, take a screen shot of the Restore Group Policy Object Wizard dialog box by pressing Alt+Prt Scr and then paste it into your Lab 21 worksheet file in the page provided by pressing Ctrl+V.

15. When the wizard is complete, click the Finish button.

16. When the restore is complete, click OK.

17. Keep the Group Policy Management console open for the next exercise.

End of exercise.

Exercise 21.2	Importing and Copying GPOs
Overview	If you want to create a GPO that is similar to another GPO that you already have, you can either import the settings to the new GPO or copy the GPO. Afterward, you can then modify the new policy and deploy as necessary.
Completion time	15 minutes

1. On RWDC01, using Group Policy Management, navigate to and click **the Group Policy Objects** container.

2. Click the GPO2. Then click the Settings tab to verify the current settings.

3. If an Internet Explorer message box opens, click Add on the Internet Explorer message box. Then click Add in Trusted sites dialog box, and click Close.

4. Right-click GPO2 and click Import Settings.

5. When the Welcome screen opens, click Next.

6. On the Backup GPO page, click Next.

7. On the Backup location page, click Next.

8. Click the GPO7 and click Next.

9. On the Scanning Backup page, click Next.

10. On the Migrating References page, with the *Copying them identically from the source* selected, click Next.

11. When the wizard is complete, click Finish.

12. When the import is complete, click OK.

Question 2	*What is the only item that did not succeed?*

13. To copy a GPO7, right-click GPO7 and click Copy.

14. Right-click Group Policy Objects container and click Paste.

15. When the Copy GPO dialog box appears, click *Use the default permissions for new GPOs*. Click OK.

16. When the copy is complete, click OK.

17. Right-click the Copy of GPO7 and click Rename. Type **GPO8** and press the Enter key.

18. Lastly, instead of always creating a new GPO, you can also link a container to a current GPO. For example, right-click Service Accounts OU and click Link an Existing GPO.

19. When the Select GPO dialog box opens, click GPO7 and click OK.

20. Click GPO7in the left pane. Click the Scope tab in right pane.

21. Take a screen shot of the Group Policy Management window by pressing Alt+Prt Scr and then paste it into your Lab 21 worksheet file in the page provided by pressing Ctrl+V.

Question 3	What are the two OUs that GPO7 is linked to?

22. Close the Group Policy Management console.

End of exercise.

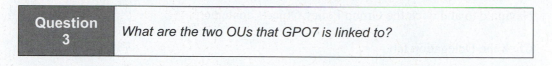

Exercise 21.3	Resetting Default GPOs
Overview	Probably the two most important GPOs are the default GPOs that come with Windows Server 2012. Therefore, during this exercise, you reset those GPOs.
Completion time	5 minutes

Mindset Question: **Which GPO has the default account policies settings including password policy settings and which GPO has the default User Rights Assignments?**

1. On RWDC01, right-click the Start menu and select Command Prompt (Admin).

2. At the prompt, execute the `DcGPOFix` command.

3. When it warns that you are about to restore the Default Domain Policy and Default Domain Controller Policy, type **Y** for Yes and press the Enter key.

4. When it says that it will replace all User Rights Assignments, type **Y** for Yes and press the Enter key.

5. Close the Administrator: Command prompt window.

End of exercise.

Exercise 21.4	Delegating Group Policy Management
Overview	During this exercise, you delegate permissions so that other users can either manage GPOs or create new GPOs.
Completion time	10 minutes

Mindset Question: **Why should you limit the ability to manage GPOs to a small group within an organization?**

1. On RWDC01, with Server Manager, click Tools > Group Policy Management. The Group Policy Management console opens.

2. Navigate to and click the Group Policy Objects container.

3. Click the Delegation tab.

4. To specify who can create GPOs, click Add. When the Select User, Computer, or Group dialog box opens, type **John Smith** and click OK.

Question 4	*A user creates a GPO. What do you need to do for that user to manage his or her GPO that he or she created?*

5. To specify who can manage an individual GPO, for example, GPO7, click GPO7. Then click the Delegation tab.

6. To add a user or group, click Add. When the Select User, Computer, or Group dialog box opens, type **John Smith** in the Enter the object name to select text box and click OK.

7. When the Add Group or User dialog box opens, set permissions to Edit settings, delete, and modify security and click OK.

8. Close the Group Policy Management console.

End of exercise.

LAB REVIEW QUESTIONS

Completion time   5 minutes

1. In Exercise 21.1, what tool is used to back up GPOs?

2. In Exercise 21.2, how many containers can a GPO be assigned to?

3. In Exercise 21.3, what command did you use to reset the default GPOs?

4. In Exercise 21.4, what tool is used to manage permissions of a GPO

Lab Challenge	Using a Migration Table
Overview	To complete this challenge, you must use a Migration Table with a GPO with the following scenerio.
Completion time	15 minutes

For your organization, you have several domains. The primary domain has most of the users and network resources. You also have a smaller test domain. You have a GPO that you have created and successfully tested on the test domain. You want to copy the GPO to the production GPO. What steps do you need to perform to use the GPO?

Write out the steps you performed to complete the challenge.

End of lab.

LAB 22
CONFIGURING GROUP POLICY PREFERENCES

THIS LAB CONTAINS THE FOLLOWING EXERCISES AND ACTIVITIES:

Exercise 22.1   Configuring Printer Settings

Exercise 22.2   Configuring Network Drive Mappings

Exercise 22.3   Configuring Power Options

Exercise 22.4   Configuring IE Settings

Exercise 22.5   Performing File, Folder, and Shortcut Deployment

Lab Challenge   Configuring Item-Level Targeting

BEFORE YOU BEGIN

The lab environment consists of student workstations connected to a local area network, along with a server that functions as the domain controller for a domain called *contoso.com*. The computers required for this lab are listed in Table 22-1.

Table 22-1

Computers Required for Lab 22

Computer	Operating System	Computer Name
Server (VM 1)	Windows Server 2012	RWDC01
Server (VM 2)	Windows Server 2012	Server01

In addition to the computers, you also require the software listed in Table 22-2 to complete Lab 22.

Table 22-2
Software Required for Lab 22

Software	Location
Lab 22 student worksheet	Lab22worksheet.docx (provided by instructor)

Working with Lab Worksheets

Each lab in this manual requires that you answer questions, take screen shots, and perform other activities that you will document in a worksheet named for the lab, such as Lab22_worksheet.docx. You will find these worksheets on the book companion site. It is recommended that you use a USB flash drive to store your worksheets, so you can submit them to your instructor for review. As you perform the exercises in each lab, open the appropriate worksheet file, fill in the required information, and save the file to your flash drive.

After completing this lab, you will be able to:

- Configure Group Policy preferences including printers, network drive mappings, power options, Internet Explorer settings, and file and folder deployment

- Configure item-level targeting

Estimated lab time: 70 minutes

Exercise 22.1	Configuring Printer Settings
Overview	In this exercise, you configure a local printer using GPO preferences.
Completion time	10 minutes

Mindset Question: **During this lab, you continue working with group policies. What can you use to configure the Windows environment so that the settings are applied once, but can be reconfigured by the user in the future if so desired?**

1. Log in to Server01 as the **Contoso\Administrator** user account. The Server Manager console opens.

2. On Server01, right-click the Start button and open the Control Panel.

3. When the Control Panel opens, click View devices and printers, under Hardware.

4. Click Add a printer and click *The printer that I want isn't listed*.

5. Click *Add a local printer or network printer with manual settings*. Click Next.

6. On the Choose a printer port page, use the existing port that is already set to LPT1. Click Next.

7. Under the manufacturer, click HP. Under Printers, click LaserJet 6L PS Class Driver. Click Next.

8. On the Type a printer name page, click Next.

9. On the Printer Sharing, click Next.

10. When the wizard is complete, click Finish.

11. Log in to RWDC01 as the **Contoso\Administrator** user account. The Server Manager console opens.

12. On Server Manager, open Group Policy Management.

13. Navigate to the Group Policy Objects container and click GPO5. If needed, click OK to close a message box that might appear. Then right-click GPO5 and click Edit. The Group Policy Management Editor opens.

14. Navigate to and click Computer Configuration\Preferences\Control Panel Settings\Printers as shown in Figure 22-1.

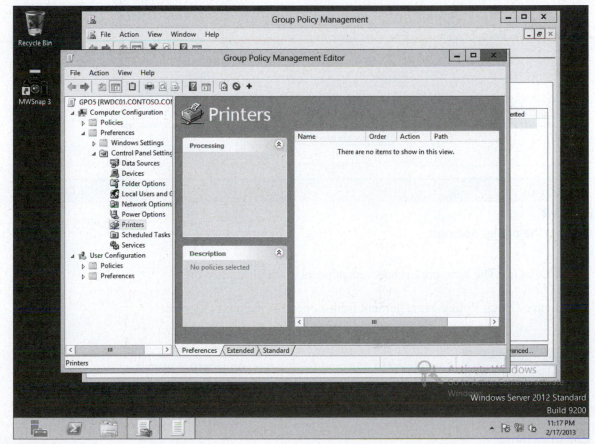

Figure 22-1

Configuring printers with preferences

15. Right-click the Printers node, click New, and select Local Printer. The New Local Printer Properties dialog box opens.

16. For Action, Update is already selected, as shown in Figure 22-2. For the name, type **Office Printer**. For port, click USB001. For the Printer Path, type **\\Server01\HP LaserJet 6L PS Class Driver**.

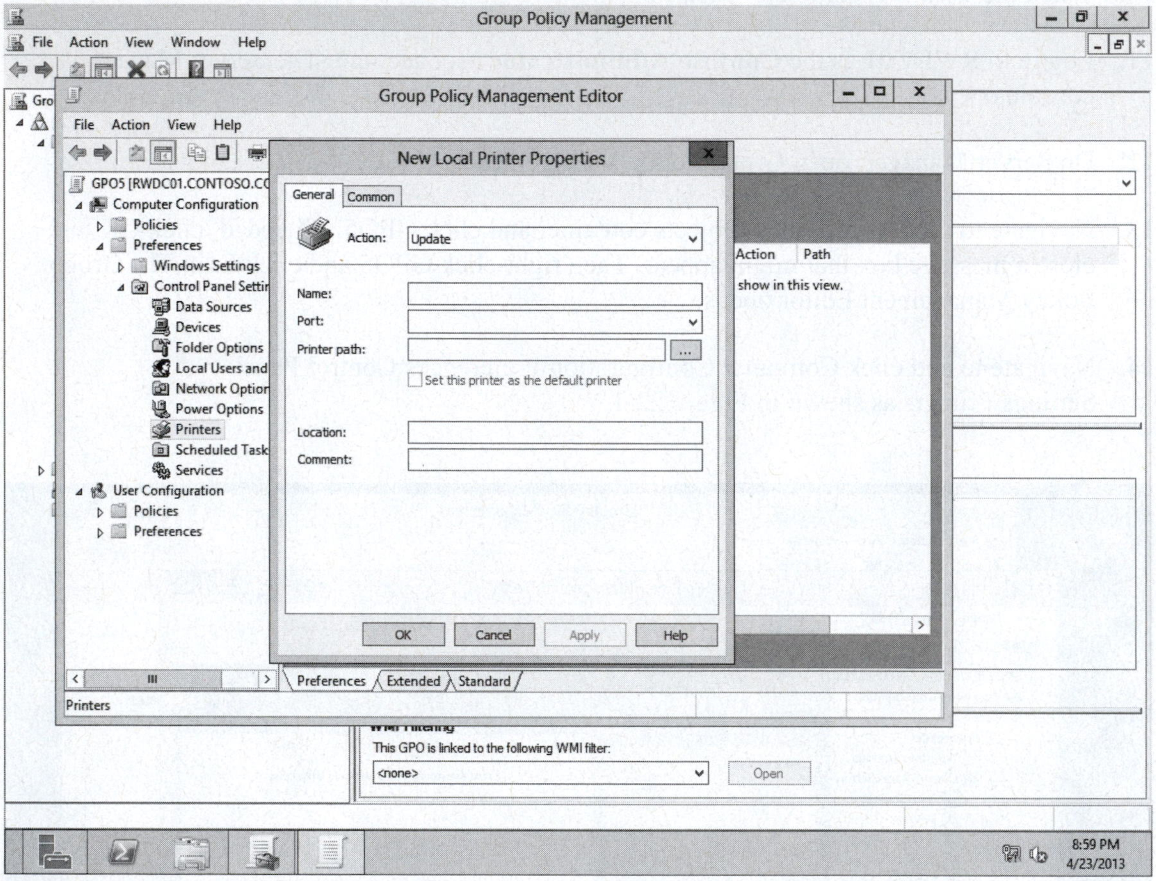

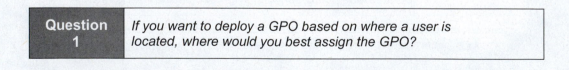

Figure 22-2
Configuring the printer settings

17. Click OK. The new preference item appears in the Printers pane.

18. Leave Group Policy Management Editor open for the next exercise.

Question 1	If you want to deploy a GPO based on where a user is located, where would you best assign the GPO?

End of exercise.

Exercise 22.2   Configuring Network Drive Mappings

Overview	In this exercise, you map a shared folder to the local I drive.
Completion time	5 minutes

1.   On RWDC01, using the Group Policy Management Editor for GPO5, navigate to and click User Configuration\Preferences\Windows Settings\Drive Maps.

2.   Right-click the Drive Maps node, click New, and select Mapped Drive. The New Drive Properties dialog box opens.

3.   In the Location text box, type **Server01\Data**.

4.   Under Drive Letter, select the I drive.

5.   Under Hide/Show this drive, click Show this Drive.

6.   Take a screen shot of the Group Policy Management Editor window by pressing Alt+Prt Scr and then paste it into your Lab 22 worksheet file in the page provided by pressing Ctrl+V.

7.   Click OK to close the New Drive Properties dialog box.

8.   Leave the Group Policy Management Editor open for the next exercise.

End of exercise.

Exercise 22.3   Configuring Power Options

Overview	In this exercise, you configure Power Options using GPO Preferences.
Completion time	10 minutes

1.   On RWDC01, using the Group Policy Management Editor for GPO5, navigate to and click Computer Configuration\Preferences\Control Panel Settings\Power Options.

2.   Right-click the Power Options node, click New, and select Power Plan (At least Windows 7). The New Power Scheme (At least Windows 7) Properties dialog box opens as shown in Figure 22-3.

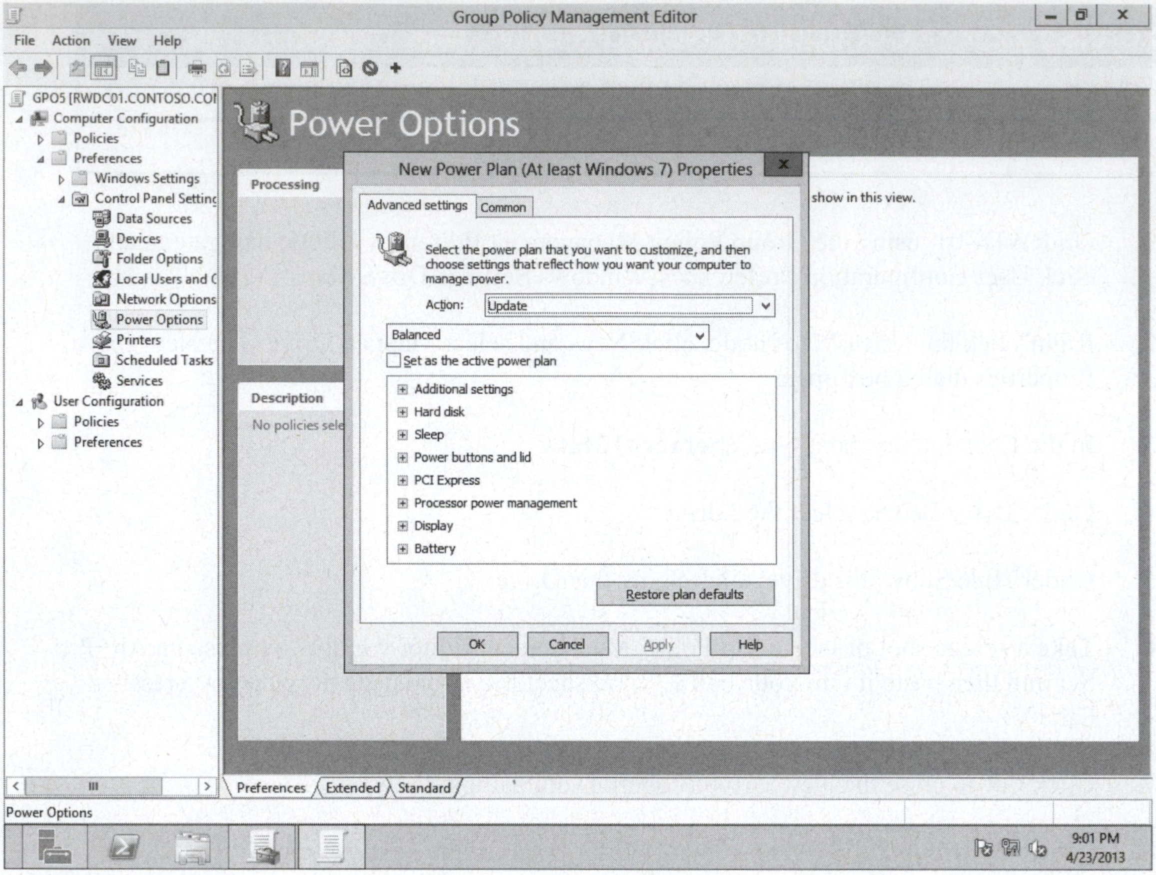

Figure 22-3
Creating a Power Plan

3. Expand Power buttons and lid, expand Lid close action and click Lid close action.
   Change the On battery and Plugged in setting of Sleep to Do nothing.

4. Expand Display and expand Turn off display after.

Question 2	How long does it take before the display is turned off when the system is plugged in?

5. Click the Common tab.

6. Click Apply once and do not reapply.

7. Click OK to close the New Power Plan (At least Windows 7) Properties. The new
   preference item appears in the Power Options pane.

8. Leave the Group Policy Management Editor open for the next exercise.

End of exercise.

Exercise 22.4	Configuring IE Settings
Overview	In this exercise, you configure IE (versions 8 through 10) with a predefined home page and pop-up blocker exceptions.
Completion time	15 minutes

Mindset Question: **You configure IE Settings and some of the options have a red dashed line under them. How can you enable all the settings that you have configured.**

1.   On RWDC01, using the Group Policy Management Editor for GPO5, navigate to and click User Configuration\Preferences\Control Panel Settings\Internet Settings.

2.   Right-click the Internet Settings node, click New, and select Internet Explorer 10. The New Internet Explorer 10 Properties dialog box opens as shown in Figure 22-4.

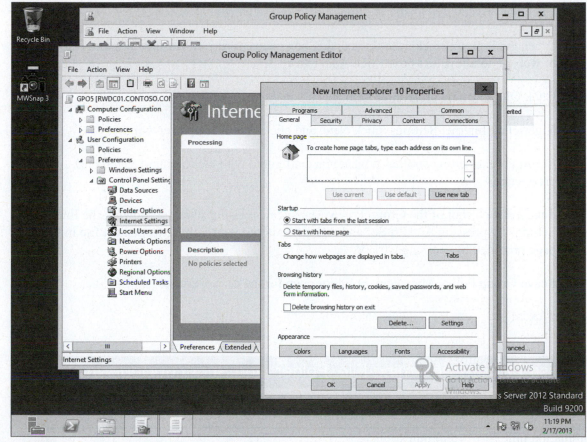

Figure 22-4

Configuring Internet Explorer 10 with preferences

3.   Under the General tab, type **http://portal.contoso.com** in the Home page text box. Click Start with home page.

Question 3	What color is the home page set as?

Question 4	What color is the Startup options set as?

4. Click the Home page text box. Press the F5 key so that the box turns green.

Question 5	What key would you use to disable the current setting?

5. Click the Privacy tab. Under the Pop-up Blocker section, click Settings.

6. When the Pop-up Blocker Settings dialog box opens, type ***.contoso.com** in the Address of website to allow text box. Click Add. Click Close.

7. Click OK. The new preference item appears in the Internet Settings pane.

8. Right-click Internet Settings, click New, and click Internet Explorer 8 and 9.

9. Configure the setting similar to what you configured with the Internet Explorer 10 preference.

10. Take a screen shot of the Group Policy Management Editor window showing the Internet Settings by pressing Alt+Prt Scr and then paste it into your Lab 22 worksheet file in the page provided by pressing Ctrl+V.

11. Leave Group Policy Management Editor open for the next exercise.

End of exercise.

Exercise 22.5	Performing File, Folder, and Shortcut Deployment
Overview	During this exercise, you create a folder, copy a file to the folder, and create a shortcut to the folder using GPO Preferences.
Completion time	15 minutes

Mindset Question: **When performing a file deployment, what is the difference between Create and Update?**

1.   On RWDC01, using the Group Policy Management Editor for GPO5, navigate to and click User Configuration\Preferences\Windows Settings\Files.

2.   Right-click the Files node, click New, and select File. The New File Properties dialog box opens.

3.   In the Source file(s) text box, and type **Server01\Data\Hello.bat**.

4.   In the Destination File, click c:\hello.bat.

5.   Take a screen shot of the New File Properties dialog box by pressing Alt+Prt Scr and then paste it into your Lab 22 worksheet file in the page provided by pressing Ctrl+V.

6.   Click OK to close the New File Properties dialog box.

7.   Navigate to and click Computer Configuration\Preferences\Windows Settings\Folders.

8.   Right-click the Folders node, click New, and select Folder. The New Folder Properties dialog box opens.

9.   For the Action, select Create. In the Path text box, type **C:\Batch**.

10.   Click OK to close the New Folder Properties dialog box.

11.   Navigate to and click User Configuration\Preferences\Windows Settings\Shortcuts.

12.   Right-click the Shortcuts node, click New, and select Shortcut. The New Shortcut Properties dialog box opens.

13.   For the Action, select Create.

14.   In the Name text box, type **Batch**.

15.   Using the Location pull-down menu, select Desktop.

16.   In the Target Path text box, type **C:\Batch**.

17.   Click OK to close the New Shortcut Properties. The new preference item appears in the Shortcuts pane.

18.   Close the Group Policy Management Editor.

End of exercise.

LAB REVIEW QUESTIONS

Completion time	5 minutes

1. In Exercise 22.1, what did you use to install and configure a printer?

2. In Exercise 22.2, what allows you to apply settings using a Group Policy once and then allow the user to change the settings in the future?

3. In Exercise 22.4, what key did you use to enable settings in IE settings?

4. In Exercise 22.5, you need to support IE 7, 8, 9 and 10. How many settings do you have to configure?

Lab Challenge	Configuring Item-Level Targeting
Overview	To complete this challenge, you must explain how to use Item-Level Targeting.
Completion time	10 minutes

You have preferences. How would you modify the GPO5 so that it will affect only laptop computers?

End of lab.

APPENDIX: LAB SETUP GUIDE

GETTING STARTED

The *Administering Windows Server 2012 (Exam 70-411)* title of the Microsoft Official Academic Course (MOAC) series includes two books: a textbook and a lab manual. The exercises in the lab manual are designed either for a virtual machine environment or for classroom use under the supervision of an instructor or lab aide. In an academic setting, the computer lab might be used by a variety of classes each day, so you must plan your setup procedure accordingly. For example, consider automating the classroom setup procedure and using removable hard disks in the classroom. You can use the automated setup procedure to rapidly configure the classroom environment and remove the fixed disks after teaching this class each day.

LAB CONFIGURATION

This course should be taught in a lab containing networked computers where students can develop their skills through hands-on experience with Microsoft Windows Server 2012. The exercises in the lab manual require the computers to be installed and configured in a specific manner. Failure to adhere to the setup instructions in this document can produce unanticipated results when the students perform the exercises.

The lab configuration consists of a single physical server running Microsoft Windows Server 2012 Standard and a number of Hyper-V virtual servers. The instructor server is called "Instructor." It will be assigned an address of 192.168.100.50.

Each student physical computer is named "Student*xx*," where the *xx* represents the student number. The first server is called "Student01," the second server is called "Student02," and so on.

Computers are connected to the classroom network and assigned an address of 192.168.100.1*xx*, where the *xx* represents the student number. Therefore, the first server is assigned an address of 192.168.10.101 and the second server is assigned an address of 192.168.100.102.

The lab computers are located on an isolated network, configured as an Active Directory Domain Services (AD DS) domain separate from the rest of the school or organization network. The lab server functions as an AD DS domain controller, as well as performing a number of other roles at various times throughout the course.

Note

For the purposes of this lab, all server and workstation passwords, for user accounts and other purposes, are set to **Password01**. This is obviously not a secure practice in a real-world situation, and instructors should remind students of this at the outset.

Some of the lab exercises have dependencies on previous exercises, as noted in the lab manual and the instructor notes for each exercise. Students should perform the lab exercises in order, and might have to complete any exercises they have missed due to absence before proceeding to the next lab.

Instructor Server Requirements

Each classroom needs a server to be used by the instructor and should be called "Instructor." The virtual lab environment, which is hosted on the instructor computer, should consist of three servers:

- RWDC01 (192.168.1.50)
- Server01 (192.168.1.60)
- Server02 (Varies)

RWDC01 and Server02 should have one network adapter and Server01 should have two network adapters.

The lab uses the following information for the AD DS and server configuration:

- AD DS domain name: contoso.com
- Fully qualified domain name (FQDN): rwdc01.contoso.com

For simplicity in a lab environment, students will use the Administrator account with the password of Password01. This document includes a setup procedure that configures the server to provide all infrastructure services required throughout the course.

Hardware Requirements

The following hardware should be used for the Instructor server:

- Minimum: dual-core x64 processors or better with support for Intel Virtualization Technology (Intel VT) or Advanced Micro Devices Virtualization (AMD-V). Quad core is recommended.
- Minimum: 8 GB recommended
- Minimum: 500 GB or higher SATA drives
- DVD drive or better
- Two network interface adapter
- Minimum: Super VGA (1024x768) 17-inch display
- Keyboard
- Mouse
- Sound card/port
- Speakers
- Internet connection (highly recommended)

Software Requirements

The following software is required for this course:

- Microsoft Windows Server 2012 Standard installation disk—Evaluation edition available as a free download from Microsoft's TechNet website.

- ISO of Windows Server 2012 installation disk—Evaluation edition available as a free download from Microsoft's TechNet website.

- Update for Windows 8 for x64-based Systems (KB2769034 Windows8-RT-KB2769034-x64.msu)—Available at Microsoft's Download Center website.

- ADMX Migrator (ADMXMigrator.msi)—Available at Microsoft's Download Center website.

- Microsoft Network Monitor 3.4 (NM34_x64.exe)—Available at Microsoft's Download Center website.

- System Center 2012 Monitoring Pack for Microsoft Windows Server File & iSCSI Services 2012 (System Center Monitoring Pack for File and Storage Management.msi)—Located at Microsoft's Download Center website.

- Windows Assessment and Deployment (ADK) for Windows 8—Available at Microsoft's Download Center website.

- Autounattend.xml file—Download from the Wiley Book Companion site.

With the exception of the Windows Server 2012 operating system itself, the software products listed here do not have to be installed on the server. You must, however, download them and make them available to the workstation on a server share. The students install each of these products at various points in the course.

Student Computer Requirements

Each student needs his or her own dedicated computer to run Windows Server 2012. Each computer is called "Student*xx*," where *xx* is your student number.

The virtual lab environment, which is hosted on the student computer, consists of three servers:

- RWDC01 (192.168.1.50)
- Server01 (192.168.1.60)
- Server02 (Varies)

RWDC01 should have one network adapter, and Server01 and Server02 should have two network adapters. The second network adapters are used to configure an external network when performing remote access exercises.

The lab uses the following information for the AD DS and server configuration:

- AD DS domain name: contoso.com
- Fully qualified domain name (FQDN): rwdc01.contoso.com

For simplicity in a lab environment, students should use the Administrator account with the password of Password01. This document includes a setup procedure that configures the server to provide all infrastructure services required throughout the course.

Hardware Requirements

The following hardware should be used for the Instructor server:

- Minimum: dual-core x64 processors or better with support for Intel Virtualization Technology (Intel VT) or Advanced Micro Devices Virtualization (AMD-V). Quad core is recommended.

- Minimum: 8 GB recommended

- Minimum: 500 GB or higher SATA drives

- DVD drive or better

- Two network interface adapter

- Minimum: Super VGA (1024x768) 17-inch display

- Keyboard

- Mouse

- Sound card/port (speakers or headphones are recommended)

Software Requirements

The following software is required for this course:

- Microsoft Windows Server 2012 Standard—Evaluation edition available as a free download from Microsoft's TechNet website.

- ISO of Windows Server 2012 installation disk—Evaluation edition available as a free download from Microsoft's TechNet website.

- Update for Windows 8 for x64-based Systems (KB2769034 Windows8-RT-KB2769034-x64.msu)—Available at Microsoft's Download Center website.

- ADMX Migrator (ADMXMigrator.msi)—Available at Microsoft's Download Center website.

- Microsoft Network Monitor 3.4 (NM34_x64.exe)—Available at Microsoft's Download Center website.

- System Center 2012 Monitoring Pack for Microsoft Windows Server File & iSCSI Services 2012 (System Center Monitoring Pack for File and Storage Management.msi)—Located at Microsoft's Download Center website.

- Windows Assessment and Deployment (ADK) for Windows 8—at Microsoft's Download Center website.

- Autounattend.xml file—Download from the Wiley Book Companion site.

With the exception of the Windows Server 2012 operating system itself, the software products listed here do not have to be installed on the server. You must, however, download them and make them available to the workstation on a server share. The students install each of these products at various points in the course.

INSTRUCTOR AND STUDENT SERVER SETUP INSTRUCTIONS

Before you begin, perform the following:

- Read this entire document.

- Make sure that you have the installation disk for Microsoft Windows Server 2012 Standard Edition.

Installing the Instructor and Student Servers

Using the following setup procedure, install Windows Server 2012 on instructor and student servers. This procedure assumes that you are performing a clean installation of the Windows Server 2012 Standard evaluation edition, and that, if you have downloaded an image file, you have already burned it to a DVD-ROM disk.

Warning

By performing the following setup instructions, your computer's hard disks will be repartitioned and reformatted. You will lose all existing data on these systems.

1. Turn the instructor computer on and insert the Windows Server 2012 installation DVD into the drive.

2. Press any key, if necessary, to boot from the DVD-ROM disk. A progress indicator screen appears as Windows loads files.

Note

The device that a PC uses to boot is specified in its system (or BIOS) settings. In some cases, you might have to modify these settings to enable the computer to boot from the Windows Server 2012 DVD. If you are not familiar with the operation of a particular computer, watch the screen carefully as the system starts and look for an instruction specifying what key to press to access the system settings.

3. When the computer loads the Windows graphical interface and the *Windows Setup* page appears, select the appropriate language to install, time and currency format, and keyboard or input method. Then click **Next**.

4. Click **Install Now**. The *Select the operating system you want to install* page appears.

5. Select **Windows Server 2012 Standard (Server with GUI)** and click **Next**.

6. When the *License Terms* page appears, select the **I accept the license terms** check box and click **Next**.

7. When it asks what type of installation you want to use, because you are doing a clean installation and not an upgrade, click **Custom: Install Windows Only (advanced)**.

Note

If the computer's hard drives are connected to a third-party controller, you need to click the *Load Driver* button to load the third-party driver.

8. When it asks where you want to install Windows, select **Disk 0 Unallocated Space** and click **Next**. The *Installing Windows* page appears, indicating the progress of the Setup program as it installs the operating system.

Note

If there are existing partitions on the computer's hard disk, select each one in turn and delete it before proceeding.

9. After the installation completes and the computer restarts a couple of times, a message appears stating that *The user's password must be changed before logging on the first time*.

10. In the *New password* and *Confirm Password* text boxes, type **Password01** and press the **Enter** key.

11. The system finalizes the installation and the Windows sign-on screen appears.

Once the installation process is finished, you must proceed to complete the following tasks to configure the server and install the necessary roles to support the student workstations.

Completing Initial Server Configuration Tasks

Before the server is ready, you need to configure the following:

- Date and Time Settings
- TCP/IP Settings
- Computer Name

1. Log on to the computer using the username/password of **administrator/Password01**.

2. By default, the Server Manager opens when you first log on after installing Windows. To click Windows settings for the Instructor server, click **Local Server** in the left pane.

3. Click the current time zone to open the *Date and Time* dialog box.

4. If necessary, click the **Change date and time** button to change the correct date and time using the *Date and Time Settings* dialog box. When done, click **OK** to close the *Date and Time Settings* dialog box.

5. If necessary, click the **Change time zone** button to change the current time zone using the *Time Zone Settings* dialog box. When done, click **OK** to close the *Time Zone Settings* dialog box.

6. Click **OK** to close the *Date and Time* dialog box.

7. Back on the Server Manager console, click the **IPv4 address assigned by DHCP, IPv6 enabled** to open the *Network Connections* window.

8. Double-click the **Ethernet** connection to open the *Ethernet Status* dialog box.

9. Click the **Properties** button to open the *Ethernet Properties* dialog box.

10. Double-click **Internet Protocol Version 4 (TCP/IPv4)** to open the *Internet Protocol Version 4 (TCP/IPv4) Properties* dialog box.

11. Enter the following information:

IP address: 192.168.100.50

Subnet mask: 255.255.255.0

If you have Internet access, add an address for the DNS server and an address for the default gateway.

12. Click **OK** to close the *Internet Protocol Version 4 (TCP/IPv4) Properties* dialog box.

13. Click **Close** to *close Ethernet Status* dialog box.

14. Double-click the computer name to open the *System Properties* dialog box.

15. Click **Change** to open the *Computer Name/Domain Changes* dialog box.

16. Type **Instructor** in the *Computer name* text box. Click **OK** to close the *Computer Name/Domain Changes* dialog box.

17. When a message stating that you must restart your computer, click **OK**.

18. Click the **Close** button to close the *System Properties* dialog box.

19. When it says that you must restart your computer, click **Restart Now**.

Preparing the Server File System

The student workstations in the lab do not require access to the Internet, as long as the software the students need to install as they complete the exercises is available on the lab server. To make the necessary software available to the student computers, perform the following steps:

1. Download all the free software products listed in the "Software Requirements" section, earlier in this document.

2. On the Instructor server, open **Windows Explorer** and create a new folder called **C:\Software**.

3. Share the **C:\Software** folder using the name **Software**.

4. Assign the **Allow Full Control** share permission to the **Everyone** special identity.

5. Copy the following to the **c:\software** folder.

   - ISO of Windows Server 2012 installation disk
   - Update for Windows 8 for x64-based Systems (KB2769034 Windows8-RT-KB2769034-x64.msu)
   - ADMX Migrator (ADMXMigrator.msi)
   - Microsoft Network Monitor 3.4 (NM34_x64.exe)
   - System Center 2012 Monitoring Pack for Microsoft Windows Server File & iSCSI Services 2012 (System Center Monitoring Pack for File and Storage Management.msi)
   - Windows Assessment and Deployment (ADK) for Windows 8
   - Autounattend.xml file

To download the entire installation package of the Windows Assessment and Deployment (ADK) for Windows 8, follow these steps:

1. Start the installation of Windows Assessment and Deployment (ADK) for Windows 8 by downloading and executing the ADKSetup.exe).

2. When *the Specify Location* page opens, click **Download the Assessment and Deployment Kit for installation on a separate computer**. Click **Next**.

3. In the Download path, type **C:\Software**. Click **Next**.

4. When asked to join the Customer Experience Improvement Program (CEIP), click **Next**.

5. When the *License Agreement* appears, click **Accept**.

Installing Hyper-V

The server will run Hyper-V, which is used to run multiple virtual machines. Therefore, you need to install Hyper-V.

1. Log on to the server using the **Administrator** account and the password **Password01**. The *Server Manager* console opens.

2. Open the **Manage** menu and select **Add Roles and Features**.

3. When the *Add Roles and Features Wizard* opens, click **Next**.

4. On the *Select installation type* page opens, click **Next**.

5. On the *Select destination server* page opens, click **Next**.

6. On the *Select server roles* page, click to select **Hyper-V**.

7. When the *Add Roles and Features Wizard* dialog box opens, click **Add Features**.

8. Back at the *Select server roles* page, click **Next**.

9. On the *Select features* page, click **Next**.

10. On the *Hyper-V* page, click **Next**.

11. On the *Create Virtual Switches* page, click to select the **Ethernet network adapter**. Click **Next**.

12. On the *Virtual Machine Migration* page, click **Next**.

13. On the *Default Stores* page, click **Next**.

14. On the *Confirm installation selections* page, click **Install**.

15. When the installation is complete, click the **Close** button.

Configuring the Virtual Environment

To prepare for the course, the following high-level steps need to be performed to prepare the virtual server environment for the course:

- Creating a VM (RWDC01)
- Configure the Server RWDC01
- Installing Active Directory and DNS
- Installing DHCP
- Creating a Software Folder
- Installing and Configuring Server01
- Installing and Configuring Server02
- Adding an External Network
- Installing Upstream WSUS

Creating a VM (RWDC01)

To create a RWDC01 VM on the Hyper-V host, use the following steps:

1. Log on to the server using the **Administrator** account and the password **Password01**. The *Server Manager* console opens.

2. On the *Server Manager* console, open the **Tools** menu and click **Hyper-V Manager**. The *Hyper-V Manager* console opens.

3. Right-click the server name, click **New**, and then click **Virtual Machine**.

4. When the *New Virtual Machine Wizard* starts, click **Next**.

5. On the *Specify Name and Location* page, in the *Name* text box, type **RWDC01**. Click **Next**.

6. On the *Assign Memory* page, for the *Startup memory*, specify **2048**. Because this is used for a lab environment, click to enable **Use Dynamc Memory for this virtual machine**. Click **Next**.

7. On the *Configure Networking* page, click **Next**.

8. On the *Connect Virtual Hard Disk* page, specify the size of **70** GB.

9. Click **Next**.

10. On the *Installation Options* page, select **Install an operating system from a boot CD/DVD-ROM**. Then select **Image file (.iso)**.

11. Use the **Browse** button to select the ISO file of the Windows Server 2012 installation disk from the **C:\Software** folder. Click **Next**.

12. On the *Summary* page, click **Finish**.

13. After the VM is created, right-click the **RWDC01** in the *Virtual Machines* section of the *Hyper-V Manager* console and click **Start**.

14. Double-click the **RWDC01** in the bottom pane to open a *Virtual Machine Connection* window for RWDC01.

15. When the computer loads the Windows graphical interface and the *Windows Setup* page appears, select the appropriate language to install, time and currency format, and keyboard or input method. Then click **Next**.

16. Click **Install Now**. The *Select the operating system you want to install* page appears.

17. Select **Windows Server 2012 Standard (Server with GUI)** and click **Next**.

18. When the *License Terms* page appears, select the **I accept the license terms** check box and click **Next**.

19. When it asks what type of installation you want to use, because you are doing a clean installation and not an upgrade, click **Custom: Install Windows Only (advanced)**.

20. When it asks where you want to install Windows, select **Disk 0 Unallocated Space** and click **Next**. The *Installing Windows* page appears, indicating the progress of the Setup program as it installs the operating system.

21. After the installation completes and the computer restarts a couple of times, a message appears stating *The user's password must be changed before logging on the first time*. In the *New Password* and *Confirm Password* text boxes, type **Password01** and press the **Enter** key.

22. The system finalizes the installation and the Windows sign-on screen appears.

Configure the Server RWDC01
To configure the RWDC01 so that it can communicate on the virtual network, perform the following steps:

1. Log in to **RWDC01** as **Administrator**.

2. On the *Server Manager* console, click the **IPv4 address assigned by DHCP, IPv6 enabled** to open the *Network Connections* window.

3. Double-click the **Ethernet** connection to open the *Ethernet Status* dialog box.

4. Click **Properties** to open the *Ethernet Properties* dialog box.

5. Double-click **Internet Protocol Version 4 (TCP/IPv4)** to open the *Internet Protocol Version 4 (TCP/IPv4) Properties* dialog box.

6. Enter the following information:

   IP address: **192.168.1.50**

Subnet mask: **255.255.255.0**

Preferred DNS server: **192.168.1.50**

7. Click on the **Advanced** button.

8. In the *IP addresses* section, click the **Add** button.

9. When the *TCP/IP Address* dialog box opens, enter the following information:

IP address: **192.168.100.55**

Subnet mask: **255.255.255.0**

10. Click **Add** to close the *TCP/IP Address* dialog box.

11. Click **OK** to close the *Advanced TCP/IP Settings* dialog box.

12. Click **OK** to close the *Internet Protocol Version 4 (TCP/IPv4) Properties* dialog box.

13. Click **Close** to close *Ethernet Status* dialog box.

14. Double-click the computer name to open the *System Properties* dialog box.

15. Click **Change** to open the *Computer Name/Domain Changes* dialog box.

16. Type **RWDC01** in the *Computer name* text box. Click **OK** to close the *Computer Name/Domain Changes* dialog box.

17. When a message stating that you must restart your computer, click **OK**.

18. Click the Close button to close the *System Properties* dialog box.

19. When it says that you must restart your computer, click **Restart Now**.

Installing Active Directory and DNS

The RWDC virtual machine will be the primary Active Directory domain Controller and the DNS server. Therefore, to configure the RWDC01 server, use the following steps:

1. Log in to **RWDC01** as **Administrator**.

2. On the *Server Manager* console, open the **Manage** menu and click **Add Roles and Features**.

3. When the *Add Roles and Features Wizard* starts, click **Next**.

4. On the *Select installation type* page, click **Next**.

5. On the *Select destination server* page, click **Next**.

6. On the *Select server roles* page, click to select **Active Directory Domain Services** and click **Next**.

7. When the *Add Roles and Features Wizard* dialog box opens, click **Add Features**.

8. Back on the *Select server roles* page, click to select **DNS Server** and click **Next**.

9. When the *Add Roles and Features Wizard* dialog box opens, click **Add Features**.

10. Back at the *Select server roles* page, click **Next**.

11. On the *Select features* page, click **Next**.

12. On the *Active Directory Domain Services* page, click **Next**.

13. On the *DNS Server* page, click **Next**.

14. On the *Confirm installation selections* page, click **Install**.

15. When the installation is complete, click **Close**.

16. On the *Server Manager* console, open the **Tools** menu and click **DNS**.

17. When the *DNS Manager* console opens, right-click **RWDC01** and click **New Zone.**

18. When the *New Zone Wizard* appears, click **Next**.

19. On the *Zone Type* page, *Primary zone* will already be selected. Click **Next**.

20. On the *Forward or Reverse Lookup Zone* page, *Forward lookup zone* will already be selected. Click **Next**.

21. For the *Zone* name, type **contoso.com** and click **Next**.

22. On the *Zone File* page, click **Next**.

23. On the *Dynamic Update* page, click **Next**.

24. When the wizard is complete, click **Finish**.

25. On the *Server Manager* console, click the **Yellow Exclamation Symbol** and click **Promote this server to a domain controller**.

26. When the *Active Directory Domain Services Configuration Wizard* starts, click **Add a new forest**.

27. In the *Root domain name* text box, type **contoso.com**. Click **Next**.

28. On the *Domain Controllers Options* page, for the *Directory Services Restore Mode (DSRM) password* boxes, type **Password01**. Click **Next**.

29. On the *DNS Options* page, click **Next**.

30. On the *Addiotional Options* page, click **Next**.

31. On the *Paths* page, click **Next**.

32. On the *Review Options* page, click **Next**.

33. On the *Prerequisite Check* page, click **Install**.

34. After the computer reboots itself, log in to **RWDC01** as contoso\administrator with the password of **Password01**.

35. Open the **DNS Manager** console.

36. In the *DNS Manager* console, expand **RWDC01**, expand **Forward Lookup Zones**, and click **contoso.com**. Then right-click **contoso.com** and click **Properties**.

37. When the *Contoso.com Properties* dialog box opens, click the **Change** button.

38. When the *Change Zone Type* dialog box opens, select **Store the zone in Active Directory** and click **OK**.

39. When it asks if you want the zone to become Active Directory integrated, click **Yes**.

40. For *Dynamic Updates*, select **Nonsecure and secure**.

41. Click **OK** to close the *contoso.com Properties* dialog box.

42. Click **Reverse Lookup Zones**. Then right-click **Reverse Lookup Zones** and click **New Zone**.

43. When the wizard opens, click **Next**.

44. On the *Zone Type* page, click **Next**.

45. On the *Active Directory Zone Replication Scope* page, click **Next**.

46. On the *Reverse Lookup Zone Name* page, click **Next**.

47. On the *Reverse Lookup Zone Name* page, type **192.168.1** in the Network ID and click **Next**.

48. On the *Dynamic Update* page, click **Next**.

49. When the wizard is complete, click **Finish**.

Installing DHCP
The RWDC01 will also be the primary DHCP server for the virtual environment. Therefore, use the following steps to install and configure DHCP on the RWDC01:

1. Log in to **RWDC01** as **Administrator**.

2. On the *Server Manager* console, open the **Manage** menu and click **Add Roles and Features**.

3. When the *Add Roles and Features Wizard* starts, click **Next**.

4. On the *Select installation type* page, click **Next**.

5. On the *Select destination server* page, click **Next**.

6. On the *Select server roles* page, click to select **DHCP** and click **Next**.

7. When the *Add Roles and Features Wizard* dialog box opens, click **Add Features**.

8. Back at the *Select server roles* page, click **Next**.

9. On the *Select features* page, click **Next**.

10. On the *DHCP* page, click **Next**.

11. On the *DNS Server* page, click **Next**.

12. On the *Confirm installation selections* page, click **Install.**

13. When the installation is complete, click **Close**.

14. Using Server Manager, open the **DHCP** console.

15. Expand the **rwdc01.contoso.com** node.

16. Right-click **IPv4** and click **New Scope**.

17. When the *New Scope Wizard* starts, click **Next**.

18. For the *Name*, type **Main Scope**.

19. For the *Start IP address*, type **192.168.1.30**. For the *End IP address*, type **192.168.1.40**. Click **Next**.

20. On the *Add Exclusions and Delay* page, click **Next**.

21. On the *Lease Duration*, change the lease duration to **1** day. Click **Next**.

22. On the *Configure DHCP Options* page, click **Yes, I want to configure these options now**. Click **Next.**

23. On the **Router (Default Gateway)** page, click **Next**.

24. On the *Domain Name and DNS Servers* page, type **contoso.com** for the *Parent domain*. In the *IP address*, type **192.168.1.50**, and click **Add**. Click **Next**.

25. On the *WINS Servers* page, click **Next**.

26. On the *Activate Scope*, make sure Yes, **I want to active this scope now**, and click **Next**.

27. When the wizard is complete, click **Finish**.

28. In the *DHCP* console, right-click **rwdc01.contoso.com** and click **Authorize**.

29. Close the **DHCP console**.

Creating a Software Folder
Because the students will not have Internet access, you must create a Software folder to hold the software and share the folder using the following steps:

1. On RWDC01, create a folder called **C:\Software**.

2. Using Windows Explorer, open the following UNC:

   \\192.168.100.*XX*\Software

   where *XX* is the student number.

3. Share the **Software** folder using the name **Software**.

4. Assign the **Allow Full Control** share permission to the **Everyone** special identity.

5. Copy all files and folders from the Software folder from the Student server to Software folder on RWDC01.

6. Close the Explorer windows.

You will then need to download all software listed in the software requirements section and place them in the Software folder.

Installing and Configuring Server01
Server01 is one of the two application servers that will host the various network services and applications. Therefore, to create and configure Server01, perform the following steps:

1. Log on to the server using the **Administrator** account and the password **Password01**. The *Server Manager* console opens.

2. On the *Server Manager* console, open the **Tools** menu and click **Hyper-V Manager**. The *Hyper-V Manager* console opens.

3. Right-click the server name, click **New**, and then click **Virtual Machine**.

4. When the *New Virtual Machine Wizard* server starts, click **Next**.

5. On the *Specify Name and Location* page, in the *Name* text box, type **Server01**. Click **Next**.

6. On the *Assign Memory* page, for the *Startup memory*, specify **2048**. Because this is used for a lab environment, click to enable **Use Dynamc Memory for this virtual machine**. Click **Next**.

7. On the *Configure Networking* page, select the network connection. Click **Next**.

8. On the *Connect Virtual Hard Disk* page, specify the size of **60** GB.

9. Click **Next**.

10. On the *Installation Options* page, select **Install an operating system from a boot CD/DVD-ROM**. Then select **Image file (.iso)**.

11. Use the **Browse** button to select the ISO file of the Windows Server 2012 installation disk from the **C:\Software** folder. Click **Next**.

12. On the *Summary* page, click **Finish**.

13. After the VM is created, right-click the **Server01** in the *Virtual Machines* section of the *Hyper-V Manager* console and click **Start**.

14. Double-click the **Server01** in the bottom pane to open a *Virtual Machine Connection* window for Server01.

15. When the computer loads the Windows graphical interface and the *Windows Setup* page appears, select the appropriate language to install, time and currency format, and keyboard or input method. Then click **Next**.

16. Click **Install Now**. The *Select the operating system you want to install* page appears.

17. Select **Windows Server 2012 Standard (Server with GUI)** and click **Next**.

18. When the *License Terms* page appears, select the **I accept the license terms** check box and click **Next**.

19. When it asks what type of installation you want to use, because you are doing a clean installation and not an upgrade, click **Custom: Install Windows Only (advanced)**.

20. When it asks where you want to install Windows, select **Disk 0 Unallocated Space** and click **Next**. The *Installing Windows* page appears, indicating the progress of the Setup program as it installs the operating system.

21. After the installation completes and the computer restarts a couple of times, a message appears stating *The user's password must be changed before logging on the first time*. In the *New Password* and *Confirm Password* text boxes, type **Password01** and press the **Enter** key.

22. The system finalizes the installation and the Windows sign-on screen appears.

23. Log in to **Server01** as **Administrator**.

24. On the *Server Manager* console, click **the IPv4 address assigned by DHCP, IPv6 enabled** to open the *Network Connections* window.

25. Double-click the **Ethernet** connection to open the *Ethernet Status* dialog box.

26. Click **Properties** to open the *Ethernet Properties* dialog box.

27. Double-click **Internet Protocol Version 4 (TCP/IPv4)** to open the *Internet Protocol Version 4 (TCP/IPv4) Properties* dialog box.

28. Enter the following information:

    IP address: **192.168.1.60**

    Subnet mask: **255.255.255.0**

    Preferred DNS server: **192.168.1.50**

29. Click **OK** to close the *Internet Protocol Version 4 (TCP/IPv4) Properties* dialog box.

30. Click **Close** to close *Ethernet Status* dialog box.

31. Double-click the computer name to open the *System Properties* dialog box.

32. Click **Change** to open the *Computer Name/Domain Changes* dialog box.

33. Type **Server01** in the *Computer name* text box.

34. Click **Domain** and type **Contoso.com** in the text box. Click **OK**.

35. When it asks for a name and password of an account with permissions to join the domain, use **contoso.com\administrator** and **Password01**. Click **OK**.

36. When the *Welcome to the contoso.com domain* message appears, click **OK**.

37. When a message appears stating that you must restart your computer, click **OK**.

38. Click the **Close** button to close the *System Properties* dialog box.

39. When it says that you must restart your computer, click **Restart Now**.

40. In the *Virtual machines* pane, right-click **Server01**, and click **Shut Down**.

41. After the server has been fixed, right-click **Server01** and click **Settings**.

42. When the settings for Server01 opens, click **Add Hardware**. Then click **Network Adapter** and click **Add**.

43. For the network adapter, click the **Virtual switch** option and change from **Not connected** to the available network interface type. Click **OK**.

44. Right-click **Server01** and click **Start**.

Installing Server02
Server02 is one of the two application servers that will host the various network services and applications. Therefore, to create and configure Server02, perform the following steps:

1. Log on to the **Student** server using the **Administrator** account and the password **Password01**. The *Server Manager* console opens.

2. On the *Server Manager* console, open the **Tools** menu and click **Hyper-V Manager**. The *Hyper-V Manager* console opens.

3. Right-click the server name, click **New**, and then click **Virtual Machine**.

4. When the *New Virtual Machine Wizard* server starts, click **Next**.

5. On the *Specify Name and Location* page, in the *Name* text box, type **Server02**. Click **Next**.

6. On the *Assign Memory* page, for the *Startup memory*, specify **2048**. Because this is used for a lab environment, click to enable **Use Dynamc Memory for this virtual machine**. Click **Next**.

7. On the *Configure Networking* page, select the network connection. Click **Next**.

8. On the *Connect Virtual Hard Disk* page, specify the size of **40** GB.

9. Click **Next**.

10. On the *Installation Options* page, select **Install an operating system from a boot CD/DVD-ROM**. Then select **Image file (.iso)**.

11. Use the **Browse** button to select the ISO file of the Windows Server 2012 installation disk from the **C:\Software** folder. Click **Next**.

12. On the *Summary* page, click **Finish**.

13. After the VM is created, right-click the **Server02** in the *Virtual Machines* section of the *Hyper-V Manager* console and click **Start**.

14. Double-click the **Server02** in the bottom pane to open a *Virtual Machine Connection* window for Server02.

15. When the computer loads the Windows graphical interface and the *Windows Setup* page appears, select the appropriate language to install, time and currency format, and keyboard or input method. Then click **Next**.

16. Click **Install Now**. The *Select the operating system you want to install* page appears.

17. Select **Windows Server 2012 Standard (Server with GUI)** and click **Next**.

18. When the *License Terms* page appears, select the **I accept the license terms** check box and click **Next**.

19. When it asks what type of installation you want to use, because you are doing a clean installation and not an upgrade, click **Custom: Install Windows Only (advanced)**.

20. When it asks where you want to install Windows, select **Disk 0 Unallocated Space** and click **Next**. The *Installing Windows* page appears, indicating the progress of the Setup program as it installs the operating system.

21. After the installation completes and the computer restarts a couple of times, a message appears stating *The user's password must be changed before logging on the first time*. In the *New Password* and *Confirm Password* text boxes, type **Password01** and press the **Enter** key.

22. The system finalizes the installation and the *Windows sign-on* screen appears.

23. Log on to the Server02 server using the **Administrator** account (local account) and the password **Password01**. The *Server Manager* console opens.

24. Open the **Start** menu and click **Control Panel**. The Control Panel opens.

25. Click **System and Security > See the name of this computer**. The *System* page opens.

26. In the *Computer name, domain, and workgroup settings* section, click **Change settings**. The *System Properties* dialog box opens.

27. Click **Change**. *The Computer Name/Domain Changes* dialog box opens.

28. For the *Computer name*, type **Server02**.

29. Click **Domain** in the *Member of* section. Type **Contoso.com** in the *Domain* text box and click **OK**.

30. When the *Windows Security* dialog box opens, specify the username of **administrator** and the password of **Password01**. Click **OK**.

31. When the *Welcome* screen appears, click **OK**.

32. When a message is displayed that the computer must be restarted, click **OK**.

33. To close the *System Properties* dialog box, click **Close**.

34. When is says that you have to restart the computer to apply these changes, click **Restart Now**. Let the computer reboot.

Adding an External Network
Some of the labs will need a second network. Therefore, to create a second virtual switch, use the following steps:

1. On Student*xx*, use the Server Manager to open **Hyper-V Manager**. The *Hyper-V Manager* console opens.

2. Right-click **Server01** and click **Shut Down**. When it asks if you are sure, click **Shut Down**.

3. Right-click **Server02** and click **Shut Down**. When it asks if you are sure, click **Shut Down**.

4. Under *Actions*, click **Virtual Switch Manager**. The Virtual Switch Manager for Student*xx* dialog box opens.

5. Click **External** and click **Create Virtual Switch**.

6. Back on the *Virtual Switch Manager* dialog box, change the name of the new virtual switch to **External Switch** and click **OK**. If it says *Pending changes may disrupt network connectivity*, click **Yes**.

7. In Hyper-V Manager, right-click **Server01** and click **Settings**. The *Settings for Server01* dialog box opens.

8. Click **Add Hardware**. Then in the *Add Hardware* section (right pane), click **Network Adapter** and click **Add**.

9. Change the Virtual switch to **External Switch**. Click **OK** to close the *Settings for Server01* dialog box.

10. In Hyper-V Manager, right-click **Server02** and click **Settings**. The *Settings for Server02* dialog box opens.

11. Click **Add Hardware**. Then in the *Add Hardware* section (right pane), click **Network Adapter** and click **Add**.

12. Change the Virtual switch to **External Switch**. Click **OK** to close the *Settings for Server02* dialog box.

Installing Upstream WSUS

Because the lab server will not have Internet Access, you will need Internet access temporarily to install and configure an upload WSUS server. Students later install a WSUS server and connect to the upstream server. Therefore, to prepare the server, use the following steps:

1. On Student*xx*, use the Server Manager to open **Hyper-V Manager**. The *Hyper-V Manager* console opens.

2. Log in into **Server02** as **contoso\administrator**. Server Manager opens.

3. Using **Windows Explorer**, create a **C:\Updates** folder.

4. Using Server Manager, open the **Manage** menu and click **Add Roles and Features**.

5. When the *Add Roles and Features Wizard* opens, click **Next**.

6. On the *Select installation type* page, click **Next**.

7. On the *Select destination server* page, click **Next**.

8. On the *Select server roles* page, click to select **Windows Server Update Services**. When it asks you to add a feature, click **Add Features**. Click **Next**.

9. On the *Select features* page, click **Next**.

10. On the *Windows Server Update Services* page, click **Next**.

11. On the *Select role services* page, click **Next**.

12. On the *Content location selection* page, type **c:\update**. Click **Next**.

13. On the *Web Server Role (IIS)* page, click **Next**.

14. On the *Select role services* page, click **Next**.

15. On the *Confirm installation selections* page, click **Install**.

16. Using Server Manager, open the **Tools** menu, and click **Windows Server Update Services**.

17. If a *Complete WSUS Installation* dialog box opens, click **Run**. When the post-installation successfully completes, click **Close**.

18. When the *Windows Server Update Services Configuration Wizard* opens, click **Next**.

19. On the *Join the Microsoft Update Improvement Program* page, click **Next**.

20. On the *Choose Upstream Server* page, *Synchronize from Microsoft Update* is already selected. Click **Next**.

21. On the *Specify Proxy Server* page, if your organization requires proxy settings, fill in the proper proxy settings. If not, click **Next**.

22. On the *Connect to Upstream Server* page, click **Start Connecting**. When done connecting (after several minutes), you can click **Next**.

23. On the *Choose Languages* page, click **Next**.

24. On the *Choose Products* page, deselect **Office**. Deselect **Windows** and select **Windows 8** and **Windows Server 2012**. Click **Next**.

25. On the *Choose Classifications* page, click **Next**.

26. On the *Set Sync Schedule* page, make sure *Synchronize manually* is already selected. Click **Next**.

27. On the *Finished* page, click **Begin initial synchronization**, and click **Next**.

28. On the *What's Next* page, click **Finish**.

29. Right-click **Synchronization**, and click **Synchronize Now**.

LAB SUMMARIES

Lab 1: Deploying and Managing Server Images

After completing this lab, you will be able to:

- Install and configure Windows Deployment Services

- Deploy Windows servers using Windows Deployment Services

- Create and modify an Autounattend.xml file using Windows System Image Manager

- Update an offline Windows image

Estimated lab time: 100 minutes

BEFORE YOU BEGIN

The lab environment consists of student workstations connected to a local area network, along with a server that functions as the domain controller for a domain called *contoso.com*. The computers required for this lab are listed in Table 1-1.

Table 1-1
Computers Required for Lab 1

Computer	Operating System	Computer Name
Server (VM 1)	Windows Server 2012	RWDC01
Server (VM 2)	Windows Server 2012	Server01
Server (VM 3)	Windows Server 2012	Server02

In addition to the computers, you also require the software listed in Table 1-2 to complete Lab 1.

Table 1-2
Software Required for Lab 1

Software	Location
ISO of Windows Server 2012 installation disk	\\rwdc01\Software
Windows Assessment and Deployment Kit (ADK) for Windows 8	\\rwdc01\Software
Autounattend.xml file	\\rwdc01\Software
Windows8-RT-KB2769034-x64.msu	\\rwdc01\Software
Lab 1 student worksheet	Lab01_worksheet.docx (provided by instructor)

Lab 2: Implementing Patch Management

After completing this lab, you will be able to:

- Install and configure WSUS

- Deploy updates to client computers

Estimated lab time: 60 minutes

BEFORE YOU BEGIN

The lab environment consists of student workstations connected to a local area network, along with a server that functions as the domain controller for a domain called *contoso.com*. The computers required for this lab are listed in Table 2-1.

Table 2-1
Computers Required for Lab 2

Computer	Operating System	Computer Name
Server (VM 1)	Windows Server 2012	RWDC01
Server (VM 2)	Windows Server 2012	Server01
Server (VM 3)	Windows Server 2012	Server02

In addition to the computers, you also require the software listed in Table 2-2 to complete Lab 2.

Table 2-2
Software Required for Lab 2

Software	Location
Lab 2 student worksheet	Lab02_worksheet.docx (provided by instructor)

Lab 3: Monitoring Servers

After completing this lab, you will be able to:

- Use the Event Viewer to troubleshoot and monitor servers

- Use the Reliability Monitor, to monitor the reliability of a server

- Use Task Manager and Performance Monitor to monitor the performance of a server

Estimated lab time: 120 minutes

BEFORE YOU BEGIN

The lab environment consists of student workstations connected to a local area network, along with a server that functions as the domain controller for a domain called *contoso.com*. The computers required for this lab are listed in Table 3-1.

Table 3-1
Computers Required for Lab 3

Computer	Operating System	Computer Name
Server (VM 1)	Windows Server 2012	RWDC01
Server (VM 2)	Windows Server 2012	Server01
Server (VM 3)	Windows Server 2012	Server02

In addition to the computers, you also require the software listed in Table 3-2 to complete Lab 3.

Table 3-2
Software Required for Lab 3

Software	Location
Lab 3 student worksheet	Lab03_worksheet.docx (provided by instructor)

Lab 4: Configuring Distributed Files System (DFS)
After completing this lab, you will be able to:

- Install DFS

- Implement and configure DFS namespace

- Implement and configure DFS replication

- Use DFS for fault tolerant shared folders

Estimated lab time: 60 minutes

BEFORE YOU BEGIN

The lab environment consists of student workstations connected to a local area network, along with a server that functions as the domain controller for a domain called *contoso.com*. The computers required for this lab are listed in Table 4-1.

Table 4-1
Computers Required for Lab 4

Computer	Operating System	Computer Name
Server (VM 1)	Windows Server 2012	RWDC01
Server (VM 2)	Windows Server 2012	Server01
Server (VM 3)	Windows Server 2012	Server02

In addition to the computers, you also require the software listed in Table 4-2 to complete Lab 4.

Table 4-2
Software Required for Lab 4

Software	Location
Lab 4 student worksheet	Lab04_worksheet.docx (provided by instructor)

Lab 5: Configuring File Server Resource Manager
After completing this lab, you will be able to:

- Install and configure File Server Resource Manager

- Use Quotas to manage disk space

- Manage files with file screening

- Use Storage Reports

Estimated lab time: 60 minutes

BEFORE YOU BEGIN

The lab environment consists of student workstations connected to a local area network, along with a server that functions as the domain controller for a domain called *contoso.com*. The computers required for this lab are listed in Table 5-1.

Table 5-1
Computers Required for Lab 5

Computer	Operating System	Computer Name
Server (VM 1)	Windows Server 2012	RWDC01
Server (VM 2)	Windows Server 2012	Server01

In addition to the computers, you also require the software listed in Table 5-2 to complete Lab 5.

Table 5-2
Software Required for Lab 5

Software	Location
ADMXMigrator.msi, NMI32_x64.exe, System Center Monitoring Pack for File and Storage Management.msi, and Windows8=RT-KB2769034-x64.msu	C:\Software
Lab 5 student worksheet	Lab05_worksheet.docx (provided by instructor)

Lab 6: Configuring File Services and Disk Encryption
After completing this lab, you will be able to:

- Encrypt files with EFS

- Configure EFS Recovery Agent

- Back up and restore EFS certificates

- Encrypt a volume with BitLocker

Estimated lab time: 70 minutes

BEFORE YOU BEGIN

The lab environment consists of student workstations connected to a local area network, along with a server that functions as the domain controller for a domain called *contoso.com*. The computers required for this lab are listed in Table 6-1.

Table 6-1
Computers Required for Lab 6

Computer	Operating System	Computer Name
Server (VM 1)	Windows Server 2012	RWDC01
Server (VM 2)	Windows Server 2012	Server01

In addition to the computers, you also require the software listed in Table 6-2 to complete Lab 6.

Table 6-2
Software Required for Lab 6

Software	Location
Lab 6 student worksheet	Lab06_worksheet.docx (provided by instructor)

Lab 7: Configuring Advanced Audit Policies

After completing this lab, you will be able to:

- Configure standard audit policies

- Configure advanced audit policies

- Using AuditPol.exe to manage audit policies

- Audit removable devices

Estimated lab time: 60 minutes

BEFORE YOU BEGIN

The lab environment consists of student workstations connected to a local area network, along with a server that functions as the domain controller for a domain called *contoso.com*. The computers required for this lab are listed in Table 7-1.

Table 7-1
Computers Required for Lab 7

Computer	Operating System	Computer Name
Server (VM 1)	Windows Server 2012	RWDC01
Server (VM 2)	Windows Server 2012	Server01

In addition to the computers, you also require the software listed in Table 7-2 to complete Lab 7.

Table 7-2
Software Required for Lab 7

Software	Location
Lab 7 student worksheet	Lab07_worksheet.docx (provided by instructor)

Lab 8: Configuring DNS Zones

After completing this lab, you will be able to:

- Configure DNS zones including primary zones, secondary zones, and Active Directory Integrated zones.

- Configure Zone delegation

- Configure a Stub Zone

■ Configure Forwarding and Conditional Forwarding zones

■ Configure Zone Transfers

■ Use DNSCMD command to manage zones

Estimated lab time: 80 minutes

BEFORE YOU BEGIN

The lab environment consists of student workstations connected to a local area network, along with a server that functions as the domain controller for a domain called *contoso.com*. The computers required for this lab are listed in Table 8-1.

Table 8-1
Computers Required for Lab 8

Computer	Operating System	Computer Name
Server (VM 1)	Windows Server 2012	RWDC01
Server (VM 2)	Windows Server 2012	Server01

In addition to the computers, you also require the software listed in Table 8-2 to complete Lab 8.

Table 8-2
Software Required for Lab 8

Software	Location
Lab 8 student worksheet	Lab08_worksheet.docx (provided by instructor)

Lab 9: Configuring DNS Records

After completing this lab, you will be able to:

■ Manage DNS Resource Records

■ Configure round robin

■ Configure Zone Scavenging

■ Troubleshoot DNS

■ Using DNSCMD command to manage Resource Records

Estimated lab time: 60 minutes

BEFORE YOU BEGIN

The lab environment consists of student workstations connected to a local area network, along with a server that functions as the domain controller for a domain called *contoso.com*. The computers required for this lab are listed in Table 9-1.

Table 9-1
Computers Required for Lab 9

Computer	Operating System	Computer Name
Server (VM 1)	Windows Server 2012	RWDC01

In addition to the computers, you also require the software listed in Table 9-2 to complete Lab 9.

Table 9-2
Software Required for Lab 9

Software	Location
Lab 9 student worksheet	Lab09_worksheet.docx (provided by instructor)

Lab 10: Configuring VPN and Routing

After completing this lab, you will be able to:

- Install and configure Remote Access Role

- Configure VPN settings

- Configure routing

Estimated lab time: 125 minutes

BEFORE YOU BEGIN

The lab environment consists of student workstations connected to a local area network, along with a server that functions as the domain controller for a domain called *contoso.com*. The computers required for this lab are listed in Table 10-1.

Table 10-1
Computers Required for Lab 10

Computer	Operating System	Computer Name
Server (VM 1)	Windows Server 2012	RWDC01
Server (VM 2)	Windows Server 2012	Server01
Server (VM 3)	Windows Server 2012	Server02

In addition to the computers, you also require the software listed in Table 10-2 to complete Lab 10.

Table 10-2
Software Required for Lab 10

Software	Location
Lab 10 student worksheet	Lab10_worksheet.docx (provided by instructor)

Lab 11: Configuring DirectAccess

After completing this lab, you will be able to:

- Configure DirectAccess

- Prepare for DirectAccess Deployment

- Configure certificates for DirectAccess

Estimated lab time: 50 minutes

BEFORE YOU BEGIN

The lab environment consists of student workstations connected to a local area network, along with a server that functions as the domain controller for a domain called *contoso.com*. The computers required for this lab are listed in Table 11-1.

Table 11-1
Computers Required for Lab 11

Computer	Operating System	Computer Name
Server (VM 1)	Windows Server 2012	RWDC01
Server (VM 2)	Windows Server 2012	Server01

In addition to the computers, you also require the software listed in Table 11-2 to complete Lab 11.

Table 11-2
Software Required for Lab 11

Software	Location
Lab 11 student worksheet	Lab11_worksheet.docx (provided by instructor)

Lab 12: Configuring Network Policy Server (NPS)

After completing this lab, you will be able to:

- Install and configure Network Policy Server

- Configure RADIUS clients

- Manage RADIUS templates

- Configure RADIUS accounting

Estimated lab time: 65 minutes

BEFORE YOU BEGIN

The lab environment consists of student workstations connected to a local area network, along with a server that functions as the domain controller for a domain called *contoso.com*. The computers required for this lab are listed in Table 12-1.

Table 12-1
Computers Required for Lab 12

Computer	Operating System	Computer Name
Server (VM 1)	Windows Server 2012	RWDC01
Server (VM 2)	Windows Server 2012	Server01

In addition to the computers, you also require the software listed in Table 12-2 to complete Lab 12.

Table 12-2
Software Required for Lab 12

Software	Location
Lab 12 student worksheet	Lab12_worksheet.docx (provided by instructor)

Lab 13: Configuring NPS Policies

After completing this lab, you will be able to:

- Create and configure connection request policies

- Create and configure network policies

- Import and export the NPS configuration

- Understand how network policies are processed

Estimated lab time: 55 minutes

BEFORE YOU BEGIN

The lab environment consists of student workstations connected to a local area network, along with a server that functions as the domain controller for a domain called *contoso.com*. The computers required for this lab are listed in Table 13-1.

Table 13-1
Computers Required for Lab 13

Computer	Operating System	Computer Name
Server (VM 1)	Windows Server 2012	RWDC01

In addition to the computers, you also require the software listed in Table 13-2 to complete Lab 13.

Table 13-2
Software Required for Lab 13

Software	Location
Lab 13 student worksheet	Lab13_worksheet.docx (provided by instructor)

Lab 14: Configuring Network Access Protection (NAP)

After completing this lab, you will be able to:

- Install Health Registration Authority role on an NPS server

- Install and configure NAP Enforcement using DHCP

- Configure System Health Validators (SHVs)

- Configure health policies

- Configure NAP client settings

Estimated lab time: 60 minutes

BEFORE YOU BEGIN

The lab environment consists of student workstations connected to a local area network, along with a server that functions as the domain controller for a domain called *contoso.com*. The computers required for this lab are listed in Table 14-1.

Table 14-1
Computers Required for Lab 14

Computer	Operating System	Computer Name
Server (VM 1)	Windows Server 2012	RWDC01
Server (VM 2)	Windows Server 2012	Server01

In addition to the computers, you also require the software listed in Table 14-2 to complete Lab 14.

Table 14-2
Software Required for Lab 14

Software	Location
Lab 14 student worksheet	Lab14_worksheet.docx (provided by instructor)

Lab 15: Configuring Server Authentication

After completing this lab, you will be able to:

- Create a service account

- Create a Group Service Account

- Configure Kerberos and Kerberos Delegation

Estimated lab time: 60 minutes

BEFORE YOU BEGIN

The lab environment consists of student workstations connected to a local area network, along with a server that functions as the domain controller for a domain called *contoso.com*. The computers required for this lab are listed in Table 15-1.

Table 15-1
Computers Required for Lab 15

Computer	Operating System	Computer Name
Server (VM 1)	Windows Server 2012	RWDC01
Server (VM 2)	Windows Server 2012	Server01

In addition to the computers, you also require the software listed in Table 15-2 to complete Lab 15.

Table 15-2
Software Required for Lab 15

Software	Location
Lab 15 student worksheet	Lab15_worksheet.docx (provided by instructor)

Lab 16: Configuring Domain Controllers

After completing this lab, you will be able to:

- Configure universal group membership caching (UGMC)

- Transfer and seize operations masters

- Install and configure a Read-Only Domain Controller

- Clone a Domain Controller

Estimated lab time: 95 minutes

BEFORE YOU BEGIN

The lab environment consists of student workstations connected to a local area network, along with a server that functions as the domain controller for a domain called *contoso.com*. The computers required for this lab are listed in Table 16-1.

Table 16-1
Computers Required for Lab 16

Computer	Operating System	Computer Name
Server (VM 1)	Windows Server 2012	RWDC01
Server (VM 2)	Windows Server 2012	Server01
Server (VM 3)	Windows Server 2012	Server02

In addition to the computers, you also require the software listed in Table 16-2 to complete Lab 16.

Table 16-2
Software Required for Lab 16

Software	Location
Lab 16 student worksheet	Lab16_worksheet.docx (provided by instructor)

Lab 17: Maintaining Active Directory

After completing this lab, you will be able to:

- Back up the System State including Active Directory

- Perform an Active Directory restore

- Configure Active Directory snapshots

- Restore a Deleted Object using the Active Directory Recycle Bin

- Perform Active Directory maintenance

Estimated lab time: 130 minutes

BEFORE YOU BEGIN

The lab environment consists of student workstations connected to a local area network, along with a server that functions as the domain controller for a domain called *contoso.com*. The computers required for this lab are listed in Table 17-1.

Table 17-1
Computers Required for Lab 17

Computer	Operating System	Computer Name
Server (VM 1)	Windows Server 2012	RWDC01
Server (VM 2)	Windows Server 2012	Server01
Server (VM 3)	Windows Server 2012	Server02

In addition to the computers, you also require the software listed in Table 17-2 to complete Lab 17.

Table 17-2
Software Required for Lab 17

Software	Location
Lab 17 student worksheet	Lab17_worksheet.docx (provided by instructor)

Lab 18: Configuring Account Policies

After completing this lab, you will be able to:

- Configure a domain user password policy

- Configure account lockout settings

- Configure and apply Password Settings Objects (PSOs)

Estimated lab time: 55 minutes

BEFORE YOU BEGIN

The lab environment consists of student workstations connected to a local area network, along with a server that functions as the domain controller for a domain called *contoso.com*. The computers required for this lab are listed in Table 18-1.

Table 18-1
Computers Required for Lab 18

Computer	Operating System	Computer Name
Server (VM 1)	Windows Server 2012	RWDC01

In addition to the computers, you also require the software listed in Table 18-2 to complete Lab 18.

Table 18-2
Software Required for Lab 18

Software	Location
Lab 18 student worksheet	Lab18_worksheet.docx (provided by instructor)

Lab 19: Configuring Group Policy Processing

After completing this lab, you will be able to:

- Configure the processing order and precedence of GPOs

- Configure blocking of inheritance and enforced policies

- Configure security and WMI filtering

- Configure loopback processing

Estimated lab time: 60 minutes

BEFORE YOU BEGIN

The lab environment consists of student workstations connected to a local area network, along with a server that functions as the domain controller for a domain called *contoso.com*. The computers required for this lab are listed in Table 19-1.

Table 19-1
Computers Required for Lab 19

Computer	Operating System	Computer Name
Server (VM 1)	Windows Server 2012	RWDC01

In addition to the computers, you also require the software listed in Table19-2 to complete Lab 19.

Table 19-2
Software Required for Lab 19

Software	Location
Lab 19 student worksheet	Lab19_worksheet.docx (provided by instructor)

Lab 20: Configuring Group Policy Settings

After completing this lab, you will be able to:

- Perform software installation with group policies

- Use folder redirection

- Run scripts with group policies

- Configure administrative and security templates

Estimated lab time: 75 minutes

BEFORE YOU BEGIN

The lab environment consists of student workstations connected to a local area network, along with a server that functions as the domain controller for a domain called *contoso.com*. The computers required for this lab are listed in Table 20-1.

Table 20-1
Computers Required for Lab 20

Computer	Operating System	Computer Name
Server (VM 1)	Windows Server 2012	RWDC01
Server (VM 2)	Windows Server 2012	Server01

In addition to the computers, you also require the software listed in Table 20-2 to complete Lab 20.

Table 20-2
Software Required for Lab 20

Software	Location
System Center Monitoring Pack for File and Storage Management.msi	\\RWDC01\Software
ADMX Migrator	\\RWDC01\Software
Lab 20 student worksheet	Lab20_worksheet.docx (provided by instructor)

Lab 21: Managing Group Policy Objects

After completing this lab, you will be able to:

- Back up and restore GPOs

- Import and copy GPOs

- Reset the Default GPOs

- Delegate management of group policies

- Use a migration table

Estimated lab time: 60 minutes

BEFORE YOU BEGIN

The lab environment consists of student workstations connected to a local area network, along with a server that functions as the domain controller for a domain called *contoso.com*. The computers required for this lab are listed in Table 21-1.

Table 21-1
Computers Required for Lab 21

Computer	Operating System	Computer Name
Server (VM 1)	Windows Server 2012	RWDC01

In addition to the computers, you also require the software listed in Table 21-2 to complete Lab 21.

Table 21-2
Software Required for Lab 21

Software	Location
Lab 21 student worksheet	Lab21_worksheet.docx (provided by instructor)

Lab 22: Configuring Group Policy Preferences

After completing this lab, you will be able to:

- Configure Group Policy preferences including printers, network drive mappings, power options, Internet Explorer settings, and file and folder deployment

- Configure item-level targeting

Estimated lab time: 70 minutes

BEFORE YOU BEGIN

The lab environment consists of student workstations connected to a local area network, along with a server that functions as the domain controller for a domain called *contoso.com*. The computers required for this lab are listed in Table 22-1.

Table 22-1
Computers Required for Lab 22

Computer	Operating System	Computer Name
Server (VM 1)	Windows Server 2012	RWDC01
Server (VM 2)	Windows Server 2012	Server01

In addition to the computers, you also require the software listed in Table 22-2 to complete Lab 22.

Table 22
Software Required for Lab 22

Software	Location
Lab 22 student worksheet	Lab22worksheet.docx (provided by instructor)